IRELAND'S EYE

IRELAND'S EYE

Travels

MARK ANTHONY JARMAN

ANANSI

Published in 2002 by
House of Anansi Press Inc.
110 Spadina Avenue, Suite 801
Toronto, ON, M5V 2K4
Tel. 416-363-4343
Fax 416-363-1017
www.anansi.ca

Distributed in Canada by
Publishers Group Canada
250A Carlton Street
Toronto, ON, M5A 2L1
Tel. 416-934-9900
Toll free order numbers:
Tel. 800-663-5714
Fax 800-565-3770

CBC logo used by permission

06 05 04 03 02   1 2 3 4 5

NATIONAL LIBRARY OF CANADA CATALOGUING IN PUBLICATION DATA

Jarman, Mark Anthony, 1955–
Ireland's eye : travels / Mark Anthony Jarman.

ISBN 0-88784-178-3

1. Ireland — Description and travel.
2. Jarman, Mark Anthony, 1955– —Journeys — Ireland. I. Title.

DA978.2.J37 2002   914.1504'824   C2002-904011-6

Cover design: Bill Douglas at The Bang
Typesetting: Tannice Goddard, Soul Oasis Networking

We acknowledge for their financial support of our publishing program the Canada
Council for the Arts, the Ontario Arts Council, and the Government of Canada
through the Book Publishing Industry Development Program (BPIDP).

Printed and bound in Canada

CONTENTS

Part One

———◆———

WANKERS AND WIDOWS
AND CHANCERS AND SAINTS

Travel is the ruin of all happiness! There's no looking at a building here after seeing Italy.
— FANNY BURNEY

The truth is often a terrible weapon of aggression.
— ALFRED ADLER

Chapter One

RECRUITS STRAPPED INSIDE
THE AMAZING MACHINE

MOVING ON A 767 IN 1997. From the get-go on the painted jet we drink hooch madly, foppishly, British Airways headphones on the so-called rock channel with some cockney DJ nattering and spinning hit singles from 1966, from my ancient grade-school history. Eight miles high and 800 miles per hour with the Yardbirds and Kinks; Ike and Tina giving me shivers with "River Deep, Mountain High"; and Pet Clark's voice booming past her white lipstick.

Some of us are bored, blasé about travel. Some of us should be pistol-whipped. My drowned Irish grandfather likely never laid eyes on a plane, was never flung through air at 800 miles per hour with "Shapes of Things to Come" crashing the hairs of his inner ear.

Shoehorned into blue seats zooming over Rocky Mountain House, Hudson Bay (I look down for Henry's lost rowboat), Baffin Island, Greenland, I cannot escape the TV screens placed overhead every few rows. I don't want to watch, but you can't *not* see Madonna's large mouth pretending to be Evita's large mouth

3

or the special-effects volcano punctuating the mindless in-flight disaster movie.

We're zooming over the real volcanoes of trendy Iceland and Sigur Rós; we're on the polar route up over the giant ice pack, but inside this finely engineered aluminum tube it's hot and stuffy, elbow to elbow, thigh to thigh. We wipe our sweaty faces with British Airways "Refreshing Tissue."

It's hot and stuffy, but crowhop out on that big wing one inch past this pane of Plexi and you'd freeze to death. You'd freeze-dry and blow off like a shrivelled maple leaf, but that's okay, that's part of the buzz, the commodity.

The British pilots, Reginald and Nigel, have such beautiful, decent accents. "Thawnks *so much* to our cabin crew."

"Long night flights are difficult, of course."

"Yusss."

The British Airways cabin crews are dedicated, are days from a strike that could strand me the far side of the ocean (not that I'd mind being stranded).

Our dedicated British stewardess, trying to cut back our impending jet lag and inebriation, ferries us round after round of water, orange juice, tomato juice, and then she hands out free bananas to go with the rivers of booze.

This pretty stew with the Sloane Ranger accent represents Europe. Whatever Europe offers, we take. We are manic tourists with wallets and Tilley hats; we are hick-yokel appetite personified, party-hearty hayseed consumers with shy eyes and back teeth floating. We're happy, *special*, and England swings like a pendulum does. We're buying an *experience*.

Soon we'll be dancing on Carnaby Street with Twiggy and the corpse of Sid Vicious, marching for a larf with Ulster's kick-the-pope brigades and the Red Hand Defenders! Yes! I'll be knocking back black garrulous pints with James Joyce and Martin Amis and Maggie Thatcher and forgetting why I came, forgetting my murky family legends and Irish errands, because Britain is a seductive stewardess and Europe is a giant theme park: castles and granite gargoyles and miniskirts and ivory beer pulls and flying buttresses a construct just for me!

But then . . . then arrives that half-drunk epiphany.

My eyes clear and I see that I'm a fool, fallen from suave *jet-set* infallibility into a Freudian pop art installation, *product.*

My eyes clear and I see myself riding an assembly line that fills Western Europe. Row upon row of inebriated tourists clutching erect bananas and waiting to be serviced.

Chapter Two

RIDING ON THE
NORTHERN LINE

MY FATHER, LEIGHTON, WAS BORN IN OXFORD. My mother, Kay, fell into the world in Dublin. I feel the magnet pull of rival kingdoms. This trip I'm visiting the two kingdoms. My mother and father met during the war in the Royal Navy. Some of the Oxford side of the family did not approve of my father's secret wartime marriage to an unknown Irish woman while on a thirty-six-hour leave in London. My grandfather forbade my father to marry my mother. All his life my grandfather loved a Catholic girl but he'd been forbidden to marry her. He wanted his son to feel the same despair.

Kay and Leighton had met just weeks before. My mother was an officer (as a nursing sister) and my father a non-com, so they were not allowed to mix. They'd slip off on separate trains to rendezvous secretly at Cheddar Gorge. They managed to be in London during the Blitz and in Plymouth when it was flattened by the Luftwaffe.

The navy shipped my father from Oxford to Ceylon in monsoon season. A big hospital in Trincomalee, for the invasion of Japan. If the Suez Canal was blocked by sunken freighters and tankers, then his convoy would have sailed the bottom of Africa, bouncing past the stormy Cape of Good Hope. I'm sure it was Gibralter and the Suez, says my aunt: He went to Ceylon early in the war; he had to come back when his twin brother died. My mother disagrees: No, he went late in the war, after we'd married; sailed to Trincomalee, Foul Point. The past is the wrong end of the microscope. My father told me of his hospital ship being dive-bombed by Stukas, but usually he didn't talk of the war. He said the monsoon rains were so hard that his shirt ballooned with water just running door to door. My English father is dead now, so I can't ask him of his wartime voyages, his fabled seasickness, the names of his ships in the Arabian Sea and the Bay of Bengal. My father is not talking to me.

My Irish mother, very much alive, is also not talking to me, even though I am going to prowl her old wrecked neighbourhoods.

In fact, she's not talking to me *because* I like to prowl her old wrecked neighbourhoods. She'd rather I didn't pry, name names, use her or the family as raw material. She'd rather I wrote nice Hallmark cards or chased ambulances. In a sense, I am chasing ambulances, chasing product at 800 miles per.

In my bedroom at my aunt and uncle's house in north London is an Irish mug with its handle on the inside. An Irish joke. Ha ha. Very good.

"What do you think of the IRA?" my English aunt asks me down in a crowded tube station. I had been looking for a trash can, but my aunt said there are none because they might conceal IRA bombs.

What do I think of the IRA?

Before I can answer, she says, "Well, what could anyone think of the IRA? They're *monsters*."

My English relatives hate the IRA and don't know that my Irish grandfather and my uncles were in the IRA circa 1916 (before it was even called the IRA); that in 1920 the Black and Tans from England were always bashing down their big door in Dublin; or that Irish relatives served the English Crown in the King's Royal Irish Hussars and the Royal Irish Lancers. I keep my mouth shut, as my English father would have.

My English relatives are kind and generous to me. I stay in their large Edwardian house, under their roof, my father's sister and her solicitor husband. Their rooms brim with pastoral paintings and china and iron farm implements pinned to the walls. They give me anything I want, chauffeur me to the tube station, lend me their London A-Z, take me to pub lunches and the roadside farm where they purchase their favourite rich cheeses and clotted cream, showing me what led to their heart operations.

"Have you seen our scars?" Matching his-and-her bypasses: the smooth breastbone breached, now ridged, now puckered, now reticulate.

They take me to their seaside cottage by the dykes and salt marshes and sail lofts of Essex, where men up to their thighs in mud push a heavy wooden boat in tidal muck and a boy sinks slowly down into tidal mud, his tiny head almost gone from the world when a rescue party finally reaches him. A child wondering if these mud flats are his last glimpses of the earth; what a strange, primal way to go, to descend into the planet.

In their cottage they show me the small upstairs bed where Andrew Lloyd Webber famously slept when he visited my cousin Judy.

You know his music, of course?

Oh. His music. Yes.

My aunt says it's like having her brother Leighton back with her. Leighton was my father. My hospitable aunt calls me Little Leighton, happily packs me a peanut-butter-and-jam lunch to take into London on my daily trips on the underground, which saves me a small fortune in restaurant bills. My aunt stocks a fridge full of ale just for me, and my uncle insists on making me giant midnight snacks when I come back from a David Hare play or *The Weir*, Conor McPherson's Irish pub play; from the Siouxsie and the Banshees reunion or a long walk along the Thames embankment; or from crawling tooth-and-nail pubs.

I am always given the same room on the second floor, with its view of the rose garden and hedges, the room's heart red walls decorated with sublime watercolours painted by my English grandfather. My aunt and uncle spoil me. I love them. Why do I feel like a spy in their house in the centre of arthritic empire?

My uncle was a bullish boxer at Oxford and is now a bullish solicitor in the City. He is big, brainy, canny, likes to chuckle at the world. We have good arguments about plays in the West End; about Thatcherite politics (my aunt ran for MP as a Liberal but loves the Iron Lady) and Lady Di and the Royal Family ("Parasites," I say); about crime in cruel Cool Britannia, pop music, landlords versus tenants (they are landlords), the minimum wage (England still didn't have one then).

"Our industries won't be able to compete with Asia."

We disagree, but we like arguing and greatly enjoy each other's company. And one or two of my English relatives wonder why I want to travel to Ireland ("There are just as many shades of green here"). Many English look down on the Irish as a gunny sack of crazed curs and wildcats.

Chapter Three

THE KITCHEN TABLE
IN THE CITY

IN DUBLIN I'M BOARDING WITH THE WILDCATS, staying at my aunt
Rose's small house near the DART line. She is over eighty but looks
much younger, is in great shape. Rose married my mother's
favourite brother, Brendan. My uncle Brendan died not long after
my first trip here in 1981. He wore an eyepatch, couldn't swallow
food. In their Dublin driveway my mother cried, "I'll never see
my brother again." We tried to be positive, tried to pooh-pooh
that idea, but it turned out my mother was right.

My aunt Rose has a bad chest cough that has been hanging
on this spring. Rose has a pleasing face and likes to laugh, still
golfs as much as she can. Some wives complain of being golf
widows. Her sons joke that, when they were kids, she was on the
links so much they were golf orphans.

Rose and I sit for hours talking in her postwar semi-detached.
Rose says my aunt Lizzie hardly came to see her own husband,
Dermot, when he was dying. Dermot was my uncle, my mother's
eldest brother, and his wife, Lizzie, does not seem to have won

any popularity contests in our family. I never met her or Dermot — I was four when he died.

"I tell you, there was something wrong with Lizzie. And I saw it. Your grandmother had a friend who had a pub down in Clogh, by the Swan, and we were all invited down for Stephen's Day. The pub had a big room in back for a party. Molly Summers played piano in the backroom. My mother took our two children for the night; I walked them up the canal to Inchicore. Jimmy was up shaving; I had my dress on, heard a knock at the door. It was Dermot. I knew something was wrong. It had all been arranged — her and Dermot in the front of the car, and me and Brendan and Tom McGovern in the back. Tom McGovern stayed in the house with your grandmother, a driver on the buses here, very nice man, loaned us a ring when we were married. Your uncle looked up to him as a father. And here's Lizzie at the last minute saying she didn't want to go to the party, and they had the only car. We had no phone and Bridie had no phone down in the Swan, and no buses were running on Stephen's Day. Tom knew a taxi driver, and we had to walk all the way from Dolphin Road to Stephen's Green to find him and he drove us down. Times Dermot would show up here needing to talk to Brendan, and I could tell he'd been crying. They lost their house because of a missed mortgage payment. I think Lizzie was sending money down to the farm.

"Well, now, Dermot was unconscious in the hospital, sure Brendan'd go and stay most of the night (he got off work at half past four then). One time, now Bridie told me this, she said, Bridie she said Lizzie arrived, she said, and Dermot *hooshed* his wife's hand away and held onto his sister Bridie's hand. *Hooshed* his wife's hand away, and he's unconscious and aren't his eyes closed, but he *hooshed* her hand away.

"Brendan always said to me, Brendan, he said, Lizzie ought to have married a docker, he said. You know dockers — they're all big and strong, and they'd put a boot up your backside. That woman! No man'd put up with what Dermot did. Dermot had a hard life."

My uncle Dermot worked as a cooper, making barrels at Guinness during the day.

"Him and another fellow opened up their own little cooper's yard in a rented garage on Prussia Street, I think, near Blackhall, the other side of the river," says Rose. "He worked until ten at night, and on top of this he cut peat in the country for extra money. Dermot was only fifty-two when he died. Hardening of the arteries, we were told."

Dermot had to help raise the family after his father, my grandfather, drowned. Dermot had to take over as the eldest male in the family, and my mother looked up to him like a father. He'd been in the IRA when he was young, was dragged out of bed by the Black and Tans and taken half-dressed to jail for interrogation.

We always laugh at this family story because his younger brother kept right on sleeping, Marty snoring away as they bang on the door and a gang of men tromp into his bedroom in their tight boots and puttees and oversize tams and pull Dermot out of the same bed, it's *funny*, but then I realize I don't know if Dermot was thrown around, if he was conked on the head, stomped and bleeding in a room in the Castle or a cell in Kilmainham Gaol or the back of a British lorry, or if he was fired from his job afterward for being arrested and missing work.

They came to the big door on the river many times, men knocking and men hiding, country men running away over the city roofs. The house must have become known as a rebel house, the safe house becoming more risky. In the basement there was an old tunnel that bored under the river toward the barracks. Republicans up from the country stayed there often, up from the Swan, Athy, or villages near Kilkenny; fellows on the run from Cork or Kerry or coming to an *ard fheis* or an IRA meeting in the large upstairs room, organizing voters or parish branches or setting up Gaelic lessons or anti-conscription pledges or a man with a rusty pistol to deliver to a Sinn Féin contact in the city.

My grandparents were both from the country (beyond the Pale), and some rural areas were more radical, more Republican, than Dublin. The big liver-coloured house on the river, close to the train station, a hiding spot for a few days, a night, a moment. My grandfather drowned, but the night-time visits did not cease. My grandmother must have been involved, must have kept going, because the bashing at the door continued.

No one in the family seems curious about any of this now. What's more important to us eighty years later is that Marty didn't wake up with all the ruckus and fighting, that Marty kept snoring away. What's more important to us is that it's worth a laugh. Thus our unreliable histories are hatched, constructed, reconfigured.

Always thin, Aunt Rose says to me, poor Dermot worked and worked and worked and didn't have time to put flesh on his bones. A lovely man, Rose says.

Skinny Dermot becomes the surrogate father of the family, but his younger brother grows up to become his protector, my tough uncle Brendan knocking opponents down hard in Gaelic football if they touch Dermot. They hit Dermot only once, then Brendan crunches them the next chance he gets. Brendan tackles them and they stay tackled — a naked warning to leave his brother alone — the athletic younger man watching out for the thin older brother who had cared for him like a father, the older brother who had lost much of his childhood, who worked tirelessly until he died in harness.

"He looked out for me," Brendan said, "so I look out for him."

And in Canada my mother phones her son's house, confused,

wanting help, and she asks for her brother.

You mean your son?

"I want to speak to my brother," she insists. "You're a bitch," she says to her daughter-in-law. "Put my brother on the line!"

Mother, I think when I hear this, your dear brothers are long dead. Perhaps my mother is going back to a time when her older brothers looked out for family, looked out for her. Her husband is dead, every brother gone, all sisters but Bridie, her friends dead, even her doctor down with the dead men. Funeral follows funeral, obit after obit in the *Edmonton Journal* or the *San Diego Union-Tribune*. My mother wears old clothes when reading the paper to keep newsprint from darkening her good outfits.

She's in her eighties and alone with her teapot and crossword puzzles, no protector now, no one to tackle the opponents, the protectors mouldering in the cold, cold ground. My mother has one sister left out of a family of ten. They rarely speak or write to each other now. Choose one from Menu A, one from Menu B. Bridie's quiet green farmland in Ireland, with turf burning in the hearth by the mineshafts pawing down, and my mother's polished steel elevator shooting up to an overheated drywall apartment in Canada — continents of glass avenues and cables and mad ocean rolling rocks between the last two sisters.

Chapter Four

JURASSIC PARK IN DUBLIN'S OLDEST GAY CLUB

AUNT ROSE AND UNCLE BRENDAN'S SON PADRAIC, my favourite cousin, came out of the closet just after my 1981 trip. He didn't let me in on his secret. And no Irish relatives were inclined to phone Canada to say, Now, did you know your man is a little light in the loafers? A whole life I was unaware of.

The entrance to the club, down a lane, seems clandestine. A curly-haired man in a black suit coat pounds and kicks at the club's big door. On tractors, on fishboats, in alleys — always the same black suit coat.

"I'LL HAVE YOU BY THE BOLLOCKS!" he bellows. I assume he's just been turfed.

A big buzz-cut doorman leans out the entrance, glowers at him. But the doorman seems willing to wait out Bellowing Man rather than lay him out on the alley cobblestones. My cousin and I sneak past Bellowing Man, through the disputed portal, politely pretending not to notice the ruckus, and Padraic pays both our covers at a wicket. Steep cover just to go in and pay more for drinks inside, but pubs close early in Dublin and you have to know clubs that are open late. This is one of them.

Bad disco plays inside, which raises the question, Is there good disco? My cousin takes me to the "traditional" Irish pub side of the club. The male bartenders are dressed in Monty Python drag, full Maggie Thatcher frump. A funny idea, but it looks like the joke gets old after a few hours of adjusting your sweaty nylon wig and being run off your feet behind the bar.

I guess now I know he's gay. The place appears to be several smoky clubs smashed together: oak panels in the first room, where we stand at the bar; tortured black steel in another antechamber; a gyrating dance floor visible through a passageway, and above it Fillmore West psychedelic light shows splay and explode on a screen. Black stairs climb up to different territories and eras and colours and codes and preferences. Older patrons prefer the trad side: Jurassic Park, it's nicknamed, because of their age, our age, because we're dinosaurs now.

Padraic gives me a tour of all the different nooks and crannies, and he explains which patrons like which parts of the bar. Padraic is popular, waving to many men. A friend asks if he's giving me a tour of the club or of all his ex-boyfriends. I don't know Padraic. Why did I think I knew him? Why is it important to me? Years ago I thought we were close, but obviously I didn't have a clue. You never know anyone — a friend, a lover, a husband, a wife, a parent, a cousin — it's *impossible* to know someone. I learn this lesson over and over, but it never sinks in.

His friends in the club are surprised to hear that Padraic was hetero when I was here years back; his friends are intrigued, teasing Padraic.

"Did a good imitation," I say.

His friends laugh loudly, but not Padraic. Padraic doesn't like this new version of the old version, this tampering with his private history. Like most of us, Padraic doesn't care to alter his past now that it's settled nicely into place. I remember his girlfriend and their secret appointment with a clinic counsellor to try to get some form of birth control, which was almost impossible in Ireland just a few years ago. Now you can get Ribbed Fantasy condoms in any bar washroom. Still no divorce or abortion, though there is talk of an abortion ship anchored offshore like a pirate radio station.

Twenty years ago Padraic spent a summer with our family in Edmonton, working construction for my brother-in-law, buying Tim Hortons doughnuts on the way to work at six a.m. (no one in Ireland believed Padraic that Canadians ate doughnuts for breakfast), rolling a huge yellow packer on a steep hill and almost killing himself, cashing big paycheques and hanging out with my friends and girlfriends at lakeside keg parties and smoky bonfires out in the darkness of the Correction Line, playing road hockey on 132nd Street under the wineglass elms, hiking in the Rocky Mountains of Montana and Alberta, exploring Jasper and Banff and Waterton and Glacier Park and the Going-to-the-Sun Highway cut through the serrated peaks (several of us bundled up in the back of Don's pickup truck for a better view) where bighorn sheep lick salt from the highway.

Giant western landscapes, giant aprons of snow on the scree slopes falling below our feet, slapping mosquitoes, sleeping in thin orange tents while brawny bears smashed past in the nightmare dark, sleeping with my knife open — not to confront the giant bears, but to cut an X in my tent wall to escape should a roaring bear claw its way inside. Padraic and my friends drinking warm beer and driving gravel roads to Wizard Lake in rusty pickup trucks with cracked glass and the Lost Planet Airmen *Live at the Armadillo World Headquarters* cranked up: *Ain't never had too much fun!*

High in Montana's mountains we climbed rubble above the treeline, hiked past mountain goats with tiny suction-cup hooves, hiked past perfectly cut blocks of striped shale the size of big refrigerators; we swam in glacial lakes, icebergs all around us, the coldest water I've ever felt, my muscles seizing like a drowning man, can't move but desperate to be clean, sick of my own funky smell after days of hiking high in petal-hued clouds and giant windows of light. I have a funny photo of Padraic clowning around in a mountain meadow of asters and forget-me-nots, a pair of purple daisies jammed behind his glasses, giant daisies for eyes lending him a demented look.

Padraic tells me in 1997 that he thought someone cruised him in downtown Edmonton back in 1980, so many sunny years before. He knew back then. Alberta two decades ago was not exactly gay-friendly. It must have been difficult to cover up, to act like everyone else. He drove on the wrong side of the road coming back up from Montana; one weekend he wanted to drive to southern California's circus act, thinking it an hour or two from Alberta.

Padraic had a goofy, open quality about him, a hollow leg when it came to eating piles of potatoes or bread dunked into the iron frying pan.

"Ah, they don't know what's good for them," he'd say to my mother, as if they'd both live forever by eating bread made familiar with bacon grease. In the summer of 1980 there is no HIV, no Alzheimer's; there is only bacon frying merrily under my parents' sunny kitchen windows.

One summer afternoon we hauled in a big trunkful of empty beer cases. Flush with cash from the empties, Padraic and I stopped at an unfamiliar lounge for a cold one on a hot day but were refused service because we were barefoot and shirtless. In the trunk of my mother's Pontiac we found two pairs of golf shoes, and two shirts came to us by our diving headfirst (*legs kicking at heaven*) into a nearby Salvation Army dropoff box. The waitress laughed as, carefully and loudly, we came clicking in from the sun to the dark interior, bare feet half jammed into my mother and father's spiked golf shoes. My cousin Padraic was fun; great craic, as they say in Ireland.

That was the summer of 1980. I also spent a lot of time with Padraic in Ireland in the summer of 1981 — hung out in his room with his brother, Sharkey; double-dated, triple-dated; walked parts of northside Dublin that I never would have known or ventured into; hiked the Howth hills and cliffs at sunset, drove Wicklow's high spooky mist, and rode a fast train to the west, the Irish equivalent of Route 66. That history seems gone now, that history wiped clean.

My cousin Padraic, in fact, seems to date the beginning of his real life from *after* those years, immediately after my visit, and perhaps more significantly, after his father died. Ireland is made anew, and Padraic is made anew. Padraic's companion of fourteen years is dead. I don't ask but assume AIDS. We don't have a chance to talk of such things, though they're on my mind, in the air in the club. I don't ask Padraic if he's HIV positive. He seems healthy as a horse.

A happy cowboy swagger to his walk, my Irish cousin shows me his club, his head high and looking all about, greeting everyone and eager to take life in. Casual clothes, not a fashion plate, not a fop.

A young man with pointy Star Trek sideburns says brightly to another man, "Tell your lover to shave his balls. It's great." He waves his hands down toward his lap, and we all dutifully look at his lap as if we possess some handy X-ray vision from the back of a comic book.

"A little bristly when it grows back in, but still, it's great." He tells us that he marks "Shave pubes" regularly on his calendar.

I try to remain open-minded but involuntarily cringe, thinking of a razor down there. The other morning I had a dream of a rat stealing a cucumber in its teeth, swimming away. I think it was a picnic or a meal and the cuke belonged to me, though dream logic is not always clear. That seems a sexual dream, but the rat's sharp teeth. . . . (*Weasels ripped my flesh*.) I want to ask the man if he uses shaving cream or an electric, but I refrain. What if you cut yourself? I hope they don't notice another shudder. They may not notice the small details. Much of the club's pierced and buffed clientele is on various controlled substances, including heroin, Special K, crystal meth, percs, pinks, Talwin, OxyContin, Ecstasy, good old-fashioned cocaine, and of course, Guinness stout, the Free State opiate.

Up in Northern Ireland it's the infamous marching season for the Orangemen (Ulster Will Fight, and Ulster Will Be Right), time for rubber bullets and the arc of petrol bombs to flaming lorries, but you'd never know it in the south, here in Jurassic Park, here in Dublin's fair city, where the boys are so pretty, where the upcoming Hollywood heartthrob or latest boy band walks down the alley and in the door and there are no girls to scream for them (in disco space no one can hear you scream). No sense of history in the new party-as-a-verb Dublin. History means little to the antsy guy who strips off his shirt on the dance floor. Here in the aisles and on the dance floor they do not discuss the venerable debate of Armalite rifles versus the ballot box.

Here a drunk man roots madly at our feet, cursing, pushing us aside.

"What are you doing?" we ask him.

"I'm asking you to move!" he shouts back. He's lost a back-pack or package; he's lost something and is furious.

One of our group quips lightly, "Well, can you look farther down the bar?"

"That some kind of joke!" His voice is threatening; he seems ready to explode. Some in our party drift away from trouble (the Troubles). "That some kind of joke!"

I'm irritated by him, by my cousin's club, almost want a fight.

Like me, he's digging for something from earlier, from the past. He's digging down at our feet. I'm tempted to boot him a good one in the head. I wonder how many friends and lovers he has buried, how many funerals Padraic and his friends have attended. How many men who were alive here in 1981 are still alive?

Billy Bragg and Wilco are in town, someone says, cutting tracks for their Woody Guthrie CDs.

"How did that Martin Ferris with the Sinn Féin get so popular?"

The drunk man finds his pack right where we jokingly told him to go look.

"SEE!" he exclaims violently, swollen with indignation and pretzel logic. "It wasn't *fiction!*"

I shout back at him over the disco deluge, wondering if we're going to have a fist fight, a donnybrook, but he leaves glowering. I am relieved and disappointed.

The others who melted away return when it's safe: What was that all about?

I don't know what it was all about. We've been drinking pints for hours, and it's hot and so smoky that my throat hurts — there are no non-smoking sections in the new Ireland, and everyone smokes like a fucking chimney. Sick of crowds and the stink of tobacco, sick of looking at guys, and I hate the overkill disco soundtrack of my cousin's club, this *vida loca.*

In *Zoo Station*, Ian Walker's travel book about Berlin, Walker contends that criticizing disco is like criticizing the weather. Good idea, Ian, but I still hate this noisy club weather, the smoke, the boring whirlwind, the techno Sturm und Drang, marching music with lasers and scratching, the bass clubbing me like I'm a harp seal, clubbing bright-eyed and dark-eyed nightmare walkers doing the Frug and the shrug and the latest brilliant drug.

In another bar, the Front Lounge, a friendly woman from

Guelph, Ontario, chats about books and the Rookes and gives me a handbill (her part-time job) for a club that stays open late, óne pound off the cover charge with her flyer, which says, "The Mean Fiddler, Wexford Street, *Alien Night Life*." Her flyer features a striking yellow-and-blue bug-eyed alien face. It's very pleasant to talk to a woman again. I ask her out for tea the next day, and she says no.

The Mean Fiddler claims to play Radiohead, Eels, Pavement, Smiths, Yo La Tengo, Violent Femmes — bands with intelligent, depressing songs and some concession to melody. Can't we go there, can't we go to the Meaner? Shoegazer versus disco. Padraic prefers the George.

My ancestors, horse riders and cattle farmers on both sides, went through the Dark Ages, Cromwell's vicious yobs, slaughters and plantations, the Flight of the Geese, the Great Hunger, the endless diaspora, the Black and Tans, the civil wars, and I'm drunkenly debating disco versus guitars as if it's the fecking fate of the free world.

A day later I watch them taking in the bad news. Afternoon drinks, the Long Hall bar, where some of Padraic's friends find they've been fleeced.

"He's gone, left the country."

"You're messing."

Their health club closed just after they paid up for five-year contracts. The owner folded his tent, fleeing the country with their money — our urban sophisticates are surprised, they knew the man, thought they knew him, a friend, one of the gang.

Health clubs bite the dust all the time in Canada, but the idea seems fresh and shocking to my new acquaintances. Their puzzlement and loss is somehow endearing, makes me like them more. Now they must seek a new health club. Must look good in a new cotton T-shirt, must look young and limber in the mirrors.

Musn't look old or weary or sick. *Slàinte!* To your health!

"Joe around today?"

"You're the footballer. Knock about with Riley, you do."

"They're all mad."

"Cracker football player. Made a few bob over there in Sweden."

"Pays well. Went to school with him. Bit of a hothead. Couldn't read or write."

"Nothing's changed." They laugh.

The Long Hall is a beautifully detailed bar on George Street, with a red tin ceiling and giant windows, stained glass and leaded glass and Victorian gilt mirrors and chandeliers, but the room still looks a bit rough, dented, which I like — not a faux Paddy pub tarted up for the tourists (for tourists like me).

The footballer counts his coins and orders a huge bottle of cider.

"When ya doing the second part of your Guinness course?" he asks the bartender.

The bartender says, "What? Speak southside English."

"Southside," the footballer grumbles.

"I denno," the bartender continues. "Rang the fecker up, supposed to be tomorrow."

The big clock is dead. The sun's white, quivering light bounces into the room from on high, but when the huge mobile wall of a double-decker bus labours past, the pub goes weirdly dark, an interior eclipse.

"American?"

"Canadian."

"Same thing."

Another night in Jurassic Park. There is no uniform look here, no solidarity, which surprises me. I see solitary men who remind me of my Tory uncle in England: bald, portly, addicted to burnt beef and Yorkshire pudding, not working out or watching their figures, not into gay gym culture, not into dancing the night away with their shirts stripped. Just sitting alone with a pint. What Prufrock thoughts and wants and regrets lurk behind those impassive, jowly masks? Whom do they miss?

Cousin Padraic: my drowned grandfather Michael is also his grandfather Michael. I forget, selfishly think of Michael as mine alone. I meet an Irish woman at the George and then wonder, If she's here, does that mean she's a lesbian or is she slumming (if you can use that term where everyone is so well dressed)? Thursday night is Lesbian Night. What night is it now? Can't recall. Have another drink, so. Padraic thinks one old bachelor uncle, Marty, a favourite of us all and now deceased, was secretly gay.

"I'm as sure *he* was gay as I'm sure *I'm* gay," Padraic insists. "A gay man can tell another gay man."

I remember reading John Rechy's *City of Night* two decades ago in my uncle's cramped apartment. Marty always called me son, stressed family, was no good at decorating, didn't notice the cockroaches. Padraic may be right, or it may be wishful thinking. I ask some of my cousins in Ireland, and they all think it possible, as do my sisters and brothers in Canada. This is probably not what the older members of our families want to hear, to *out* someone after his death. He would be furious at me for asking or talking about it.

My aunt in England became good friends with Marty during the war. "I used to babysit for your parents in Oxford, and Marty would stay and talk with me for hours." In her London rose garden she says to me, "Marty never married."

I decide to risk mentioning Padraic's theory, and she holds up a finger as if to stop me, admonish me, but instead she says, "Back then I was told he had a secret friend in Oxford. I never knew what was meant."

As children we were given the story of our favourite uncle's wartime heartbreak: Back home on leave, didn't he catch his girlfriend with someone else? Marty turned away in sorrow, turned away in shock and anger, and re-enlisted in the US army. He was in Hawaii during the war and in Berlin later, during the Cold War airlift. A family rumour that he left the army in Germany under a cloud, something about missing mess supplies and the black market.

Marty had a history of marching to his own drummer, a history of losing jobs. Burning barrels at Jameson's Whiskey, his skin breaking out at the New Jersey farm and nursery, waving his cook's knife at a customer bothering a waitress at the Philadelphia Automat. His sister Josie adept at any job and Marty fired or storming the exit.

Confirmed bachelor for eons, small apartment full of books and newspapers, minimal furniture, reading constantly and smoking like crazy, non-filter Chesterfields, along with twenty-five cups of coffee a day (if I'm lying, I'm dying), artificial creamer rather than milk or cream, salt slathered on everything, even salt on his toast. Marty favoured gravy, greasy food, coffee cake, shunned vegetables, and he lived into his eighties. Overly generous, like his mother, Mary, in Dublin — if he had money he gave it to you, never saved, gave his nephews and nieces American cash, brought piles of presents to my parents over the years, visited them often in Oxford and later in Canada, gave them a silver tea set, and forced them to the Italian liner when my father balked at leaving Oxford for the New World and his new job at the clinic in Edmonton.

My uncle hated the Kennedys, had the family Irish temper, its explosions of grumpiness about the world at large: "THESE DAMN BANK MACHINES PUTTING PEOPLE OUT OF WORK! THEY'RE ALL BLOODY NOOTS! LOOK AT THESE EE-JITS!" Marty never gave a damn what others thought, and Padraic liked that about him.

"Marty always told it like it was," Padriac says. "The only one in the family who did." Yet if he had a secret, then he did give a damn about that, didn't tell it exactly like it was. But who could blame him.

Our uncle visited us every second year in Canada to take us out for blue steak and talk a blue streak at the Boiler Room, slip us five-dollar bills, ten-dollar bills, US twenties, American presidents (even though he had little money); every second year my aged uncle riding Greyhounds across a blurred continent with his sore feet getting worse, furious when he was no longer allowed to smoke his Chesterfields on the bus.

Marty bought a car once, way back when, reportedly a Model T Ford.

"I stalled the damn thing on a hill and I gave the car away to a friend, never drove again." The years he didn't travel to Canada he went back to Ireland, alternating: one year going west across giant rattling cornfields, one year going east across the sea.

Which year, I wonder, was my uncle's final trek on the Greyhound? The care home, the end of mobility, end of something. His father slips under the canal; my cousin slips away to Miami, Barcelona, Greece; my uncle slips away, another lost highway. I miss his visits, his blarney, his rage. Who was his secret friend in Oxford?

The funny thing is that even if he was gay (and I don't know), my grumpy uncle would have hated this place, hated our bartenders in frumpy Margaret Thatcher drag and a disco-inferno herd jumping around like a right bunch of headers to a Village People revival (or the Chemical Brothers or retro jungle or Nine Inch Nails) and glittering boy-men chatting merrily of the many clear advantages of taking a razor to their balls, of riding bareback, of daring the monster, daring the death warrants. Jurassic Park would not be a haven for my dear old uncle in his thick glasses and rumpled corduroy suit the colour of orange peels.

A tall man leaving Jurassic Park kisses me quickly on the mouth. This surprises me.

"I think I want a son," Padraic says. He has seen what having a son has done for his brother, Sharkey. "Changed him completely. A new man," Padraic claims, impressed by Sharkey's transformation. We're all transformed, all new men. Jurassic men. I remember us hiking in Montana, high above the treeline and monkey flowers, sleeping at night with an open knife. I wonder about Padraic's future — wonder if Padraic will live long enough to have his son, wonder if Padraic will escape the bear coming in the thin tent.

Chapter Five

COUSIN SHARKEY'S
REDNECK SECTION

PADRAIC'S YOUNGER BROTHER, SHARKEY, drives me anywhere I want. Sharkey's busy, has a job and a growing family, but he finds the time. He's a good guy, salt of the earth. He's a garda, an Irish policeman.

Sharkey the garda says he heard a joke. "A teacher asks her schoolkids to use the word 'beautiful' in a sentence. A girl says, 'Last night the sunset on the Wicklow hills was beautiful.' 'Very good,' teacher says. 'Now then, can anyone use it twice in one sentence?' Boy puts his hand up, says, 'Me sister said she's pregnant, and me father says, 'Beautiful, just fooking beautiful.'"

"SHARKEY!" protests his mother, Rose, from the backseat. "You never heard such language in *our* house. Where did you pick it up? You use it and don't even *know*!"

This is true, but there is some irony here, since Rose uses the word "thing" in almost every sentence and doesn't know. How was the movie? Oh, it was *thing*. My mother has always been the same way: Mrs. Thing called.

Both my Irish cousins are funny, both with the gift of the

gab, a certain mischievous charm and easy grins, the ability to tease and the ability to butter you up. Both enjoy taking you for a pint. A few slight differences, though.

Padraic is a single nomad, globe-trotting to Miami, San Francisco, Spain, Brussels, Bath, Bristol. He likes art and books, sketches old doorways and iron gates around Dublin, works in heritage architecture and is fixing up a brick Victorian rowhouse in north Dublin's city core, not far from the James Joyce Centre. The northside is less fashionable than the southside. Padraic doctors his tiny hedge with an electric trimmer and cuts through the orange extension cord and worries about his walled garden lacking water in the summer if he's gone away (Going away? But I've just arrived), worries about spots on the ivy he has planted in the back.

"Ivy is pretty tough, isn't it?"

"Now if it's Padraic's ivy, it'd be very sensitive," his brother, Sharkey, joked at Rose's house — this before I knew for sure that Padraic was gay. Was Sharkey hinting?

Neglected northside Victorian tenements are more affordable than Georgian buildings, which are more striking and solid and so were gentrified first. So many lovely buildings fell into neglect over two centuries after the Act of Union and the flight of the fops, so many felt the wrecking ball or burnt or crashed down on their poor tenants. I must ask Padraic what they call buildings that are pre-Georgian. Gothic? Restoration? Late Viking? Stone Age Revival? The cost of Dublin real estate is through the roof and no sign of stopping. Better take Victorian if you can. Padraic's long-time partner is recently dead. They bought the brick house together, worked on fixing it up.

Padraic both denies and admits his role as family clown. They like me in that role, he informs me, so I'll play the clown if that makes them happy. But it's not really me, he implies. He talks of this casually, as if he is above it all, suave, mature, but I can tell that the childhood reputation irritates him.

It's not really him, but I have memories of Padraic almost crashing the family car several times when my mother was here years ago, my mother terrified and mad behind us in the backseat. It's not him, but Padraic cuts the orange electrical cord into smaller and smaller pieces, and he keeps us all waiting for hours at Rose's house. He bounces in the door and says sorry, he was "lifestyle shopping" for a trip with a friend to Spain. He parks his car for us to use while he's in Spain but neglects to leave the car keys, blocking the drive and his mother's garage, so no one can move *any* of the cars.

Sharkey's life is a contrast: a job with the gardái, plain-clothes; a pretty wife and small boy and another baby on the way. He is rooted in the postwar suburbs: a cozy house on the same street as his mother's, the street he grew up on, except these semi-detached houses originally worth 20,000 Irish pounds are now worth 200,000 or more, which is similar to what happened to my parents' bungalow in the Alberta oil boom. Two Irish brothers, same womb, same parents and grandparents, same city, but living on different planets.

In Sharkey's cozy house we listen to 2-Tone, Madness blaring, and get nostalgic about ska while messily staining stairs and doors and eating and drinking like bachelors with our take-out cartons and big green box of Heineken. Sharkey's wife is out of town visiting her family in Wexford, and Sharkey and I are supposed to be renovating while she's gone, but it's become a bit of a last-minute effort, since we tend to go out on the town more than we stay in to work on the house.

Sharkey likes golf with his boss, making sure his boss wins. Sharkey has little in the way of books or art in his house, likes TV, music, a pint at the local, makes a beautiful, carefully sliced BLT, which is just the ticket after a late night at the Dollymount pub by the Bull Wall. In some respects Sharkey is *more* conservative than Padraic, but in his own way Sharkey is *less* conservative, more irreverent, freewheeling.

In 1981, their father puzzled by both brothers: Padraic failing the summer courses that he was taking because he had failed his spring courses; the once-proud backyard garden now a neglected ruin, a kingdom of weeds; Sharkey working a flex-time job where, because of his sleeping late in the morning and golfing in the afternoons, he was so far behind in hours that it would take a century or two to catch up.

"I don't understand," his father would say. "You're never at work."

Work was certainly not like that when their father started a job. In fact, Brendan lost his first good job because he was put in jail after some march or protest, and his forceful mother, Mary, had to intervene at the office to get his position back. Brendan became much more conservative after that scare; it changed him.

Sharkey eventually lost his flex-time job and became a policeman, something his father disapproved of. His father wanted Padraic in the sciences, but Padraic hated the courses and wanted to take literature and art. As a teen Brendan had a scholarship but had to give it up and go to work. He wants his children to get ahead, do what he didn't.

A hard-nosed father puzzled by both of them, and it looked desperate as he lay dying in 1982. Now one son is designing and fixing buildings and architectural projects, one son enforces the country's laws and doctrines, and both walk through solid lives with vocations, pursuits, friends and partners, houses, respect, and joie de vivre. Both travel the world, both are well liked, well thought of. Nothing is fixed, nothing what it may seem.

Their father, Brendan, dies too young — like his father, Michael, like his brother Dermot — and their father doesn't see how well his sons have done. A lesson. I must remember this when my three sons are maxing out my credit card and crashing my car through the world's back fences.

Chapter Six

SHITE AND ONIONS
IN THE NATIONAL LIBRARY

AUNT ROSE AND I HUNCH INSIDE DUBLIN's National Library, torturing our eyes, poring over myopic rolls of microfilm, searching the cylinders for Michael, my drowned Irish grandfather.

My mother always told me that Michael drowned the very day of the huge funeral procession for Michael Collins, the famous Irish revolutionary and commander-in-chief of the government's war council of 1922, shot in a rural ambush. This is part of my morbid interest. So I have a specific date to check in the newspapers of the time.

In the National Library my aunt and I filled out forms and sat in an office and were granted permission from a genial nun, moved into different chambers and more forms and staff, and finally were sent up the marble stairs to wreck our eyes at the spinning wheel. Cacophony of drills, buzz saws, and jackhammers from renovations to the old building; men hammering in the hallway, men moving on the roofs.

The microfilm is in a temporary room — a fireplace mantle as tall as my head, lovely tilework surrounding a huge iron grate and hearth. Bright summer sunlight makes it almost impossible to read the murky screen. Both our heads are bent inside an ancient low-tech microfilm projector, a big black box with the front open and a white surface on the bottom. Rose drapes her black coat over our heads to block the sunlight, and leaning into the box, we resemble nineteenth-century photographers.

I have no letters from my grandparents, no bits of furniture passed down, no pocket watch, very little by way of stories or mythology. They're a blank to me, ciphers. I have almost nothing. I possess just one photo of my lost grandfather, Michael, a turn-of-the-century family portrait taken when Michael and Mary had only two children, not the nine he left when he drowned (they had ten children in all, but one daughter died before he drowned). In the photo they look young and happy, and they dress well, look good in their clothes. Michael's eyes playful, a contrast to most dour portraits of the era.

I can see his bemused face in my mind without looking at the old photograph. His head tilts slightly, a calm half-smile on his face, the confidence of a physical man comfortable with the camera and the wait, with his rough suit and vest, comfortable with himself or deft at hiding his doubts. Maybe the photographer was telling jokes, knew them.

Michael's hair is cropped close, and a hawk nose juts out over a big moustache. His collars are high, Edwardian, and under his coat is a fancy waistcoat. He's a hard worker in good shape: no fat at his neck or stomach. His dark tough hand rests on his wife's shoulder. Both from the country, but they met in the city.

My grandmother Mary Doyle looks pretty and buxom in her high-necked blouse with a tight waist, her thick hair tied up loosely in a chignon. The two young children must be Kathleen and Dermot. Kathleen has a pudgy moonface, short bangs, wears a loose sundress, bare calves above little leather lace-up ankle boots. Kathleen who dies at three, soon after the photo; my mother, Kay, unofficially named after her. (Her parents, too superstitious to legally name my mother after a dead child, supplied two other official monikers for the birth certificate but called her Kay at home, and the tag stuck.) And Dermot, a smiling baby with pudgy cheeks, quizzical raised eyebrows, and what looks to be a nascent Mohawk haircut. Dermot who becomes the man of the family after Michael drowns; Dermot who works and works and has a hard life and dies at fifty-two. And here he is an unknowing baby. All of them in the photo handsome and dying too soon.

At the time of the family photo they still had to be living in the artisan's cottage on Malachi Road in Arbour Hill, since they couldn't have moved to the big doomed house on Usher's Island until 1915 or 1916. I had assumed they lived at 11 Usher's Island for a donkey's age, but a Thom's City Directory lists number 11 as an iron merchant's until 1916, when it is termed a tenement. My mother born Easter 1916.

Did he ever think that, a full century after he joked with the photographer and stared at the lens, a callous grandson would come snooping through his addresses and backpages? Just two children in the old photo, a small family compared with what was to come. He can't wait to get his pretty wife home, her top open, the bride stripped bare. They must like each other. My mother was sick during every pregnancy with six children — years of nausea in Oxford and western Canada. I wonder if it was the same for my grandmother in Dublin with ten children. She looks so young compared with later photographs. Later, Mary always wore black. She became bigger. What they call "a fine woman."

I sense that Michael — like Padraic and Sharkey, like my own five brothers and sisters — can be a funny man, that he doesn't take the event of the portrait seriously, but I'm sure he can be deadly serious, has light and dark, has the family temper when crossed, has a hand hard as the oak he cuts. He liked books and reading, but he'd laugh at my soft hand, my avoidance of hard labour and punching a clock.

I know his hand is tough and hard because he was a master cooper with the St. James's Gate Guinness Brewery, once the largest brewery in the world. "Working for Uncle Arthur," he termed it, after Arthur Guinness, who, with a 9,000-year lease, took over a failed brewery in 1759, the same year that Wolfe and Montcalm were shot and bleeding to death across from each other on the Plains of Abraham in Quebec.

My grandfather Michael made oak barrels with his bare hands and a blade like a machete, transforming heavy planks of English oak and Quebec oak into flawlessly curved staves, his blade whacking close to his muscled skin like a meat cleaver hitting hard and sure, listing the stave, carving a square into a curve, measuring those precise cuts with his eye, using no nails, no screws, slicing those oak pieces into a watertight fit, a perfect circle of sticks. Adze, drawknife, hollow knife, driver saw, cleaver, iron jigger, maul, croze, and men crowded together in shirtsleeves, hammering hoops in clouds of steam, the high roof of iron and skylights like a train station, big fires and the aroma of wet oak being heated. Years and years to get the knack for it, apprenticing up to seven years with a master. Hard to get in, but a very good job to have in those days, the cream.

Uncle Marty never did get the knack, apprenticing as a cooper for Jameson's Whiskey across the river. Wrecked more barrels than I made, Marty joked, and then the cooper teaching him was picked up for being in the IRA, and that was that.

At Guinness, Michael uses a steam bell to cover the barrel, to make the hard oak moist and pliable, and a windlass cinches one end at a time to allow the iron hoops on — several iron hoops pressing the staves tightly together to give the barrel its shape, its bent stripes, its sublime curves. Michael collects and burns oak shavings for a fire on the ground to char, or blaze, the inside of the new cask, to seal it, tilting the cask to heighten the draft as the smoky flames roar up through the wooden circle.

Dark wood, different sizes, some monstrous barrels higher than a man: Firkins and Kilderkins, Ale Puncheons, Union Butts,

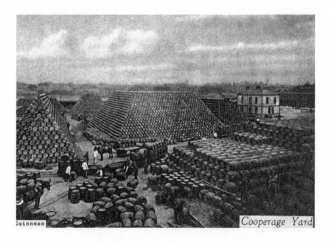

Cooperage Yard

Porter Butts, Barm Hogsheads, London Hogsheads, or Bosnia Export Hogsheads. The Stave Yards, the Coopers' Dressing Shed, the Branding Room, the Broken Cask Yard, the Cask Cleaning Shed. Need a man with a good nose to sniff out barrels that have gone sour.

We clean about 12,000 casks daily by washing scrubbing and steaming.

Yards of lumber in neat stacks, towering stacks of oak and mountains of barrels, flat-topped pyramids of barrels three or four storeys high, like temples, giant Mayan pyramids of barrels in the yard, shipping barrels full of stout down the River Liffey, barges two deep at Victoria Wharf, and launches and steamers and schooners rolling to the far ends of the earth from Michael's hard hands.

The brewing of porter is extensively carried on, and the number of hogsheads exported in 1909 was 539,773, in addition to bottled stout exported, 67,384 barrels and 11,835 cases.

My grandfather Michael belonged to the Regular Dublin Operative Coopers' Society, 5 Blackhall Street, Dublin (its charter granted by King Charles II in 1666). My cousin Peggy in Philadelphia says on the phone that Michael's father, our great-grandfather, was also a cooper. At least two of his brothers were coopers.

Coopering — building and repairing barrels, from the Middle English *cowper* or Latin *cupa* for cask or cup — was likely a profession older than shipbuilding. A hard profession to get into — it helped to be a cooper's son — and a hard craft to master, though easy to lose; a link to the bustling guilds of the Middle Ages, back to the first people to work with wood and fire.

In sepia photographs of wharves or warehouses or storefronts, oak casks everywhere in the background, in doorways, in the side alley, out back, perhaps similar to the way we employ and discard pop cans and boxes. Salt, salted fish, flour, molasses, tobacco, gunpowder, stinking whale oil, drinking water, whiskey, brandy, rum, wine, India Pale Ale. Northside Dublin has a Cowper Street. Every shack or mansion has casks; every general store, every pier, every prairie schooner crossing the wastes, every cellar, and in the deep hold of every ship, big barrels or butts laid on skids, bungholes up and free of the dirty bilge water. The term "scuttlebutt" comes from the sailors' gossip at the ship's drinking-water barrel, or butt, like office talk at the water cooler.

How many oak casks did Michael char? How many created or restored, planed and shaved? Have I seen one of his barrels travelled to a polite patio, with scarlet flowers waving in its circle? All his precise work gone, history now; a ghost's craft, lost with their stiff leather aprons.

"It went very fast," says my cousin James in his Mercedes. "Only took a year or two to kill the trade." Dermot witnessed its death throes before he died in 1959. The Dubliners sing a song, "Rare Ould Times," that laments the loss of a cooper's trade, his house, and his love. It could be about my uncle.

Metal casks, then the newer metal kegs, doomed this society, drowned this ancient craft. It vanished quickly. Barrel staves on the Phoenicians' sunny shores and casks on Roman piers and in Black Plague alleys flowing with gin and fleas and Norwegian rats running to a child holding a purple plastic Gameboy, the quiet eye of the late twentieth century, the end of the line, except for Ye Olde Pioneer Village theme parks (Hey, kids, look at these extremely fascinating barrels!).

James says, "Guinness kept some of the coopers on to make a line of wooden furniture until the last lads retired."

In Dublin's National Library the 1922 newspapers are full of raids and ambushes, snipers at the window, shots from the hedge, shots in the hot head, dragged from the warm bed as my IRA uncles were dragged from bed in those years, dragged to fields, killed in a dark, flea-bitten cinema, bullets and smoke in the flickering light, or one man shot four times, yet somehow their metal missed the essence, somehow he survived to tell the tale.

Michael might have known some of the names, where the bodies were buried. Why am I so interested in Michael, the drowned man? No one else is. I suppose I seek something official instead of the shifting, murky family versions of his death.

The Dublin version: Rose and other relatives were told that Michael drowned right in town, drowned in the River Liffey saving children, a hero giving his life to Anna Livia. In Philly they also heard a river in the city, but my mother always told me a canal in the country.

Some versions mentioned a fast whirlpool in the water pulling him down, and some suggested that alcohol was a factor, that a few of the men had stopped at pubs out in the country and were paloothered, paralytic, and had gone for a quick dip on a warm day and slipped under, but my mother says that her father didn't drink, that she didn't see it in the house except when someone visited and they'd call out for a bottle to be brought in.

Another version: my mother believes her father's heart stopped from the shock of cold water, and a doctor tells me this does happen. *Cardiac arrest causes many deaths attributed to drowning.* My mother wants me to see a doctor to have my heart looked at, just in case. Nearly everyone over the years agreed that Michael couldn't swim, yet Aunt Bridie tells me she thought him to be a good swimmer. It'd be nice to know more. The contradictions and different versions made me curious as a kid, and the fact that he drowned the exact day of Michael Collins's extravagant funeral made it stick in my head. To me the two Michaels were inseparable.

Because of my grandfather's death by drowning my eye is now drawn to tales of water in Dublin's National Library's old newspapers: swimmers, ships sinking, bathtubs, drownings. It seems so easy to drown, to just disappear in the alien world of weeds and wake, the unuttered words, the lungs going to gills. The body wants to go a few inches under.

Steamer Goes Down Over 200 Drowned Terrible Tragedy of the Sea

Man arrives home 10 a.m., gone two hours, cottage locked and smoking, 2 beds on fire and 2 girls, two and four, drowned in half-full tub. Wife left at 9:15, wanted in connection with incident.

The Liver Is the Road to Health

Children in Bath Looked Asleep
"I Done It," Woman Sobs in Dock

Scrolling the old Irish newspapers takes forever, is dizzying. Digging up the past is harder and more tedious than I expected. The past won't cooperate. Drowning is so much faster, maybe ninety seconds, a few minutes.

My aunt and I struggle to make the big baulky machine focus its lens, struggle to thread and scroll old metal reels, scanning torn pages of newsprint converted to film, tiny articles and headlines and banns and ads and comics, blurred print and photos, weird fonts swimming, miles of pages looking for that one name, Rose and I looking for that one entry that means something to me or the family.

King's County Burnings
Fine Mansions Given to Flames

Woman Directs Ambush

Saved from Drowning Fishing for Crabs
Fell in Strong Current

Prompt and Plucky Action

Gored by a Bull

Ten Rules for Longer Life

An older man, two projectors to our right, bellows: "SHITE AND ONIONS, CAN SOMEONE HELP ME WITH THIS BLOODY FILM?"
A librarian shows up, tries to soothe him.
"IF YOU SEND ME DOWN THOSE BLOODY STAIRS ONE MORE TIME!"
Drills, grinders, and hammers and white-haired researchers shouting, "shite and onions": This is the wildest, most raucous library I've ever been in. Ireland seems inherently noisy, lively, crazed, more so since I've come here directly after seeing rather (*rawther*) reserved relatives in England. I try to keep reading, searching.

Michael Collins Lying in State in General's Uniform

Hands Hold Crucifix & Beads of Rosary

"Aren't the Boys Great," He'd Say

43

Canada Wants More People, Less Government, Reduce Debt,
Says Mackenzie King

In the library I am seeing the same articles and headlines
reporting Michael Collins's assassination that my Irish grandfather read at his home on Usher's Island, at his leisure after
walking home from work at the Coopers' Shed just down the road.
We inhabit the same roads, the same century. He's the same age as
I am. He looks a bit like my eldest brother, a bit like my younger
brother. I wonder if he has a favourite chair. Mary and Michael
live at what was once a good address, a gentleman's house in 1850,
though it's on its slow way down by the time of the Irish civil war.
My grandparents are not rich, and the buildings on the quays are
a little scruffy, but Michael and Mary may be seen as social
climbers, with shelves of books and a prized rosewood piano,
fanlights and plasterwork, generous rooms and massive beams and
doorposts and newels, silver and china, iron rails and tiny black-
and-white tiles outside the front entrance, and domestic help,
though this likely is in exchange for room and board rather than
any grand salary.

At sixteen my grandmother Mary came to the city to work as
domestic help for the Cleeves, who had a dairy; a slavey fresh
from the farm and few jobs around for females, especially a
culchie from the country. Now she's hiring girls as help, moving
from below the stairs to above the stairs.

There is no equivalent in our time to the status a cooper
enjoyed in Victorian or Edwardian times. There is no job like it
now. Michael apprentices as long as a doctor. Michael could be
considered working class, but his job is the absolute top, one of
the best to be had in Dublin; he is almost prosperous. Guinness
has liberal benefits and a medical plan ahead of its time. My
mother does not go without shoes, though many neighbourhood
kids are barefoot in all seasons. His taxes are far higher than what

labourers or dockers pay. Men in the trades didn't mix with labourers at the pub after work.

My mother rides a brown scooter (only choices then are black and brown). Mary is famous for buying beautiful oak and mahogany furniture at the many pawnshops and auction houses on the quays, at a time when such fine old furniture is not valued, entire dining room and bedroom sets going for a song. When her children grow up and marry, she sets them up each time with a household of auction furniture. She set up Bridie and Josie with a boarding house of their own, but their hearts weren't in it.

Mary's large house on the Liffey is only blocks from the Liberties and the Coomb, some of the worst, vermin-ridden tenement slums in Europe, where a hungry family of twenty may live in one room in a chopped-up building full of such smelly rooms, no plumbing and chiggers bite you red and raw in your straw mats, and you pawn and redeem your worn, worthless clothes every week in a kind of strange shell game and the pawn-shop is your savings and loan.

Where the tenement stairs, once carpeted and grand with Georgian lords and ladies, are rotting through and insect cities hide behind inches of damp wallpaper and the buildings occasionally collapse on their landlord's massed tenants or burn up and burn down from the hundreds of lit candles and oil lamps and coal fires.

Where TB and typhus and diphtheria sweep through like express trains to take off tiny children or whole families. Where neighbours and shopkeepers and shawlies and barflies chip in for coffins and a decent wake with whiskey and a bite to eat. Where all of them help out with what they can, stretching a penny. My mother's grim three-storey tenement is a palace compared with the Liberties.

In his palace I see Michael Lyons sitting by a lace-curtain window, late-summer light moving like wind up the glimmering river, smoking his pipe, popping open a corked bottle of black porter or hop-bitters, reading his buff-coloured newspaper after work, as I like to do, reading of the Irish civil war's mayhem, the daily murders and reprisals, Mutt and Jeff comics at the top of page five, just above the prisoners tied to mines and blown into shreds of flesh.

City Ambush — Bullets in Chest

Woman on Trial in London

Smoke Irish Cigarettes

Illness After Eating Sandwiches

Eleven Bombs, Railway Line Torn Up Again

Harnessing the River Liffey to Cost £1,000,000

Light and Power for the Whole City

The girls are noisy playing on the wide wooden stairs; the turkey cock cries from the big backyard, where it chases one of the many boys, and a train whistles and steams at nearby Kingsbridge Station. With so many children born to Mary by 1922 it must have been a lively household, especially since they all sang and danced and played instruments. The ruined, cheerless house I look at now was once lovely and lively. I imagine Michael apprenticed under his father, but I don't know how he made the move to the city and Guinness. I'm told over and over in Dublin that Guinness looked favourably on only those Catholics with military connections. Was it easier because his father and brothers were coopers, or was it because his brother Patrick was in the British cavalry? Funny that his brother was British cavalry and Michael was IRA — an odd mix, yet common in many Irish families. Athletic associations and Irish-language groups might have led to the IRA, that was common enough, but I also think it was the family connections to the farming country he and Mary hailed from.

In Ballsbridge I pay a visit to Leo, a woman with a man's name, a good friend of my mother's from nursing. Leo was a Fleming before she married, and my grandmother knew her family well. The Flemings ran a pub and a factory near Mary's childhood farm. My aunt Bridie knew them in the Swan when she moved down there with her husband, Willie, who drove a truck for the factory. The factory drivers from the country stayed at Usher's Island.

I ask about the house on Usher's Island being a safe house during the Tan War and after. There is no hesitation. "Mary was friends with the Flemings down in the country. All of the Flemings down there were volunteers and IRA," says Leo's husband, Liam, in a placid voice. Wearing a tie in his own house, a tie and a blue pullover sweater, Liam has the slightly formal look of a retired banker or executive. In their well-appointed house near Sydney Parade, it's odd to hear them talk calmly about the IRA and "fellas on the run" staying at my mother's house. The old IRA, a long time ago, a different galaxy. Now the IRA is in Colombia doing coke. Now the IRA breaks your leg with bats or a nail-studded board. Now they're considered thugs (A bunch of t'ugs, vicious vigilantes) who shouldn't be invited to the table for a democratic election.

"Uncle Paddy was IRA," says Liam. "He was sentenced to death, though he escaped execution. Paddy wrecked his cell, wouldn't wear prison garb. 'Committed no crime,' Paddy said.

They had him in a straitjacket, tried to force him into prison garb, but he wouldn't wear it. Cell named after him in Portlaoise Prison."

Leo's daughter is back home with two sons after fifteen years in Canada. "I want to go back to Canada, feel more Canadian than Irish now," she says, telling me that Dublin business circles are still a little old-fashioned regarding women.

"I used to visit Ma Lyons at Usher's Island," Leo says, "and your grandmother, she always made me two boiled eggs mashed in a cup with salt and pepper and a bit of butter mixed in and good bread; I loved the way she did up the eggs for me." I remember liking this same dish as a child.

"I knew Ma Lyons before I knew your mother, Kay. I was interested in nursing, and she put me in touch with Kay, who was already in London. Kay was a great help, got me started, took me under her wing. We trained in the same place, Putney, and we remained friends ever since. Wrote each other a long letter every Christmas. I had no reply this Christmas, and I wondered. Kay was very good to me." This is the reason for my phone call and visit, to explain that my mother is having trouble writing a letter now, is losing her memory.

"Ma Lyons used to air out her brown habit, a Franciscan habit, like a monk's, a tertiary. I think she was with St. Francis on Merchant's Quay — this brown habit and a Franciscan scapular that goes around your neck. This is what she'd wear when she was dead, and she'd have it hanging up there to air it out a bit. Ma Lyons lived on the second floor at that time, had her own bedroom and a great big living room and a little kitchen up there with a gas stove and her brown Franciscan habit and scapular."

Leo and her husband give me cake and tea and Heineken. My grandmother's scapular reminds Leo of a time she was down in the country during the war.

"I was back visiting and there was a man who was quite ill,

and as a favour I was asked to give him his injections. This was a 'friend of a friend' thing, but not really a friend who asked me the favour, if you know what I mean. I didn't want to, but along I went. It didn't help, as the old boy died," Leo says.

"Now there was a man in the county who would come into your home and prepare the body, and would I help him too? This was my holiday, my leave. So I got soap and water to wash the corpse. In the hospital we used Dettol, but soap and water is fine at home. You wash and plug — stuff wool or cloth in the nostrils, ears, any opening; plug up the holes to keep the fluids from coming out later. I turn away to my basin of water, and doesn't the man heft the body off the bed and lay him on the floor. What on earth is he doing?

"'Easier that way,' the man says. I put a chair against the door so the family doesn't see this. They had a special tin trunk full of sheets, tableclothes, crucifixes, everything you needed for last rites. Most people had this prepared. Down on the floor we get the man's body in his habit and then put the scapular around his neck.

"'Musn't forget his pash-port,' the man says in his country accent. He smoothes the scapular over the corpse's chest. 'Musn't forget his pash-port.'

"The family gave me a glass of sherry and a sweet biscuit in appreciation. The next day I went back to the war."

I had thought this visit might be depressing, a solemn duty to my mother, but I greatly enjoy meeting Leo and her family, enjoy hearing of her visits to the house at number 11 and her cup of mashed eggs and salty butter and tea with Ma Lyons up on the second floor.

It's likely that Michael heard about the big house at work, since Usher's Island is so close to Guinness, but his IRA connections might have led him to the house or helped with it. A tunnel could be handy, as would the proximity to the railway station to the country, the roads and the river, the many rooms, and the rooftop exit. And Michael did make a leap from a small artisan's cottage to a rather large building. His IRA links would be a secret in his new city neighbourhood.

This was before independence and the Irish civil war. Was it a secret from his brother Patrick in the British cavalry? Perhaps his IRA associations led in some way to Michael's death in the country during the civil war. My gut feeling is that this is not so, though Dublin was infamous for its informers and revenge killings. His tenement was a safe house for a while, but eventually they were raided. Lorries coming up the river and stopping at your address and men jumping off. Raided once, it went on and on; you could expect boots in your hallway every few nights.

WARNING TO CITIZENS
Action by military authorities this evening.

Irregular forces are to make attacks on certain places in Dublin this evening and to-night.

The Public are warned that they should remain indoors as far as possible.

Michael admires his brick house; he's come up in the world. A rough farmboy come to the city and made good, a big rectangular brick home on the riverside, close to Arthur Guinness and close to the Four Courts, Dublin's legal centre.

Designed by James Gandon, the Four Courts' beautiful landmark dome was a smoking ruin after it was shelled by the British in Easter 1916 and then shelled again by the Irish in June 1922. Windows broken, pillars black, and walls giving way; both times my mother's childhood street in an uproar, and both times my grandfather's side losing.

But in 1922 a new twist to the dramatics: in 1922 the

Republican munitions dump inside the Four Courts catches fire and blows sky-high, blows right under the archives, the Public Records Office exploding, the massive pillar of smoke a roiling, soot-dark mushroom cloud riding high over Dublin and the river, as if half the city is hit, the wide pillar of smoke visible for miles as Ireland's legal records and documents burn and float out like blossoms to the streets and roofs, and they can't put out the fire and the explosions continue and the church won't allow last rites to Republicans and the escape route in the sewers is blocked by the high tide coming up the river and the men burn up inside or stagger out to surrender while a fascinated Dublin crowd watches from the bridge on Winetavern Street as if at a game of Gaelic football (no CNN or television then).

The anti-treaty garrison surrenders, June 30, 1922, at 3:30 p.m., but the fire alive into July, the firemen can't get close to the conflagration, the firemen can't stop it, and above the city James Gandon's landmark copper dome burns silently, melts away like the dream of a united Ireland. The battle ends, but the civil war starts across the rest of the country, the civil war starts across the narrow river from my grandmother's house, a war that leads to the deaths of the two Michaels, a war still being fought, a war still looking for an ending.

This is the view from my grandfather's front windows, my mother's window — one war right in my mother's front yard the Easter day she slides bawling into this world and is evacuated in a pram full of loaves, the 1916 Easter Rising her birthright, and then another war in her street in 1922, another war under her nose before she is six, before they have picked up all the pieces from that Easter and battles after.

Family friends dead, friends on the run, friends in prison condemned to death. Henry Adams said that chaos breeds life, but it must have been an odd way to grow up, it must affect you (strife better than boredom).

Little wonder that Yeats thought it the end of the world — exactly which rough beast is this crawling toward him in the rubble of Dublin? The start of something, the end of something; six strange, tense years of strife — centuries of strife, if you go back before Cromwell and Strongbow — and the small island left with a paralyzed economy, destroyed railways and bridges, scorched earth, charcoal buildings, no assets or money, and staggering debts, including annuities owed to Great Britain, its former tenement landlord. All those centuries the Irish never gave up, but there must have been times of doubt, of wonder at the signs.

My grandfather has less than two months to live, hasn't had supper yet, looks forward to a good meal with strong tea and sugar and after supper a slice of pungent farm cheese in the drawing room, to finish his exciting, depressing newspaper.

Child's Strange Death — Scalded by Water from a Motor Radiator

Ship's Fireman with 4 Bottles of Cocaine

Weissmuller the Human Hydroplane

Hanging Follows Attempted Drowning

He hasn't drowned yet (he's come up in the world), but the canal water is getting close. July here, and in August he dies. In August he reads of the rifleshot in the country valley. Giant black headlines about Collins being killed, the huge dark headline taking the whole top half of the page.

GENERAL MICHAEL COLLINS SHOT DEAD
Romantic and Popular Figure
No Details Are as Yet Available as to the Exact Circumstances

He reads the paper. I read the same paper. I'm the future coming back to tromp through the past, the wild colonial boy who desires a dark pint with his dead grandfather.

Many Who Passed Through the Chamber of Death Deeply Moved by the Scene Which Met Their Gaze

5,000 Per Hour at City Hall

Uniformed Guards and Six Tall Candles

Bridges Black with People, Windows and Curbs Filled as Far as Eye Can See

All Hotels Closed NOTICE: "Cessation of Work"

This last detail intrigues me; I've found something. Everything *closed*, a holiday of sorts. I realize this notice, this "Cessation of Work," kills my grandfather. Michael Collins's official day of mourning kills my grandfather.

If he'd been at work at Arthur Guinness's Coopers' Shed that Monday in August he'd have lived, had another ten kids with Mary.

Women and Girls Gave Way to Their Sorrow

Sad Relics: General Collins' Bloodstained Coat & Cap

Austrian Fails Channel Swim

Fruit Stealing

Impure Milk

I almost give up searching the reels of old newspapers —
there's just too much on Michael Collins's death and the war, his
bloody clothes and other deaths, other drownings — but then I
find him, find a tiny article, glimpse my grandfather and his
smaller, less celebrated death.

IRISH TIMES
Tuesday, August 29, 1922
DUBLIN AND THE PROVINCES
News from All Parts

Drowned While Bathing

Michael Lyons, aged 42, of 11 Usher's Island, an employé
of Messrs. Guinness and Co., was drowned while bathing
in the Grand Canal, Dublin, yesterday. He was unable to
swim, and went beyond his depth, and the efforts of two
others to rescue him failed.

Three lines in the National Library.

Here is my drowned grandfather, Michael. Same age as I am.
This is what I came for, why I flew the polar route to Heathrow,
got paloothered, held a free banana in a sunlit 767.

Why did their efforts to rescue him fail? Those who could
tell me are dead; those in the water, those who saw him, had him
in their hands, his reflection in their eyes.

No one knows exactly where he drowned. No one in the
family has ever looked for the spot in the country or even knew
which canal (the Royal and the Grand both go west from Dublin),
or knew for sure that it *was* a canal.

I want to chase the place down, possess it somehow — a
tanned tourist believing he has the right to a summer souvenir.

I was told that my grandfather drowned the very day of the

funeral procession for the famous Michael Collins, but I never heard about the civil war raging at the same time, an epoch of horrific bloody anarchy and arson, adrenaline and revenge. Torture, mutilation, and murder, a depressing and fascinating era of roving gangs and gangsters and punks and flying squads, when the Irish maimed and castrated and used hammers to get information, hunting each other down, a price on your head no matter which side you took — those accepting Michael Collins's peace treaty with the English versus those who refused the treaty, saw it as a sellout of all they'd fought for, all who'd died the past six years and more.

Families torn up like Christmas wrapping, men and women gone to ground and gone to new graves, snipers on the roof, in the church tower, snipers in the hills, chases across the bog, and killing prisoners, eye for an eye, the Irish killing far more Irish than their old enemy, the slow Brits, ever managed. And in the civil war no right side; it gets past that.

Yet in our family we were never told this sad part, of the Irish killing one another once the British had left the south. My mother talked of the Brits shelling the Four Courts in 1916, but not of the Irish shelling it again in 1922. And I read Joyce and Yeats and Synge and O'Casey and somehow missed the gist, the drift, the details. What was Joyce doing during the civil war? In Paris publishing *Ulysses*? Teaching in Trieste? He never came back. Did he care what went on? He must have. Mayors shot, judges shot, steam locomotives detonated, railway tracks torn up, stations and bridges blown up, shops and pubs and prominent houses exploding or ablaze because someone might have voted the wrong way or taken the wrong side, looked the wrong way. Executions and retaliatory attacks, guerrilla warfare, concentration camps; old neighbours and good friends suddenly at one another's throats, and they are not willing just to forgive and forget later on.

A historian told me that these bloody months were deliberately not taught in school, that it was Eamon de Valera's policy, once out of prison and in power, to excise this from the schoolbooks, unlikely as that seems. Many writers and accounts blame de Valera for the civil war, suggest that he seemed to want to start it, seemed to call for bloodshed. Did he start it and then try to cover that up? This weird war waging when my grandfather drowns, but I wasn't told about that part, the context.

My mother doesn't like the idea, doesn't believe me when I mention an Irish civil war, yet she lived through it. My mother seems blissfully unaware that the Irish fought the Irish in the south and west, Irish killing each other right in her neighbourhood, her dear city. Who am I to tell her? Maybe she's lost that bit of memory, the way she's lost other bits. Men in uniform shelling men in cloth caps and suits and belted coats, the long coat lingering in memory as a symbol of the conflict. My mother was seven when the fighting ended. She says she remembers the British soldiers and police touts and Black and Tans, the lorries in the road, Irish men on the roofs escaping the British. Us versus them in 1916, in 1920. But a time coming very soon when the men on the roof of her house will not be able to escape one another.

My mother remembers the *before* but not the *after*; she doesn't remember what followed hard on those Tan War days, doesn't remember what, to me, seems more memorable because it seems much more miserable.

An Ennis election poster from 1923 — President Cosgrave's pro-treaty candidate, Eoin MacNeill (co-founder of the Gaelic League), opposing the IRA and de Valera, a violent contest for de Valera's old seat in County Clare:

WHO . . .

LOOTED YOUR SHOPS?

ROBBED YOUR BANKS?

DESTROYED YOUR BRIDGES?

MURDERED YOUR SONS?

VOTE FOR M'NEILL

My mother worries that I'll get in trouble for saying the wrong thing, that I should be careful, as if I might make the wrong parties mad, get knee-capped by the IRA.

Where did you hear this? she whispers on the phone, as if someone is listening in.

You better check that, she mutters worriedly when I insist that it had to be Irish forces pounding her big door when her mother was a widow, since her father had drowned in August of 1922 and the British were gone in January 1922 and the Black and Tans and the auxiliaries left even before that date. My mother used to laugh, imitating her mother putting on the poor mouth at her big front door, trying to delay the soldiers so the men upstairs could escape through the third-floor skylight.

"Ah, I'm only a poor widow, and you're after waking all me babies."

If Mary was a widow, then it was after the August 1922 drowning, and so it had to be Collins's bunch rapping at the Dublin door, the IRA chased down by the IRB, the Free State. It wasn't the British at the door after 1922. It was the Irish bashing at the door.

We have no time for trucers. For goodness sake aim straight.

I don't know about that, my mother says in a dark, nervous voice. All agree the Black and Tans were dirty bastards; all agree on that.

Convicts, my mother says; British emptied the prisons to let them all sign up, to set them like dogs upon the Irish. Emptied the jails, my aunts agree. Is this a myth? Ex-soldiers and sailors, the dry official histories say.

I find this article in *The Globe* from July 29, 1920 (*2 Cents in Toronto and Hamilton, 3 Cents Elsewhere*):

SINN FÉINERS TO BE MET BY MOST
BE-RIBBONED FORCE IS BRITAIN'S LATEST PLAN
Men with Distinguished War Records Posted to Irish
Constabulary — Will Get a Pound a Day
(Special Cable to The Globe and The New York Times)
The government's plans . . . stamping out the Sinn Féin
campaign of murder and terrorism . . . frustrate the Sein
Féin murder clubs. . . . Great enthusiasm shown by the
candidates. . . . The most decorated force in the world. . . .
Many are well-to-do men who are taking on the job in the
spirit of duty or adventure.

Strange that after the carnage of the Great War, of the Somme and Passchendaele, newspapers of the day, with a straight face, still bandy about notions of duty and adventure in a uniform. This beribboned force will bash my mother's door down, will, in their "great enthusiasm," jail mayors and burn Cork with petrol. Were the writer and editors being deliberately blinkered or naive, or did they think the public couldn't handle reality? I'm amused by the optimism, the boosterism, their blind bias toward empire and authority and their "latest plan." There was an economic crash after the Great War: did none of the Biggles-type candidates apply to keep from starving rather than in a spirit of duty or adventure? Not exactly hard-hitting journalism.

Yet we're not that different, for all our irony and cynicism and reality TV and surgical strikes. We're just as much in the dark. Good guys and bad guys, white hats and black hats, murder clubs versus great enthusiasm. The article is almost comic to a contemporary eye, yet at the same time it's ineffably sad.

When, I wonder, did the Black and Tans disband? Was the end fast? So infamous in Ireland — a hurtling force on the roads, a law unto themselves, bullies, vandals, arsonists, killers — and yet little information about their sudden disappearance from the records, from the map. Now just the name of a drink you order in a fake Irish pub by a ski hill, a pub owned by a consortium of dentists in Denver or Calgary.

The British handed over barracks and garrisons to Michael Collins in early 1922. Did any Black and Tans stay on to live in Ireland, the way German POWs fell in love with Canada, the way Cromwell's conscripts stayed on?

Some Tans stay on to train new armoured-car drivers on the Rolls-Royce Whippets with Vickers machine guns, the boxy Lancia armoured cars, and the heavy Peerless with twin turret guns. Did some Tans join the constabulary? Get hired by Guinness? Marry an Irish sweetheart, or pegeen? Or did the Tans take the train south to Cork and sail the Irish Sea, sail back as fast as they could over the windy winter water to England for black tea and crumpets and a pipe and a pint of your second-best bitter and the odd anecdote about their time in the Troubles, kidnapping Catholic lads and shooting them in the back of the skull, burning villages on a whim, doing a Cromwell in the ould sod in the spirit of adventure?

I am reminded of my English uncle's polite but vocal belief in England's legal claim to Ireland. *Legal?* I am fond of both sides, related to both sides, don't think either bunch is on the side of angels, but it seems to me that Cromwell's English armies, with superior weaponry and numbers, marched town to town in 1649, killing thousands of innocents in their homes, plundering and burning and knocking down castle walls to take over, since might is right. Does this mean that Adolf and his blitzkrieg bop version of the Roundheads had a legal right to Poland and other choice bits of *Lebensraum*? Might is right only when it goes your way.

My ancestors in the seventeenth century can't own land in most of their own country, can't own property on the sea or a river in the west, can't lease bogland, can't own a horse worth more than five pounds, can't hunt, can't own a pike or a half pike, can't catch a fish in the landlord's salmon stream even if they're starving. Offshore fishing rights are sold to the Dutch by the Crown. Irish churches and cathedrals taken over and Masses made illegal, their priests and prelates hunted down. They're kicked out of jobs and kicked out of homes. They can't sell grain or corn or wool or cattle to the colonies, and no cattle to England. English taxes and tariffs and penal laws. They can't vote, can't speak their own language, can't go to Trinity for university. Step out of line and get deported to the West Indies as slaves. Plot for freedom and you'll be "legally" killed like a dog, called a bogtrotter, a savage.

If you're English you can pick choice areas for "Plantations," parachute in farmers from other countries to replace the grumpy Irish population eating bonnyclabber. It's to hell or Connacht for you if they want your land.

Fast forward a few centuries and Black and Tans roar around in their Whippets and Crossley tenders, breaking glass and Irish doors and breaking Irish heads, shooting up houses and streets, destroying villages and farms, cottages and cowsheds in a scorched earth policy to systematically break the Irish economy and break the Irish resistance: destroy Irish factories, livestock, barns, crops, hayricks; destroy dozens of dairies and creameries; and perhaps the *pièce de résistance* in December 1920, douse downtown Cork in gasoline and torch it. Rebel Cork, where two Lord

Mayors die: one is murdered in his house by British hitmen, and one starves in a British prison.

Bullies, criminals, riff-raff pulled out of prison, bastards, devils, gangsters. In London my English relatives complain of Irish riff-raff, and in Dublin my Irish relatives complain of English riff-raff.

A British brigadier general ordered some of the worst Tans sacked, and his orders were ignored — the Tans did what they wanted in 1920, no checks and balances, running amuck like an ultra-violent stag party costumed in puttees and tams. Murder in order to get murder by the throat. Then our villains disappear into the woodwork — *poof* — vanished from the country and into job lines and front parlours and clerking desks, into bland footnotes on a page.

In an English living room talk of English law, of a "legal" right to govern, talk condemning Irish acts of violence (That's not cricket. . . . These Irish are animals. . . .). A convenient amnesia regarding England's own animal acts, its long centuries of the imperial sword and rack and flogging to death and a whiff of grape and transports and keelhauling and burning tar on the scalp and gallows and firing squads and iron artillery and decapitated Irish rebels and overheated Gatling guns biting into darkies coming over the ridge.

Like the US, England wants to throw its weight around, knock heads, but it still hopes, like most of us, to be popular, and both insular countries are genuinely puzzled if they're not liked while exercising their "legal" right to topple foreign governments, to murder foreigners — puzzled or stunned to find themselves attacked.

There is a Creole proverb: Those who hit forget; those who have the scars remember. *Je me souviens* stamped on the Quebec licence plate: I remember.

Now why are these Irish always on about their history? Why

can't they just forget what we did to them and follow Manchester United or *Coronation Street* or the NBA or a good murder mystery on the telly?

Soldiers Break into Prison to Kill Prisoners

"A Fugitive" Injunction Against de Valera

Mr. John McCormack Famous Singer Now in Ireland

Had Piles 40 Years Now Cured

Hanging Follows Attempted Drowning

My mother says that she hates politics because she had so much of it as a child in the 1920s and 1930s.

My mother laughs about her mother coming in the door with her jaunty hat as battered and crooked as her red lipstick and her black umbrella destroyed from fighting women and police in some political fracas in the street, coming back home from rallies, by-elections, clampdowns, town-hall lectures, parades, protests, secret and not-so-secret executions. Mom tells me that her mother, Mary, went every year to Wolfe Tone's grave at Bodenstown, a politically loaded pilgrimage for the IRA.

My grandmother marching first against the Brits and Dublin Castle, and then marching against Michael Collins and his dictatorial regime; against Cosgrave's subsequent dictatorship, the Special Branch, the Special Powers for executions; and marching against the Public Safety Act allowing those in the new government to do what they want, detaining thousands and thousands of prisoners and executing scores of them. Later, my mother's mother marching for the suffragettes, and later still, marching against the dour de Valera when he clawed his way back into power. And my mother had her fill.

In 1923 women march with placards "In Honour of the Murdered Republicans," since the names of the dead were not public knowledge (the fog of war). These brave women list the names of the dead, marching the crowded streets to name names when the papers are not allowed or don't know or refuse to do what the noisy women try to do.

Harry Boland Murdered in Balbriggan

Noel Lemass Murdered on the Dublin Mounts

The new Free State in '22 and '23 was a little too free with executions, killing seventy-seven Republican prisoners, cynically freeing itself of future opponents but making bitter lifelong enemies, a bullet-happy Machiavellian move.

In 1916 the blundering British made martyrs of a handful of Easter Rising leaders and changed popular sentiment from one dead set against the badly planned uprising ("Ireland's Darkest Day," said one Dublin newspaper) to an outpouring of sympathy and support and hatred of the foolish British executioners. My mother just born. Yeats wrote poems in London about the Easter martyrs, surprised to see people he loathed — naifs and drunks and wife-beaters — elevated to sainthood, Yeats stunned by their instant hagiography.

Seven is a lot, seventeen is a lot, but seventy-seven! The Free State executed seventy-seven captive prisoners and countrymen. They didn't die in battle or in an equal fight but were escorted from their cells and shot by Irish hands, disposed of like dust into the bin. Did Yeats write a poem for them, or did he just give up and go back to his Ouija board and his Fascist blueshirts and his affection for Mussolini and pretty young women?

In Dublin my grandmother and other angry women march with their names of the dead — women in flapper hats and long dark coats and black gloves marching the city carrying placards and babies, typing up broadsides against censorship and murder, on hunger strikes outside the jail entrance and on hunger strikes inside the many old jails.

What did my farmboy grandfather think as he read the madness of the evening newspapers? Fighting so close to his house, rifles and artillery firing right down the street, and him on the wrong side, the losing side twice. Death for others so close in the city and then Michael dies out strolling in the country, dies of a holiday instead of a war, a holiday because of the war (the old blues tune: "Death don't take no vacation in this land").

This reminds me of my railroad job years ago, a dusty Canadian National warehouse where my duties entailed shipping crated coffins to small towns in advance of long weekends and holidays. People who would soon lie in my coffins were still alive and at work, talking about football and movies and the weather, unaware that I was roughly shoving their coffins off the forklift and loading dock and into the back of CN trucks and Freuhauf semis en route to hamlets around the wild rose province. The coffins would be filled over the long weekend, always a taker, the holidays dangerous.

We're driving a red Rambler, a rakish smile cruising between the ditches, going sailing in the ripply estuary, going fishing for char up north, hooks in a hat, a good chat, a drunken shotgun wedding in the country, a grad party, a high-school reunion, a family do, a ball game, stepping in a canoe with a snort of rye and one eye on the sister-in-law's derrière, one hand on the wheel, a cowboy boot pushing down on the lower strand of barbed wire and passing the loaded gun through, packing a red

Eskimo cooler with booze, doing the Australian crawl toward the distant island, pulling the cord on the Evinrude outboard in the late sun, pulling out blind into the passing lane near Ma-Me-O Beach or Gunn, and our coffins moving toward us where I push them into place on a CN truck.

And this reminds me of an Irish wake in 1981, where the elderly man's body lies on a door across two chairs. The room more and more crowded, until finally two relatives move the body out of the way, stand the dead man up against the wall — still on his door, mind you — lean your man in a corner so as to free up the two chairs for the living, and we carry on with the wake with the dead man standing in the corner, head tilted to one side, a man of few words, this counsellor now most silent, most grave, watching over us as we eat and drink for him.

Sometimes the Irish seem good at laughter and good at death. My English father saying that death doesn't mean as much to the Irish; they're so used to it. My mother so upright and unblinking after my father's death in California.

Tough Irish, they said in California. Was this her public mask?

"Depressing," she says, "to be alone all the time. Doesn't get better," she says, "gets harder each year." She was never the same. My English father was her ambassador to the outside world, a diplomat.

I may have had the last completely lucid conversation with her. She took a taxi from her apartment to the hospital, was in some pain. Nurses said on the phone that she was delirious and making inappropriate responses, and that she had a urinary tract infection that was causing her pain, but she pulled it together one more time for my long-distance call, mind hanging on by dental floss, asking about my boys, commenting on the summer weather. But she travelled over the edge immediately after that conversation. Doesn't know me after that late phone call. I fly to Edmonton, and from her hospital bed she breezily introduces a black security guard as her driver.

"Now, you might think it queer," says my aunt Bridie to me on her farm near Wolf Hill, "but tell your mother I say a prayer for her every night."

I remember a few years back my mother praying for God to take her older sister when she was gone to Alzheimer's. It's my mother's turn now. Does Bridie, the youngest, worry about her turn coming up so soon? I wonder about my turn on the ride, being left on the iceberg.

Bridie, I don't think it queer, and I'd be happy if you say a prayer for me as well, if you care to.

Polish Pogrom — Barbarous Treatment of Defenceless Jews

Every Man Who Dies Before 100 Dies by His Own Knife and Fork

Couldn't Lift Girls from Tub

My aunt Rose and I decide we've had enough of 1922, of Dublin's topsy-turvy library. I'll come back up the marble stairs another day to wade through more papers (cities could have ten daily newspapers then). With some relief I exit the wild library and the men on the rooftops, exit the violent past like I flee the cloistered air of a hospital, so nice to get outside into the palpably pleasant present to relax and move and stretch out my arms and shoulders and breathe fresh air and tourist-bus exhaust.

My aunt has an errand, so we wave goodbye to each other outside the Kildare Hotel. I think she had fun looking at the old newspapers.

See you later tonight, I say.

God willing, says Rose.

I need food and drink after my Irish death trip, and I need silence after the raucous library. The Kildare Hotel pub is quiet, but thirty seconds after I order a pint the place fills with a shouting after-work crowd, tilts from empty to full, alters animus, and a crowing, happy crowd drives me out. Exit stage left, wondering when I became so anti-social.

I find on this trip that I have a pathological aversion to the mob, to my fellow pilgrims, an aversion that is worsening as I get older and lumpier and grumpier. Maybe I need help. As my mother was only too happy to point out at some inevitable breaking point in her eventful visits: "My, you have a bad temper! And you used to be such a sweet little boy."

This formerly sweet boy flees past the bustling Tara Street Station toward the sea, following the river to the spectral City Quay, across the Liffey from the Customs House and the Royal Canal, tall-masted clippers gone like ghosts, soft sea air noticeably cooler, fresher. What happened to that sweet boy? He and I see an old-fashioned brown Guinness sign in the distance; he and I stumble on an empty pub, run by artists and no television blaring and no shoppers and no office crowd — a pub not yet renovated, though it will be soon. Like my phantom grandfather, I move away from blathering crowds and packed bridges, driven away to seek private refuges.

In the Funnel Bar I drink in peace (the liver is the road to health) and stare at the empty river, where forests of schooners once shouldered each other at the busy docks, where dockers sweated in the holds, where idle draymen gambled in the pitch-and-toss schools, coins and bodies lying on the quay in a scrum while keeping one eye out for the police. Now the Irish police have more on their minds than poor men gambling for a few coins on the sidewalk; now they have bigger fish to fry.

I drink and think about the frustrating search, the fractious blood relations, the drowned man who eludes me. I'm not a detective, feel I'm failing. Sick of myself and my head, I am lacking in the *joie de vivre* department; I am less keen than mustard.

"Which way to the toilet here?"

"Dunno," I say. "Sorry."

"Which way to McDonald's?"

"Dunno," I say. "Sorry."

I read the paper, eat an oyster sandwich, guide pints of ale to my mouth, catch up on my journal, and write postcards home. I am a flea on Ireland looking for a bit of blood, a clue. I am losing confidence, impetus, worrying about worrying. Portishead plays "Wandering Star." Their sad music makes me happy. I hope that

Visa bills run up here in Europe will not find me in distant, pink Canada, a small-enough wish, and I stare at Gandon's Customs House and the Liffey's murky moving water (Anna Livia) and the mouth of the Royal Canal, not knowing I am staring at the guilty canal.

Chapter Seven

AUNT BRIDIE IN COUNTY LAOIS

MY COUSIN JAMES PICKS ME UP AT ROSE'S front door early on a Sunday morning in Dublin. We drive out of town, past the well-intentioned high-rise projects; drive Circular Road, seeing more slum kids on their grey horses from the Smithfield Market; drive a broad new highway (EU money, ta); drive southwest toward Kilkenny, down to a coal-miners' church, where we will meet Bridie at Mass.

Rose is my city aunt and Bridie is my country aunt. I want to visit with Bridie and any relatives she can introduce me to, see the family farms, see the lay of the land, since my grandfather and grandmother and my great-grandparents all came from the landlocked country around Kilkenny City, Johnswell, Muine Bheag, Wolfhill, Shanrath, Athy — a quiet area where four counties, Kildare, Carlow, Kilkenny, and Laois, bump into each other, with their zigzag lines cutting up the map.

A coal mine nearby at Castlecomer once employed a number of men: good anthracite burns very cleanly, with no smoke. I imagine miners by the slag heap and face, miners with suspenders and small pickaxes and big drooping moustaches that make them look serious and tiny lamps on their helmets, lamps wider where the bulb points light down over their eyes and the narrow end up like a pointed spike, making their helmets look Prussian. Walk underground at the same time, shower together in a noisy group, stride home together, work clothes torn and filthy, especially the dark knees, where they crawl in the shafts. Black faces and sky at the top of the well so bright.

The well gone dry, the mine closed now, the face played out, though past a stone wall and a wire fence you can still see the tipple and the square building — grass grown around it, windows bricked in — where the men cleaned up after their shifts underground. The many local flour mills and distilleries and linen factories and marble quarries and breweries and corn stores and abbeys and hotels all closed long ago and now seem a soundless dream, something glimpsed in a reflecting pool. Dark coal miners built this pale stone church on an endless hillside in the trees and foxglove and lonely pastures.

Bridie's husband, Uncle Willie, drove a truck for Fleming's fireclay factory in the Swan and later drove a coal truck down narrow local lanes and humped bridges, grinding gears and delivering coal to his steady customers, to local businesses and convents. This is a lovely corner of Ireland, good for wild rhododendrons and nice cheeses and sausage, but it is not striking, not rich, not full of diesel tourist buses and Italians and Germans. Red cattle moaning and roaming stony pastures, hunchback birds beating glossy wings in the wide hedgerows, and little in the way of cash crops or obvious drama.

James's father drove a coal truck, but James pilots a new Mercedes. Cousin James pulls over to give a lift to two men walking to church in ancient dark suits, men on foot in a sudden rainstorm and grateful for the ride. The men climbing in with us have strong country accents, old-fashioned sing-song voices, and

James effortlessly bends his city voice to match theirs — James works in the city in a starched white business shirt, but he used to be a country boy, a culchie.

"You're all well?"

"We are. We're not too bad at all."

"I'm not unwell. Thanks for asking."

"Ah, the weather's turned nasty."

"Aye."

A sexy female voice on RTE Radio One says, "An organized band of rain clouds will hit the country Monday."

"I'd say we're getting tomorrow's rain today," says one dripping man.

"Gale warnings Tuesday," adds the radio, then segues into the song "There's a Guy Works Down the Chip Shop Swears He's Elvis" and my ears perk up: a 45 I bought here in 1981.

"And is your mother well? Tell her I was asking. Ah, sure I'll see her. Ah, sure Bridie'll be up here today."

"God willing."

At the coal-miners' church the men climb from our car, and both say, "I thank ye."

Such a different world from the George pub in Dublin, so different from the beautiful, cool, self-aware patrons of the Front Lounge on Parliament Street. I greatly enjoy how the word "ye" sounds so natural in these two men's mouths, reminding me of Hardy's ploughmen or Synge's *Playboy of the Western World* or outports in Newfoundland where the word survives as well, even in the mouths of fourteen-year-old girls who watch MTV and dress like barrio pop singers.

How ye making out, b'y?

Yet in Banff, on Wolf Street, I hate the new sign for Ye Olde Irish Pub. Is there a difference between "ye" dropped from a human mouth and "ye" painted on a brand-new sign in a tourist town in the Rockies? I will impose an executive-type decision and say there is a difference.

Huge arches above our hair: a spacious, light church where you need a coat on your back for the chill. The walls of quarried stone once masked with plaster but recently stripped clean to show off the miners' frank walls of naked stone. Churches always make me think of frank, naked women. The church pews are half empty, and I wonder if the congregation of faithful is dying out. Not a priest-ridden race anymore.

In Dublin steeples needle up every street, but the priests are aging and churches are closing or are converted — to community centres or aromatherapy and self-esteem workshops or condominiums or bars. By the Guinness Brewery I see an old stone church has become Lighting World, a new way to see the light. Another church I walk past is now a software business. More boobs and money, and less and less the narration of church bells. Fewer people lighting votive candles, and your man is not bothering with Stations of the Cross or climbing the Reek on a pilgrimage; whisht, it's desperate, so close up shop, sell off the church pews and deacons' benches to a new life in a pub or a rock star's mansion.

In this, Holy Ireland is becoming like much of Europe, joining the club or perhaps going back to an ancient pagan past, back to the snakes. Everyone except me went to church Sunday morning when I was here twenty years ago. I was allowed to sleep in, had my aunt and uncle's house to myself while the family was out. I like to stay up late, hate getting up early. I was the heathen future come for a quick visit. I should have gone to see their church. Perhaps the fights with my own parents over church were too fresh in my memory. Maybe there was no room in the little car.

Like Rose in Dublin, the country priest has a terrible cough; we wonder will he get through Mass, and I sense I will soon learn this cold everyone has lingering like a spirit in their lungs. The service is more streamlined than I remember — Catholicism lite. When I was a child, Mass seemed to take forever (if ye had any patience on ya).

Aunt Bridie's farm is just down the hill from the church, on a bit of a plateau with grand views of the sloping green valley and big sky to the south. She is in her late seventies but is still my mother's baby sister, the last child to issue from that union of widow and drowned man. She never knew her father.

My mother says that Bridie was the baby in the family, was spoiled. After Michael drowned, Bridie got anything, my mother claims, had dresses delivered, let Kay do all her homework. Seventy-five years later my mother still resents this. In the hospital my mother takes to calling my sister Maria Bridie. Maria does not appreciate this. Kay and Bridie don't seem to write or call each other, despite being the last two living children from this large, loud brood. Bridie is both funny and stern. She doesn't seem spoiled to me. She has a no-nonsense face, thick glasses, and strong and vocal opinions; she shares this last trait with my mother and grandmother and most of the clan. They all look like each other, and yet all look like different creatures.

I wonder if she knows that our cousin Padraic is gay. Bridie and Rose may be wondering whether I know. None of us talks about it (the love that dare not speak its name). My mother returned from one trip mentioning suspicions about Padraic, but I assumed she was just being critical. Ireland is a good place to be gay, I'm told, and the family in Dublin all seem great about it, though his father, the footballer with the temper, might not have been so agreeable if he was alive.

Bridie's daughter and son-in-law live in a house across the farmyard from Bridie. Years ago I had a big meal at this farm — but my memories are fuzzy. Maybe it was after the rock-fest at

Macroom, the singer from the Undertones like a spider climbing over the outdoor PA towers, singing "Teenage Kicks" and "My Perfect Cousin." Padraic, his girlfriend Sally, and her friend Bernadette were there with me. In 1981 we also did a road trip to kiss the Blarney Stone. I remember these two farmhouses a stone's throw apart, mother and daughter and grandchildren and cats and dogs all close together. Sun in the windows and in the sun a startling white cloth draping a long table, and Bridie's daughter, Mary, singing — my cousin sings old Irish ballads with a lovely sad voice — and the tablecloth like a glowing shroud and I talked with Bridie's husband, Willie, tall and thick with white hair and big hands. We didn't have a lot in common, but I liked him, talked briefly about my grandfather's drowning.

Now wasn't it a whirlpool that opened up and pulled him down into it, and how do you fight it, a champion swimmer can't get out of those, terrible like, must have been a sad thing for everyone, family all in bits.

Yes, I agreed, yes — though in 1981 I wasn't hugely concerned. I was thinking of Bernadette's derrière. She had crimped her hair for the rock fest and it looked good. Add the whirlpool to the vague list in the back of my head. Willie liked a game of cards, like to dance with Bridie in his arms, liked to smoke

Players, but they made him cough, so he switched brands. Or maybe he switched to Players because the other brand made him cough. I can't be sure now and should have paid attention and now our Willie is a dead man in a grave beside this church, the grave we stand at after Mass in a misty rain. Rain at a funeral means that the deceased is in heaven.

Bridie's sweetheart down there in the ground like in a mineshaft, and we shift from foot to foot like pit ponies. Where does a man's memory go, that information, lexicon, those opinions, that big white Irish head that took in so many jokes and pints and potatoes and drove so many trucks of coal to the solemn convents? His lungs worked and then his lungs didn't work. Bridie was there, holding his hand. Lowered into our stony earth, lowered into Ireland and its endless seasons of rainwater hitting like coins in the lush grass, lines of silver pouring from the heavens over our head.

Another feisty widow in a world of widows. I take tea and more tea with widow after widow with the knowledge that I'll leave a widow someday; the question is *when*?

CIARA IS A BIG NOSTRILLED SLUT. I see this written on a wall. I believe it is a better class of graffiti you'll find in Ireland.

I pick up a tiny religious card off the ground, The Miracle Prayer: *Say this Prayer faithfully, no matter how you feel, when you come to the point where you sincerely mean each word, with all your heart, something good spiritually will happen to you. You will see.*

I'm trying sincerely to mean each word with all my heart, but Sharkey says to me, "Why don't you give up this literary stuff and write something I'd like to read — lots of shagging."

Mary has me mixed up with another cousin from Canada, brings out a snapshot.

"No, that's not me," I say. "That's David."

"Your face has gone fat," says Bridie.

"Don't be saying that to him."

"Well, it's just what happens. Sure you didn't have a beard then," says Bridie.

"David was the one with the beard," says Mary.

"No," I insist. "I had a beard then. Ran out of razor blades in 1977."

"You didn't."

"Your face is fatter."

I guess my first visit was not memorable for them. A lentissimo parade of dorky strangers from abroad in bright rayon and lenses, high-rise backpacks and yahoo accents.

"Are you hungry? Thirsty?" As well as the small farm, my cousins run a combined pub-post office in a nearby town. In other Irish towns I have seen a number of combination post office-grocer-antique store-pubs (with your pint a view of Kellogg's Corn Flakes and Bird's Custard and Sweet Aftons and Omo detergent), a combination barber shop-bar, and my favourite, a combination undertaker-pub: throw back a whiskey while getting fitted for a fine coffin, an example of sharp target marketing (a good many of us are thirsty, and apparently some of us are going to die).

I climb behind the narrow, busy bar at the noisy pub-post office, and Mary and Michael teach me to pull pints of Guinness, which makes me nervous but is a lot of fun.

"Nice and easy does it. That's got it, that's the knack. Very good. Now wait and let that settle a bit. The English can't wait; the English will not wait. A desperate race." The stout in Mary's pub tastes far better than that at the Guinness Brewery in Dublin, the brewery bartenders pulling too many pints too quickly for the impatient foreign tourists in the crowded sample room. A pint of Guinness needs time and the right touch of disdain; you mustn't just wank away at it like you did in grade seven.

On the Guinness Brewery floor in Dublin I found extra

coupons for pints, more than I needed, so I shared them with two guys from North Carolina. At a table we talked of their new hockey team.

A blond German approached the sample room bar: "TAKE ET BACH!" Insisting they take his pint back. Each tourist in the room staring at him. "POUR ET OUT!" he yodelled.

I thought him a nutter, but now, tasting an excellent pint in Mary's pub, I realize the German nutbar had a point. My pint at Mary's is rich and lively, though the foamy stout leaves a huge moustache. I wipe this foam on my sleeve and the rest of the evening wear a chocolate-coloured stripe on my white shirt. A lesson.

Three smiling sisters, my great-aunts, ran this pub when I visited the first time. Nance ran the pub and cooked — a good cook, says Rose; Jenny ran the post office — she was "delicate." Lily was the youngest; she was shy and ran the house and kitchen and died first.

These sisters planted Michael Collins in my brain because they had a shrine to him in the pub: a book displayed, faded newspaper clippings and brown photos of the man and an armoured car and news of his death — their handsome hero, their doomed rock star. It was here I first noticed worship of the man, but I didn't pay much attention. It was just something to look at while the older people talked. I didn't know who he was, though I did know that the last song on Jethro Tull's *Benefit*, a favourite grade-eight album of mine, mentioned Michael Collins. I knew the name. It wasn't until years later that I learned anything about him.

Nance is still alive, very old, and she has passed the pub on to my cousin Mary. Mary, I say, I'd like to take a picture of Nance, the last sister; Nance who used to get up first and deliver the mail around the village and was a great worker. She appears briefly but doesn't know who I am, looks confused by my camera, waves a hand up by her head and runs and hides behind a door. I can't explain to her and feel rotten. I don't see Nance again, and I know I never will. Once Nance was young with a crush on a handsome man in uniform who was shot in the head in the valley of blossoms. She holds up her hands to her head. Don't shoot. My cousin Mary and her husband, Michael, still keep the old framed photo of the Big Fellow under the Guinness clock, a photo that has been there forever. Nance runs away from me, and I can't tell her she planted Michael Collins's assassination in my brain.

Mary's pub doesn't look like a franchise Irish pub — it's more 1960s smooth Scandinavian. Most pubs don't fit tourist stereotypes, but Irish workers are busy expanding and rebuilding all over Ireland, owners and publicans and Irish banks dropping big bucks and puffing them up and tricking them out with clay jugs and whiskey mirrors and old typewriters and black-and-white photos of writers no one reads so the rooms look like what we *think* must be a proper, or "real," Irish pub. A real pub mutates into a weird fake pub so we blow-ins can rest assured that the fake pub we choose on our once-in-a-lifetime trip is indeed real.

Once a quiet pub this — no beer taps or pints, just a few bottles to choose from and a few Formica tables far apart. Now there are many tables, many beer taps; now a roaring trade, the small white rooms noisy and crowded. My mother disapproves of the conspicuous spending and boozing she witnessed on her last trip.

"Hasn't it changed?" everyone asks me, eyes shining.

"Yes, it has."

"Now, give my best to your mother, will you?"

"Ah, I remember your father well; he was a good man."

"Well, I hope the weather improves for you."

"Ah, the weather this year. Won't make up its mind."

There was no modern bathroom when I was last here:

I think the jacks were outdoors. Or was that on the Aran Islands weeks later? Memory is so faulty an instrument, wooden and chipped and needing putty or duct tape.

"Whose shout is it?" people yell, wondering who will buy.

Buckshot, a talkative local character, latches on to me and buys me pints, porter and palaver flowing, and my cousins are amused watching.

One woman says, "Ah, there's nothing like a fresh man."

"Did you say a fresh ram?" asks another woman. "Well, which is it?"

And the two women squeal with laughter and lean into me but don't make eye contact.

I laugh — *heh heh heh* — not 100 per cent sure what they're on about.

"He's a bit thin on top there."

"That's from all those U-turns under the sheets."

"Paul, that girl is looser than a pile of soot on a windy day. Tell me now, what are you going to do with a streel like that?"

"So aren't I just attempting to explain myself, and my ex-wife asks, 'Murphy, would this be a long boring tale or a short boring tale?'"

"She's just messing with you."

"Married the wallet, she did."

"Nothing in the wallet now."

"I still have my little divvy."

"Back door's open, Gretta!"

Gretta looks back and smiles, does up the zipper on the rear of her skirt. "Ta."

"Ah jayz, I'm all done in. Ya haven't seen my cap there, no?"

"Whose shout is it?"

"What are you drinking? Harp? Harpic."

The women protest when Bridie takes me out, but not vehemently enough for my liking. "Goodbye so."

Pints are much cheaper in the country pubs: 1.85 Irish pounds, versus 2.70 pounds in Dublin. I estimate about a two-dollar difference on each pint of beer, which is a lot over a lifetime.

Behold the heretofore little-seen scientific side of my mind: Say I am born here in the country and, starting as a strapping baby, drink just three quick pints a day and live eighty-odd years, which I won't. I'll save $165,200. At age eighty, happy as Larry, I can buy a nice little farm and dappled cows with big pink udders to put my mouth to — just with the money I've saved on each pint of porter in the country. But you must drink or you won't save a penny. I can't keep up with these fine ones, like Sharkey and Buckshot, who knock back nine pints of heavy stout, though I'm liking it more and more. Those fine lads save about $495,600 over a lifetime. Drink twenty pints a day in the country and you save more than a million dollars. Lucky so-and-so's.

Three or four pints a day and a new dairy farm as a reward is about right for me. I've no need for a million dollars; it'd just turn my head.

Guinness stout used to be served warm, room temperature, but it is far colder on tap now, this fairly major cultural change in Holy Ireland a slow process over many years.

"A bit colder each summer," my cousin Sharkey tells me. He doesn't like stout this cold and keeps his hands on his pint the whole time to warm it. "Any shite better if it's cold, because you can't taste it." Sharkey says that younger bar patrons began ordering colder lagers in summer, and porter sales dipped noticeably. A sensitive corporation must respond; rust never sleeps; Europe turns American.

Padraic had a summer job with Guinness in 1981 and was paid in big bottles of porter as well as salary, quart bottles that we drank warm in his backyard, trying to work on his father's prize garden gone to ruin. Wolfe Tone slit his throat in prison with his pen knife, a small thing. My father kept his beer in a closet in our Edmonton house, not in our fridge. We would borrow Dad's beer and never pay him back, and now it's too late.

"Ah, this rain!" exclaims my aunt Bridie in Kilkenny City. "My hair'll be a *boosh*!"

Bridie has lived in Ireland for more than seventy-five years, and you would think she is encountering rain for the first time.

"A squib coming! It's spilling out of the high heavens! We'll be drowned!"

Sometimes I feel I'm onstage in a melodramatic Synge play or stumping through Flann O'Brien's comic masterpiece *The Poor Mouth*, where it rains so much that all the locals are bald from the torrents and it's so wet that fishing boats pass overhead at night and lift their sheep in nets.

"I'll be drowned. Don't want to get wet today. If I get wet it'll dry into me and I'll catch a cold. Won't be able to go up to Dublin with youse."

I hadn't thought of it that way. And her family, *our* family, does have bad luck with water, with the Dog Pond, the obelisk, the sombre canal leading away from the familiar city, brooding sirens calling, the tiny white sun gone, the damp, bad luck with drink, lifestyle shopping, the rain in Spain. *It'll dry into me.*

As children, Bridie and my mother knew a morbid dread of TB and pneumonia and consumption and Liffey fever, random mortal diseases that decimated families crowded in the Dublin tenements. Solve an old disease and there's a playful new one.

Bridie's driving is comic. She comes to a stop in fourth gear and then tries to start up again while still in fourth. The car stalls.

"It's been doing that."

Bridie tries third gear and attempts to start up again. No dice. She tries reverse instead of first gear. We start hopping backward like a demented frog.

"Now, would my driving be making you nervous?"

"Ah, not at all," I lie. I'm glad for a lift, and I enjoy spending time with her.

"Well, some say it does."

In the centre of Kilkenny she finds the city traffic a bit much and starts bashing curbs and medians and missing obvious driveways, as if she has lost control of her hands on the steering wheel. Bridie pulls over to recover in front of the castle on the river.

"When I get nervous I get het up."

She is much more adept on backroads, comfortably pointing out this and that while zipping along the loose chippings.

My aunt sits in the shelter of her car while I walk alone through Kilkenny, a pretty medieval city and Ireland's centre of power in the Middle Ages — until Mr. Cromwell showed up in 1649 to put an end to dancing, to put down the "barbarous wretches" who would not pledge lifelong fealty to a revolving door of upper-class twits and madmen across the water. Cromwell was here only about nine months, yet 350 years later you can't escape his shadow, his nine-month gestation. (*The Roundhead rascals; I wish I had my sword in their stomachs.*) The bishop tied to the rock on the beach, the tide flowing up. Cromwell and his cutthroat Roundheads deliberately massacre entire cities for psychological effect, for bad PR, so subsequent Irish towns are much more likely to surrender quickly, not to fight back or drag out a siege, though he massacres some populations anyway after they surrender. Supposedly this is a mistake, over-zealousness, not their intent at all. Oliver's army plunders and kills and confiscates land and holdings from those Irish without "constant good affection" to him or the Crown (though the English Crown is not exactly constant or good in these times or any times).

English preachers warned their flocks to guard against

popish plots and the lust of savage bogtrotters, warned of daughters ravished by goatish monks and smaller children tossed upon Irish pikes whilst your own bowels are ripped out and holy candles made of your grease.

On which side of this unreal divide were my ancestors? No idea how long they've been in this area. My grandmother was a Doyle, which to my ear sounds very Irish, but apparently Doyle means "dark foreigner," to distinguish the dark-haired Danish Vikings from the blonder Norwegian Vikings. The Doyle symbol is a stag, a symbol of permanence: *I was, and I will be.* I'm related to Phelans, Irish for "little wolf," Kennedys, whose name means "ugly-headed," and Flemings, a name that comes from Flanders and the wool trade between Ireland and continental Europe.

I always thought Lyons, my grandfather's name, sounded French or Norman (*Lyon-la-forêt*), but it turns out to be a common name that can be traced to the Irish names Laighean (spear) or O Liathain (grey), as well as having the French connection. No way to know. The Irish name (Doyle) might be foreign and the foreign name (Lyons) Irish.

Lyons was a famous biscuit maker, and you can still buy boxes of Lyons tea; Michael Collins had a teacher named Lyons, and Joyce's aunt three doors down at 15 Usher's Island was a Lyons. The Sacred Heart Order nun raped and strangled in Ballbay was a Lyons. I see it on the names of grocers and pubs in the west, especially around Louisburg and Westport. There are Lyons silk curtains in the drawing room of Lord Leighton's Moorish brick mansion in Holland Park. It's all mixed — my mother's last name, my father's first name (Leighton), and my English cousin's trendy London neighbourhood. Could my ancestors north of Kilkenny have been brought in as part of the plantations of James I? They're Catholic, though. If they were low enough on the social radar, they might have stayed on the land without trouble, almost as chattels, or they might have moved here after the invasions and massacres were over.

How long do you have to be here to be a *true* savage bogtrotter, to be truly Irish? Is there such a thing? How do you prove who is genuinely native Irish and who is *not* Irish? What is or isn't Celtic? The subclavian artery wears a groove across the first rib. This pretty island has a pretty habit of assimilating conquering foreigners and visitors, from St. Patrick to exiled bad-seed Vikings to Roundhead soldiers of fortune to Spaniards to French Huguenot farmers to cloistered Wiltshire monks to the prosperous pince-nez Ascendancy to German tourists — a cliché, but they become more Irish than the Irish.

And if your parents leave for a while for work? Then you're out of the will, so to speak.

On a broad walkway beside the River Nore I pass below the towering dark cliff of a giant wall that is Kilkenny Castle, pass sublime swans with feet the size of army boots, pass leafy grounds and rose gardens, all belonging for six centuries to the prominent Anglo-Norman family the Earls of Ormond, who sold out Bishop Plunkett, later made a saint, but in 1679 not a saint, in 1679 falsely accused of running a popish plot, and after his show trial in London, Bishop Plunkett had his thumbs tied together and a white mask placed over his head by the hangman Jack Ketch, and as the Lord Chief Justice decreed, "You shall be hanged by the neck, but cut down before you are dead, your bowels taken out and burned before your face, your head shall be cut off and your body to be divided into four quarters, to be disposed of as his majesty pleases."

I have to look around the town briskly, as Bridie's waiting for me. The views around the castle walls and river are quietly melancholy, arranged stone and weapon slits and beautiful vistas and birdsong managing to convey what once was.

Under sulphur butterflies and the sward canopies of oak and cypress and chestnuts and plane trees I wait out brief pounding rounds of rain; under the dripping roses serene swans drift to me on the water, drift past the ruins of a mill beside a rippling weir and the weir's water pressed flat and the colour of green peppers. Richard II stood here in 1399. In 1920 the Church decided Plunkett was in heaven.

"I'm going to shop at Dunne's for a few things," decides Bridie at her car, so I have a few more minutes to cut through tiny winding streets and black limestone passages to Irishtown and St. Canice's Cathedral, the church that Oliver Cromwell used to stable his army's horses — Cromwell, Lord Protector of the Commonwealth of England, did the same to St. Patrick's Cathedral in Dublin. The Irish kicked out of their own churches, their own farms and fields, their own houses. Kilkenny streets and walls where Jonathan Swift walked and meditated as a bright student; where my grandfather Michael walked to hurling matches as a country boy in a cloth cap, in a light rain tree to tree.

When there is more time (there is no time) I will explore the zigzag maze of lanes and steps and gateways and stone pubs, Butter Slip, Smithwick's Brewery, the Black Abbey, the round tower on the hill, Norman tombs, the Famine Church, the ruins of St. John's Priory (smashed by Cromwell and his English army). Time enough to stop for a beer, find where the witch's maid was burned at the stake (though apparently the witch wasn't burned, just the maid — a hazard of the service sector), to look again for black marble and sheela-na-gigs, their exaggerated genitalia decorating stone passages, perhaps a sexual fertility goddess who led to the adoration of the Virgin Mary, and in my head P. J. Harvey's frantic song: "Sheela-na-gig, you exhibitionist!"

Chapter Eight

HORSE ARTILLERY

BRIDIE IS FUN. SHE IS GREAT CRAIC and a good guide: she hauls me into many pubs, takes a drink herself, and chauffeurs me to many relatives' houses and farms north of Kilkenny, trying to help me talk to relatives I haven't even heard of, family who don't know me from Adam but fill my belly with food and drink.

Eat, eat, eat.

Let's have a fry. Oodles of time for that; first, let's sit and eat. Can I get you a drink, pet? Bring him a drink, will you. How about a bite to eat? Have you eaten? You must be famished.

Fifteen pounds I put on in a week or two. My first day in the country I must have been given five or six good meals before sundown. Eat toast and tea with Rose in Dublin, then drive to church in the country to meet Bridie. After Mass, Bridie puts on a fry: blood pudding, bacon and eggs, fried tomato, toast, jam, orange juice, and strong tea. The honeyed, milky Earl Grey I drink at home is a different creature entirely from this muscular tea; this is my mother's dark tea, my grandmother's dark tea. As Rose says, country tea so strong you can skate across it, bag after bag crammed in a tiny pot; as my grandmother used to say, black as the hobs of hell.

We drive a few minutes to a huge old farmhouse just outside Kilkenny to visit two sisters, Mary and Kitty, who I gather are daughters of my grandfather's brother Patrick. In Mary's big green door and escorted immediately to chairs at a table of roast beef, roast potatoes, mashed potatoes, cauliflower and other vegetables, Yorkshire pudding, gravy, butter, beer, juice, milk. Not yet noon and tucking away my third meal. The women must work hours to make this every Sunday. The food is delicious.

"Nice colour on him," Mary Phelan says. I thought Mary was referring to a baby beside our table, but she means my summer tan, rarer in Ireland than in Canada. Mary Phelan and Kitty are my mother's first cousins, but Kitty was also a wartime friend in nursing. Kitty worked in England for decades but now lives a few miles away, right beside the tiny cottage where my grandfather was born with the nine others. My mother has told me that she didn't see this side of the family much; she just said they were farmers by Kilkenny, and that was about all she knew. I wonder about a split of some kind between two brothers.

"Mary's had a hard life," Bridie whispers. "Her husband's will allowed her to stay in the house, but she was left nothing. Everything goes to the son."

Mary is instantly likeable and makes me feel very comfortable in her home. I like her roomy, ancient farmhouse and am glad I'm related to her.

A new house stands half built and hard by the old imposing farmhouse, I mean very close. The son married a woman half his age and was building his new dream house when his young wife fell away from the tree, started seeing a married man.

Fine for *him*, the women snort.

His young wife took a flat in town. He stopped building his

house beside Mary's farmhouse. Six months later the ex-wife hanged herself. I associate women with pills, not ropes. The son sold his bit of family farmland to suburban developers, took the money, and moved farther away, but the half-house stands as a reminder.

I meet him this day, but he doesn't talk or make much eye contact, and he doesn't stay long. He likes horses, which runs in this side of the family. The half-house there in the corner of your vision, waiting for no one; horses running past the window, his wife waiting on the end of a rope, his half-life left hanging also. You're alive, you drive the sad new roads, you boot up and your computer blithely informs you it's creating an error log.

After eating one of our meals we stroll into their backyard to a tiny cedar gazebo, squeezed in among the roses. Kitty and Mary smile optimistically, eager to talk, but at first their answers to my questions are vague.

"Well now, I don't know about that now."

"Da didn't talk about such things."

"We didn't ask questions. Older people never said anything to us, and we never asked."

"Back then, you just didn't."

The two women in the gazebo now regret not asking more questions when they were younger, and I know the feeling. Mary says she asked her father if he ever saw a play.

"Saw better plays than you'll ever see" was his reply. Was Patrick in Paris? London's Strand? Patrick wouldn't say anything more. Paddy travelled the world and marched to war for a king — Paddy on shore leave in drunken foreign ports, loading horses in boxcars, riding nervous trains to the front — but he didn't talk of his travels to his children. You didn't, the way I don't ask Padraic about HIV.

Mary wears a bright red sweater and a long skirt. Kitty has a nice pale blue sweater and brown skirt. Bridie looks smart in a black jacket and white skirt. Did they dress up for me? Once my aging aunts were tiny children in wool booties. Mary and Kitty's father, Patrick, stayed on the farm while the others left for Dublin or England or America. Paddy is my great-uncle. I've never heard of him until today.

"He was British Army, Royal Horse Artillery. Good with horses, took care of a rich man's horses not far from here. After the war Paddy was cheated out of some land; someone else got his land because he was connected to the right political party. Paddy was on the wrong side. Patrick's mother, Catherine, died giving birth to her tenth child, Mary."

This is all news to me. This means that my grandfather Michael lost his mother when he was young, and then, to make it harder, Michael thirty-five years later left his family without a father. Did the daughter feel guilty that her mother died delivering her?

"The father's sister was a nun, and she came out of the convent to take care of the children." One of whom is my grand-father. I had no idea. All of them crammed in a tiny cottage, more and more children coming, and then the mother dying of childbed fever or uterine rupture, hemorrhaging in a pallet, a cottage full of blood and smoke; how did so many manage to survive? Tougher than us wimps.

"I blame her," say Mary and Kitty. "The nun was too strict on them, did more harm than good. No noise, no music allowed. There were two concertinas and a big box of sheet music passed down from someone in the family, someone musical, but they weren't allowed to play them. No cards, no dancing. Had to bow and scrape in front of a church." This was my mother's father's world, the world Michael left behind.

Michael and Mary's house in Dublin, by way of contrast, sounds like it was very musical. A beautiful piano at Usher's Island — they sold the upright and bought a baby grand, and they had a concertina, a melodeon. Maybe because such things were forbidden to Michael when he was growing up. Bridie says my grandmother Mary was musical: button organ, harmonica (I play harmonica). Dermot played violin and bagpipes and was a lovely singer. Brendan a singer, my mother and my aunts step-dancing and playing and singing.

"Remember the *times*, though," Mary and Kitty say, regarding the nun. "The times were very different then."

"Now, Mary Phelan has a beautiful voice," says Bridie.

I realize that few people play or sing or dance any more, or make their own entertainment. As the cartoonist R. Crumb asks, Where has it gone, all the beautiful music of our grandparents?

"Patrick fought in the Great War," the friendly women in the cramped gazebo tell me, but I think to myself that the Boer War makes more sense if he was older than Michael. Perhaps he battled in both, handsome cavalrymen with brown, jittery horses waiting for their opening while young infantrymen from the colonies are slaughtered in mud and lice; horses wait while an empire's bodies dutifully pile up on the wire and new machines cut them to pieces. The bodies open so easily, but the fabled opening for the charge of Paddy and the mounted men doesn't come. Paddy'd have to be more than forty years old during the Great War. An older officer, perhaps; a career, eyes in his head, seen a few things, close-mouthed, following orders.

Patrick leaving his bride at the train station or the North Wall, no idea if he'd be back alive or with both of his two legs, fighting for the English overseas and his very own brother Michael fighting against the English in Dublin (THE CALL TO ARMS: IRISHMEN DON'T YOU HEAR IT?). There was an active anti-conscription movement during the Great War, Irish wanting to fight for Ireland on Irish soil and not for another country. In 1815 the Royal Horse served in the carnage of Waterloo, repulsed

grenadiers à cheval and cuirassiers. There might have been friction
in the family, but everyone is dead who would have known both
brothers. The cavalry had Guinness to drink at Waterloo. The
Royal Irish Lancers, the Irish Horse, the Royal Inniskillin Fusiliers,
the King's Royal Irish Hussars: Irish and British causes and
personal histories tangled, not easily differentiated, like miles and
eras of old wiring hiding in the walls of an ancient house.

IRISHMEN!

MORE MEN ARE WANTED NOW.

ENLIST TO-DAY.

GOD SAVE THE KING.

GOD SAVE IRELAND.

     (1914 recruiting poster)

Patrick's military link might have caused friction, but it
might also have helped his brother Michael get hired by
Guinness. My mother doubts this: "My father was very *efficient*,
and he depended on no one."

In my mother's Dublin neighbourhood I stopped once in a
tiny storefront for juice and six dust-coated, sun-faded postcards
of the west, postcards that looked as if they'd been there since
Cromwell. I was intimidated by the tough locals from a housing
project but mentioned that my mother grew up around the corner.

The grocer said, "The houses there fell down or were pulled
down — trucks shaking the quays and foundations wet from
the river."

"My grandfather was a cooper for Guinness," I added as we
talked about the neighbourhood.

"Guinness hired only Protestants," a man said. "Guinness
hired only British." I couldn't understand every word said in
the store, but I felt the bristling memory and resentment from
generations before.

"My grandfather was Irish and Catholic," I insisted.

"Must have been in the army, then. British or army; hired no one else," they said, and that was that. A woman at the James Joyce Centre insisted on the same thing. I suspect this is a myth but it is a prevalent myth. I had never heard of Michael being in the military. The failure to get hired in this neighbourhood might have been a class issue as much as a religious one. Some of the neighbourhood corner boys have their wrong-part-of-town address etched on their tribal faces, on their clothes and red hair, in their accents and words. No thanks, Guinness would say. Not hiring right now.

Parts of the original city wall are near this shop, Viking artifacts under our feet. Outside you can see graffiti and wildflowers filling vacant lots and newer places built atop ancient walls and foundations. The housing projects were not a good idea.

"There's a man named Lyons living in the flats," says the proprietor. "Go in and have a chat with him. And one old boy used to work for Guinness. He's old but has a good memory on him."

"Go see the jail," a friendly man with a shaved head says. "Kilmainham, well worth a visit. Where are you from? I was going to fly to America last year, paid £3,000 for travel, hotel, a Porsche, got to the step of the plane and started vomiting blood and was in the hospital for two weeks. I won't fly now for a million pounds." He says this all in remarkable good humour.

The tough-looking lads all call out, "God bless!" when I leave the little store. This surprises and charms me. They alter the way I perceive these old parts of town.

A savvy horseman and farmer after the army, my great-uncle Patrick lived to be seventy-six, very good for a male in our family. How much time passed before he received the news of his brother's drowning in the canal outside Dublin? Mail was swift back then — five deliveries a day in Dublin — and they had telegrams, send a wire. I doubt they had a telephone anywhere near the farm in 1922.

In the gazebo Mary says, "Another brother, John, a tailor in Manchester, used to send *News of the World*, and as kids we enjoyed reading it, but Patrick was strict and he stopped that."

Perhaps that was part of the Irish revival that discouraged foreign sports or songs or newspapers. Or the nun's childhood influence on him? My grandfather Michael would seem to have been more good-humoured. "He was strict," my mother says of her father, "but no more than the time. Not jolly unless a party or some event."

"Brothers all over the globe, so," says Mary. "A brother Laurence immigrated to America and was a cooper for an American brewery. Laurence, he went to Mass every day and said the rosary at bed. Now, his American boss got to like Laurence and tried to play matchmaker with his daughter, but the boss's daughter wanted nothing to do with him. 'You can keep your Irish greenhorn,' she said.

"Now, one black, rainy night Laurence went into church to pray to the Lord for guidance: Should I stay in the USA or should I book a ship back home to Ireland? Didn't the boss's daughter happen to be at church praying for her father, who had taken ill a bit. There was the daughter, waiting at the big church doors, storm lashing, rain pouring off the eaves, but Laurence now had a rolled umbrella and the two of them shared it; the two of them decided to go from church to visit her father in hospital.

"The boss on his sickbed told her, 'You'll be sorry if you don't marry,' but still she refused. They didn't marry right away, but Laurence, now he'd be your great uncle, decided to stay on in America, and eventually the boss's daughter said yes to him and they had nine children — three daughters became nuns and one son a priest." They did missionary work in the wilds of India and Atlantic City.

So few of us in the family even go to church now, an amazing change in such a short time. I had not heard of my great-uncle Laurence before this story. Westmont, New Jersey. Larry in Joisey. Another family link to beer. I wonder what brewery he worked for in the States. It likely doesn't exist any more, bought up by the giants.

Mary and Kitty say Michael's eldest brother, James, ran a pub in Coolcullen, raised fleet greyhounds, and was a great hunter, a good shot. He must have known the country well. He had no children. There is a family mystery concerning a great-uncle and great-aunt's daughter, also named Mary. A family full of Marys.

"She ran away and was never heard from again. They were hard on her, and there was a fight with the mother or father." The prodigal daughter went out the door and didn't come back.

I was thinking 1800s: Dickens, George Eliot, Hardy. It takes a moment, but I realize Mary would have been Kitty and Mary's first cousin, the same age when they were young, in the same world — driven away in the 1930s or 1940s. As if my mother dropped off the map when young. Was Mary pregnant, I wonder to myself. Was she shunned or punished, no room at the inn?

"Killed him, didn't it?" asks Kitty.

"No," Mary Phelan disagrees. "Her father was cross as. . . . The family searched the world for her, but she was never found. No one knows where she went; Mary just disappeared. There was a small inheritance she never received." A daughter lost to them, lost to us; no funny stories about her, no fatted calf. She could be alive this minute, with her own big family, my lost cousins, or Mary might have died young, one of those unsolved cases, a lifeless body in an industrial city where no one knows who she is.

Mary Phelan says, "Three of the brothers were coopers, but one brother, Tommy, a tall one, quit a good job in Dublin. And didn't he walk all the way back to Kilkenny through the fields?"

I'm reminded of a Howlin' Wolf song: *I walked all the way from Dallas*. Why do my aunts always remind me of old blues songs?

Laughing, Mary and Kitty repeat this bit to me; they clearly enjoy telling this wee tale. Oh, a bit of a wild one, he was. All the way from Dublin to Kilkenny, walking through the fields! I wonder what Michael thought of his younger brother Tommy giving up a good job, leaving the city. I hope he laughed too, the way Mary and Kitty laugh.

Tommy the wild one had a little cottage right beside the church. It's gone now. "No loss," they say easily. "A great-aunt left Tommy the cottage," says Kitty. "The church bought it after."

The wild one had no children and helped at the church as caretaker. Did Tommy the wild one outlive his wife, Kate Reade? I don't know. I visit women and hear about men. Michael and Tommy's sister Caddy was a housewife in Kilkenny, Bishop's Hall, had two or three children. The women in the past sometimes seem anonymous. Or perhaps Mary and Kitty assume I want to hear about the men.

My great-uncles lived almost to the year I was born — we are separated by only days, and at the same time we are separated by two centuries. They're from the nineteenth century, and I'm sneaking into the twenty-first.

My great-uncles strike me as almost Falstaffian: oak casks of dark porter, greyhounds coiled, oiled shotguns aimed down, Patrick's big horses swaying their heads in tiny stone stables, Patrick in a ship sailing to the Western Front, James the eldest hunting wet fields, hunting for a brother's lost daughter, Tommy crossing hundreds of fields to get home from Dublin,

Michael's cloth caps full of orchard apples, Michael with a forked stick dowsing for water to dig a neighbour's well, dozens of brothers clomping their boots at open-air dances on grass or a rutted road, courting their long-haired women, coaxing their favours, their long, complicated dresses and petticoats, their brown eyes, their blue eyes, the solemn, mirthful anticipation, the wooden doors and stairs, my great-uncles working miracles with wood and fire and metal, alchemists working with their tough beefsteak hands, working wet peat bogs, working the bar in cloistered, windowless pubs, rows of ceramic beer taps raining porter's rich bonnyclabber, skimming off the spongy beehive foam with a wooden paddle, men to men in the smoke, leaning to talk to chilblain drunks raising a dark jar to Charles Parnell or Dynamite O'Rossa, furtive shawlies sneaking in with a tin can to be filled with drink, or women of the evening, the unfortunate country girls of the Monto flash houses (this could be where our lost daughter, Mary, ended up, a Mary Magdalene washing a man's feet with her hair).

Silver coins snick dark counters, light sneaks in hardwood snugs, light sits in thick mirrors and green-and-yellow bottles while ham hands roll noisy barrels into the cellar and up from the cellar, wood groaning, and outside a racing sun, big feet walking furlongs of wildflowers' fat air and grain buzzing and buteo hawks giving you the evil eye, great moustaches on the men, leather boots, rough waistcoats and unlaundered trousers, Patrick's stiff cavalry uniforms, posed photos on steamship decks, days between ports, engines vibrating metal underfoot.

One brother, Michael, and his sons fighting England at home and one brother, Patrick, marching off for an English paycheque, a farmer fighting farmers in South African dust or French mud or a Turkish beach, losing more friends to bad water and disease than to snipers, the survivors shunting back home with rusty bayonets, red garters, and a handful of ribbons and medals clinking like coins in a dovetail drawer closed tight as a mouth.

My great-uncles ride with noisy hounds and wage war with horses and heavy leather saddles and curved blades and bullets singing. In my world a beige machine tells me it's low on toner. I feel a bloodless bureaucrat, an amnesiac cut off from the visceral, violent, puzzling world my great-uncles walked through easily just the other day, walked just the other summer.

We don't walk.

Mary stays at her farmhouse, but Bridie and Kitty and I drive sunny backroads to Johnswell and an ancient mortar cottage with blue window frames and tin sheeting where once sat a thatched roof — the archetypal tiny white-limed cottage in a shady glen on the right side of the road driving east, the cottage where my grandfather was born and where his mother died in childbirth, a place now empty and damp, though the thick white walls still look solid in the sunlight. A few rooms: where did ten or twelve of them sleep? No plumbing, no electricity, no waterbed, no shower, no CD player or VCR or SUV or Amex card.

Mossy stuccoed walls pen a yard between the cottage and a long, low shed for pigs and cows and maybe in the shed a spot for a cooper to work his magic for a few coins. Walls everywhere — thick, angular walls enclosing small spaces or corrals. Mortar and stones raised up centuries before, and tiny windows to pull a bit of light inside but avoid an old luxury tax on glass.

When I was young my father mentioned a glass shortage during the war. He said the Irish were gossipy, nosy, and despite any shortage, they had to have even a tiny window to have a good gander at who's after going past.

Two modern houses perch the sunny hillside hard above the old cottage, and Bridie and Kitty and I chat above the cottage in the shared driveway. Michael grew up here, lost his mother here.

The house he went to on Usher's Island is five times larger.

"A house goes downhill fast if no one is living in it," allows Bridie. "No one's turf fire keeping it warm and dry."

Kitty stands with a tiny smiling creature the size of a muscular squirrel — her tiny dog on a leash, and Kitty hunched over and buttoned up in her blue sweater on a warm day. Both Kitty and my mother were smiling nurses in wartime London, but my mother didn't come back from the war, from her new edge of the world. Kitty worked in England, but eventually came back home by the old cottage. The eldest daughter. Kitty's newer house is white, an iron gate is painted light green. I realize I don't know if she has any children — there seem many children, grown and young, but none associated with her. Perhaps the smiling dog is her child. She doesn't ask us inside her house, and this rankles Bridie.

Kitty says Mary Phelan wants to run a bulldozer through the old cottage. I think the cottage is rough but beautiful. Kitty wants to keep it. My mother's friend. Kitty is on drugs; Kitty is dying.

For token exercise after all the meals I wander uphill to two deserted farms on a shady lane, climb higher for a better view of the countryside. I need to walk, but no one else wants to go climb with me. Climbing this hill is travelling back in time. Cattle stare my way from leafed trees and rutted fields. Mortar on one old farmhouse wall has fallen away to reveal mismatched bits of stone split and stacked as if bricks, some stones blue and some white and some the colour of sand. And slate tiles above broken and slate falling from the roof and the roof with giant holes and trees growing up from the kitchen floor.

I peek in and angular birds fling out past my ears, scaring the bejesus out of me. Stonework and walls and stone lintels and doorjambs overtaken by green plant life.

A wringer washer rusts on its side in busted struts and loops of metal. These ghost-silent relics were thriving farms with big families, sisters and brothers and best friends and neighbours and enemies and hired hands and smelly, noisy animals and my dead grandfather a tiny boy lying back on a hillside dreaming of Fair Day under these same sunlit cumulus clouds, these blue-and-white skies and green pastures. Prettier country when the sun lights it up like a bright slide inside a magic lantern.

I have to laugh. Downhill at the whitewashed cottage Bridie grumbled, "Kitty should have invited you in for tea or something to eat," but I am happy for a few minutes without eating.

Any height in this country brings a good view. Far to the north of us, this side of the Royal Canal, are bogs and heather, but to the northeast I can make out the Wicklow Mountains and hills around Dublin; the Blackstairs Mountains jut up to the east, toward Wexford, and the Sieveardagh Hills roll to the west, toward Tipperary. Unremarkable country, but I like the dependable look of the landscape, like to think that it looked this way in the Middle Ages, looked this way to Cromwell on his steed, looked like this to those many men and women forced to go elsewhere. Its slopes and violets and lime-washed walls collecting light and held in each emigrant and exile's sad, mad eye.

Back downhill by the ancestral cottage Kitty and Bridie talk to a tall man who shows me a family tree he's worked on — my grandfather just one branch, one of many brothers, many branches, possible pasts and futures. The tall man has the same high hairline as I do, the bigger nose and ears of my younger brother. He is Mary and Kitty's youngest brother, Patrick, son of Patrick. Michael would be his uncle. I am meeting so many people at once.

I can see from his family tree that my grandfather Michael is older than Patrick and not the other way around, as I thought I heard in the gazebo — Michael is older by a year and a half. Michael born in 1876, while Custer was riding his tired nags into

Little Bighorn's slippery slopes and the drinkers in the pubs sang "The Hat Me Father Wore."

So Patrick the cavalryman would be twenty-two years old for the Boer War and thirty-six when the Great War erupts and trains start rolling over Europe and Patrick calms his big chestnut mare and they'll be done with the Hun by Christmas of 1914. He married at thirty-one, his wife, Rose McDonald; their firstborn, Kitty, came in 1917, after eight years of marriage. Four children. In 1922 Patrick would be forty-four when he hears that his older brother has drowned just days after his birthday. Paddy has one more son in 1925, but he names the last son Patrick, after himself. Does not name his son after his dead, drowned brother. This son is the tall man I meet on the time-travel hillside.

The family tree shows that my great-grandparents' names were Daniel and Catherine; hence Michael's naming his eldest son and daughter Danny and Catherine, then the name Catherine (or Katherine or Kathleen, depending on which piece of paper or gravestone you consult) bestowed unofficially on my mother after the older daughter dies and my mother is born. The youngest daughter, Mary, is born in 1887, so Michael would have been eleven when his mother died in the cottage giving birth, Patrick nine.

There is a Laurence born in 1872 and a Laurence born in 1883. I assume it's the same as with my mother's nickname — a child dying, then passing on the name later. Passing on the names, the big heads that tear apart your mother's womb, the moon faces and laughing eyes, good with animals, the hair-trigger temper. Until I saw this family tree's neatly typed names I had no idea my brain was related to the brains of Kennedys and Phelans and Mannings and Murphys and O'Mearas and Byrnes and Nolans and Purcells and Slatterys and Brophys and Dwyers. Bridie is good for doing this for me, taking me around the unknown countryside. All these crowds, all these Marys and

Paddys and Danny boys, my tribes, my viruses, my virtues, what is carried within me all these long years like quiet passengers in seats without my knowledge or choice.

"My wife will be sorry she missed you," says the tall, laconic man with the family tree. Bridie says his wife is younger than he is, and I see on the family tree that he married when he was forty-four, when my grandfather already knew of ten children. Perhaps the Irish tradition of the country bachelor marrying late. "She'll worry that I neglected you somehow, didn't give you a decent meal."

"We've had lots, thank you," I say. He holds the paper down in the wind and I take a photo of the family tree, since Patrick doesn't have any copies.

He poses for my camera by a flowering hydrangea, all of us squinting downhill, his white hair and white shirt glowing in the sun as if he's about to fly off the hill, white houses moored around us like glowing clouds.

The rural setting fools me, for it seems rustic, Old World, agrarian, but then the lanky man mentions that his daughter works in Los Angeles.

"She does animation for Disney. She married a man from Montreal." He doesn't ask me if I know him. His daughter must be in her twenties, I guess from their date of marriage. The two farms intersect with Quebec, California, Australia, Russia, Spain.

No longer are the Irish forced to join another country's army or sort coal on the foggy docks or emigrate to be charwomen in Liverpool or lose their hair and teeth shovelling fertilizer or pitch in a ship's hold or lose their arms to a machine in an English mill town or die tamping sleepers on an American railroad on a burning plain (*Tamp 'em up solid*) or malarial swamp or frostbitten avalanche zone (*Tamp 'em so they won't come down*). Marty and Josie sponsored by their Aunt Jennie in America, scared teens seasick on a ship with no idea what lies ahead for them. My grandmother's younger sister, Jennie, went to Philly as a domestic for an auctioneering family. My mother on the night boat to England (Kay likely thrilled) during the Depression.

Now you can leave your home or you can stay in your home, and the economy is a tiger. Now you can jump on a plane to Hollywood, as Patrick's daughter has done, or go climbing in Nepal, like my cousin Feargal in the west, or fly to Miami or Greece, like Padraic. Now we like to pretend we're free, free to be anyone (at least until the next high-tech downturn).

Chapter Nine

DRUGS SEND YOU STUPID

HIGH HEDGEROWS AND WE MOTOR DOWN in the purple gap, green shadows and violent yellow light flicking on our faces peering forward. Bridie steers us back once more to the Phelan farmhouse, where Mary tells us we must have a fry before we leave.

Meal #4: iron pans of quivering eggs, back bacon, blood sausage, and fried bread served along with tea, coffee, juice, tall cans of beer, triangles of blackberry pie, apple crumble and whipped cream. Someone points at the burnt top of a loaf, calls it the Protestant part. Have some!

Later we will motor to my cousin Mary's pub-post office for snacks and four or five pints of stout. And Bridie will offer a late meal back at her farmhouse. "You must try this marmalade with homebrew poteen in it." I am all appetite, love to eat and drink, but after this marathon I feel as massive as the Michelin Man. And you can't say no.

I'm not sure who everyone is at Mary Phelan's farmhouse, whether the people are related by blood or marriage or not related a whit. I can't always tell who is a great-aunt and who is a friend of a friend. Someone in the TV room runs a string of mares; someone in the kitchen owns a little mini-golf or pitch and putt. Mary Phelan's son has a garage and petrol station. At meal #3 of the morning an older man and younger man argued about the European Union, the collapsed Russian market, and agricultural subsidies, farmers versus small business — who works harder, who gets more government funding.

"Feck all for the farmers!"

"Come away, the farmers are always getting some damn handout!"

"Jay-sus, now that's a load of shite. I wish that were true."

They argue and swear loudly at each other. Joe is a gruff older farmer. The younger man has been out in the world, lived in Australia, travelled and come back across the water, and set up his own business in Ireland.

Joe says, "I gets no favours as a farmer and damned if I'm going to kiss arse to get something thrown my way."

"I have to kiss arse at my job," says the younger one.

"Not me," says the older man.

"Well, you're blessed!" he says, voice rising. "You're a lucky man, Joe, because I tell you I have to lick arse every day of the week."

I like the younger guy, the intelligence revealed in his admission. Joe seems to enjoy being abrasive, a point of pride, his talent he must share with us. I also sense that Joe is skeptical of me, suspicious or jealous of the attention I get from the women here. I am a coddled interloper, waited on hand and foot. He's not going to coddle me, by gar!

The younger man's wife says jokingly to her little girl: "Joe's bold. Slap Joe." The little girl refrains from slapping Joe. There is an air of vague disappointment all around.

The men stop arguing and swearing at each other, and it's as if it never happened; they move on happily to the hurling match.

My mother is like this — she loves to argue but seems to forget it immediately and is soon happy to make up and get along, eager to do some favour for you. Not everyone forgets and forgives so easily — say me, for example.

Kitty is not here. "Your mother wouldn't believe the change," Mary says to me. "Asks something and half-hour later asks again. Aged terribly in a short time. She's gotten stupid." She uses this word "stupid" calmly, a different shade of meaning than in Canada.

"Them drugs they give you are the divil, send you stupid. Asks something and half-hour later asks again."

I don't tell her that my mother does the same thing, or that Mom's sister in Philly no longer knows who she is, though she knows all the words to the old songs. Josie used to come back home every year. On her last trip she looked at Rose, turned to Bridie, and asked, "Who is that woman?" Someone she'd known half a century.

"Something's wrong with Josie," Bridie said. Bridie was upset at Josie's state and upset again when my mother was diagnosed. When her son James picked me up in his car, he cautioned me: "Don't be too graphic about your mother's condition."

My mother went to visit her sister in Philly and thought everything seemed fine, but Jo woke up in the middle of the night, shouting, "Who's this woman in my bed?" You have the same name, the same face, but something inside is altered, parts go missing. In Dublin my mother travels in from the airport with someone else's suitcase.

Or my aunt and uncle in their eighties, Josie calling out for Marty and he crosses the hall and holds her hand, both unsure where they are, what the year is, wary of the world but somehow knowing they're brother and sister, back to being children, holding hands somewhere in New Jersey, far across the ocean from the big Dublin tenement they left in the 1920s after their father died, the big house on the River Liffey.

Marty has skin rashes on his feet, complains, "They took away my shoes!" He always told me he'd save pills for when he's infirm, kill himself rather than live that way, but Marty doesn't save the pills; Marty forgets that part of the script. They found him on his floor, something felled him, but he got up like a boxer off the canvas. In an American nursing home Marty and Josie hold hands and wait for whatever it is. Tough Irish.

"Family," Marty'd say years before, "it's all you have." You need a hand in yours at the end (*hooshed it away*).

And now my own mother in a Canadian hospital wondering who I am, wondering if I can tell her where she lives. The hospital staff give her pills for her pain, but the pills constipate her ("travel always disrupts my *system*"), so the doctor gives her more pills and a needle in the stomach to try to undo what they are doing with the first pills. She was walking until she met the hospital bed; they helped her to stop walking. The ward appears bent on destroying her with some speed, is marvellously efficient at this task. A guard in a rent-a-cop jacket to make sure she doesn't get any exercise. It's called a university hospital, but she's held in a giant warehouse really, a jail; she's doing time, and the warden is invisible. My mother cries every time I walk in.

Do you have my address? she wonders. If you could give me a clue, my mother suggests, as if it's a game or a quiz show. And that damn Bridie won't give me my money. You mean Maria?

This seems scary to me: to not know your address or your bank, to not know your brick house teetering on the ravine or your last high-rise apartment with its view of the river valley. It must be terrifying to not know the way home. She asks me in a concerned voice, Is my mother still alive in Dublin? Saves these questions for me, knows that I know some of it.

In grade four my son Kelly had an assignment to interview a grandparent. All dead but my mother. I took Kelly's assignment for my own purposes, adding what I had heard over the years and what my mother could tell me over the phone. A year later she remembers almost nothing. A last interview, a last gasp, a lost world.

A few years ago she prayed for God to take her sister Jo. What do we pray for now? There is no coming back from this. And this is what is waiting for me in my head — runs in the family, gallops in the family, some quiet tenant inside your bright green brain eating your favourite grapevines and dendrites, and I find myself wondering every time I can't think of the right word. Someday they'll take away my shoes, my teeth. It's *thing*.

Chapter Ten

BLOOD PUDDING

MARY PHELAN BUILDS UP A FIRE OF PEAT AND WOOD in her white-washed house. I'm very warm, as it's July and sunny outside, but the older folks are cold, even in their long sweaters. Both Mary and Bridie have two stoves, an old turf-burning one and a newer electric range. A pleasant smell to a turf hearth, different from wood or gas. There are three or four generations mingling in this house. Some watch hurling on television: Wexford is playing Kilkenny, an important game for the locals. Everywhere along the roads I saw flags displayed for the Kilkenny side. Our side loses.

The long two-storey farmhouse was built centuries ago: it's tidy and pretty, with whitewash and green trim under the windows and a shining green door surrounded by flowerpots on a square of bricks. In a high window sits a white milk jug full of daisies. The dining room where we ate our meal was once a utilitarian side section of the building, used for storage: kerosene, turf, coal, porter, milk, cheese, meat on a hook, and other sundries. No fridges back then. The younger man who's been to

Australia tells me of drilling through the room's two-and-a-half-foot walls to run a cable — he couldn't get through, stopped cold by a barrier of giant boulders locked in mortar.

I can glimpse newly built suburbs just beyond the corner of the barn — the city edge creeping up on the farms; the working farms becoming urban space, ornament, tiny yards, fresh pavement. Mary Phelan and Bridie admire the California look of the new houses, the rectitude of sidewalks, the tidy lawns the colour of dragonflies.

Mary points to a high hedgerow with poppies blossoming in it.

"They'll clear this and widen the road, straighten the corner so," she says. "It'll be beautiful."

They want suburbia, concrete, vinyl; they want Levittown instead of their pastoral meadows. I don't know how to tell Mary and Bridie that their corner is beautiful the way it is, that it's a mistake to bulldoze their corner. I can't tell Mary and Bridie that I hate the stark new houses, their aluminum geometry and prefab lines — that I prefer the rough farmhouse walls concealing boulders and bones, my ancestral cottage up the road, where my great-grandmother died in some pain and where Kitty is about to die. Prefer the poppies strung inside the huge hedges like coloured Christmas lights and the crooked lane's corners.

"Here looking for your roots, are ya?"

"Uh, no. Yes. No."

Uncertainty is my meat. No idea what I'm looking for, but I'll know it when I don't find it.

"You Americans, now, you t'ink we all have pigs in our parlour."

In the farming country near Kilkenny I studied my relatives gathered to eat meat at Sunday dinner, and I mused about the kinetic, genetic zigzags of family and tribe and the sheer *range* of what makes you, of what can be punched into the mix, what is available — the code selected like a random, messy jukebox. We run out of phone numbers, but we don't run out of faces.

Why is it I don't feel that these people passing me generous platters are true family? *Who are they?* I don't see familiar faces. They aren't me. We have no letters or links or past visits. The family name and farmland and pubs and photos and history handed to strangers over centuries: related but not really linked because I went away, even though I wasn't alive at the time, was never here. You went away.

A Scottish man on a plane once complained of just that, told me he has an amazing life in Vancouver — fascinating friends, a good job, good nightlife in a giant city, likes the outdoors, skis Whistler, climbs mountains in the Coastal Range, climbs the world — but when he arrives back at the old village in Scotland someone might ask, And how was the flight? And that's it.

You could be from Mars, he says. They know nothing of my life. They don't care.

Is it a lack of curiosity, I wonder, or that they haven't been out? Or do they not want to know? They have difficulty with someone who comes jetting back like a spy. You're made very welcome, but something troubles them.

He keeps going back to Scotland to see a woman. She flies to see him in Vancouver as well. She's not from Scotland but wants to live there. He's from Scotland and doesn't want to live there. A math problem.

My relatives mix me up with some other cousin, some other foreigner. You went away; you live in some inhospitable frostback nation. Someone went away. But then a child comes back from outer space. They have trouble placing you, imagining your time travel, your vague minor betrayal.

Too many traits and markers are fluke: lines on a postwar

map, ration books, an ad in the paper, famine memories, Irish butter, the whitewashed store, the distant shores, *Lebensraum*, love and marriage, a baby carriage full of hard discs of bread under the riddle of fine masonry and gunfire, the smoking copper dome, the basement munitions dump on fire and blowing up under the archives, pages gone like pilgrims, Ireland's lost tribes, lost records, the theatre of history still playing, playing the marked cards of culture, accent, eye colour, which church, which lane, which side of the dirty river, which side of the ocean.

Too many traits are conditioned by your specific era and your aching birthplace. Rationing still on in England in 1952, and an Italian ship with a berth open for a family migrating, a train across empty Canada to a tiny rented rowhouse in Edmonton and then your very own blue-and-white house, then the yellow brick home and wondrous witty wintry upbringing in the New World by the snowy ravine full of poplar and magpies and the muddy yellow river that flows to Hudson Bay. That poor lost man Mr. Hudson stalled in the ice so far from home and his son into the rowboat and jets hauling us overhead in constant lines of vapour back to Europe. The *Discovery's* mutinous crew lost some weight and lost their teeth, but they made it back to Ireland to pawn their anchor and rope and then sailed the rest of the way home to face the music and rope in England and we go back to visit and take snaps of the queen in her gold carriage (*always shouts out something obscene*).

I have a good sleep in my aunt Bridie's spare bedroom. No rooster on her farm, so a big cow's head mooing right outside my window at ten is my alarm clock. Nice. Feel a long way from leafless, noisy Soho or the rubber bullets and Orangemen bagpipes and fife-and-drum kick-the-pope bands or Padraic's crowded nightclub scene. Padraic and Sharkey haven't been down here in years and years, they say; can't remember the last time they saw the farm or the cousins' pub-post office.

Once people lived by a landmark and saw it all their lives — a steel steeple, a kiln chimney, a mountain the colour of a dark plum — your life tethered within sight of that landmark. One white bay or one mountain's strange stare all your smelly days. Now it's the opposite; now you travel away in a monoxide traffic jam, travel away from your landmark to Amsterdam, Madrid, Miami, San Francisco, jump smiling on sunny rocks in Greece, collect air miles for some vague future. See your landmark in your dreams, sell it back to yourself like perfume.

At night my aunt's booming voice: "I'll leave the light on — sure someone'll be going in!" She pokes her head in the bedroom door, saying, "Here's a drop of holy water," flinging some drops into my bedroom.

"Thanks," I say. "See you in the morning."

"Please God," she answers.

Rose says that Bridie inherited her farm from Joe Kenna. My grandmother Mary's mother was a Kenna. I don't know if it's the same family. Then Peggy in Philadelphia says it's John Kenna and he was my grandmother's first cousin. Find tiny bits at a time. Bridie was good to him when he was old, running errands and doing his wash. A neighbour had his eyes on it, put his horses on the field. The priest got Joe to make out a will and leave his farm to Bridie. Willie, her husband, never showed much interest in the land. They had different apple trees: apples for cooking and apples for eating. Limestone hills and limestone buildings. Coal once pressed in the ground and iron squeezed into the farm's drinking water; iron often close to coal mines. Willie was anemic but stopped taking the doctor's iron pills after moving in here, didn't need them any more. The kettle is brown with iron, the bathtub and commode and sink streaked brown with iron. No bottled designer water in Wolfhill or Shanrath, no tofu or sundried tomatoes, no sneaker pimps or cool-hunters.

My aunts Bridie and Rose at times remind me of my mother, and they also remind me of my aunts in Philly. I forget who is who, who I'm talking to. The rolling, uncertain countryside reminds me of the lake our family went to, the same rocky penury and big ice-cream cumulus of my childhood summers on the Great Plains.

Time seems fluid, plays tricks, is out of joint, and I get dislodged, forget where I am, who I'm with, what year it is. The smell of peat burning, pictures of Jesus and Mary cupping her sacred heart, oilcloth, warped linoleum, stained sinks, a giant tin kettle with a black handle and black button lid and long snout, an old black stovetop with white enamel sides and iron legs, the cord hung high over the stove to dry towels or clothes — clearly I'm in the Old World, far back in the past, and then on Bridie's old radio a new song by Guided by Voices from Ohio via New York's trendy Matador label, a song from the future confusing me. How did they manage that? How did they send that song backward in time to me? One peasant peers out of Hardy or Synge and utters, "I thank ye," and another colours toons for Disney in Malibu. Ireland's motoring fast into the future, and I'm yanked on a clothesline into the past. The tangents osculate once in a while; the tangents kiss.

I chop wood for Bridie, happy to smash something hard, happy to do something physical after so many meals with different relatives and strangers, so much blood sausage and rashers and Irish lamb and beef and blackberry pie and brack and pints of stout. Famine here once, but we're well stuffed now.

I love my dictionary's definition of blood pudding (or blood sausage or black pudding): *an article of food composed of swine's blood, coagulated by cooking, intermingled with particles of fat and usually stuffed into skins.* Oh, honey, please pass the coagulated swine's blood intermingled with fat.

The axe's wooden handle is broken and the remnant is sharp, so I wear pink plastic dishwashing gloves and feel ridiculous. But chop wood I must, for I am stuffed into skin and my waistline girth has intermingled prodigiously with swine's blood and vast particles of fat.

I chop stumps and clouds on speed over the stone stables, shadows rush over the red iron gate with the fleur-de-lis on top, the square gateposts, the cows and the white Charolais calf and the two dogs. The yellow stone stable has an arched entrance and what look like narrow rifle slits each side of the low archway. In 1981 I took pictures of my cousin Padraic in that same archway.

Bridie's son-in-law, Michael (pronounced Mee-haul), finds his big bull dead on a gate. A ripe heifer in the next enclosure. The prize bull tried to get over the steel gate and got hung up, its own huge weight pressing down until it suffocated. The steel gate too sturdy. Desire killed the bull. It died alone. Michael Mee-haul found it, his face flushed with the news. Aunt Rose says, "Michael has put a Trojan effort into the farm."

Bridie is sad about the bull: "A big, beautiful bull. It was fine with its own cows, but someone else's — go through fences and ditches to get at them."

She's sad about the dead bull but happy I've cut her some sticks for her fire.

Chapter Eleven

Because They Hate Us

That night my aunt Bridie takes me to Pedigree Corner, a refurbished crossroads pub. New money seems evident in its many mullioned windows and yellow-and-green designer paint job and high-wattage rows of outside lights. Several televisions in the big pub's bright rooms. It would not have looked this way in my grandfather's day. My grandfather survived without rubber-backed carpet and multiple colour screens nattering day and night (if I was dictator for a day, TV on for no reason would be illegal). Joyce called his country the sow that eats its farrow. Now it seems reversed; now the young new Éire attempts to devour the remains of frugal old Ireland.

Nirvana plays on a jukebox, and a young woman sings along drunkenly in another room. Not all Irish are blessed with a natural voice, not all sing like a lark.

Bartender looks in the direction of her voice, waits a beat, says, "Kurt Cobain'd die *again* if he heard that."

The affable bartender tilts his head to show me a scar in his short hair.

"Hit on the head with a bottle and then five lads beat me. I'd kicked out one or two from the bar and then refused to give up my newspaper. *One*: reading it. *Two*: they were acting smart."

The young barkeep kept reading his newspaper, and a lad smashed a bottle into his bent head. Over a paper, fighting over a straw. Then kicked him when he was down, his buzz cut bleeding into the new rubber-backed carpet.

"Lucky it wasn't worse," he says. "Could've *died*."

The courts gave one year to one assailant and two years to another, then on appeal changed that to nothing and six months. One of the droogs was convicted later in England for stealing £1,500 sterling.

I am reminded of a Dublin man, brother of a politician, who was cut on the head in a fracas at Padraic's gay club and wanted compensation, but he didn't want his name used in a public lawsuit because of his brother, didn't care to be identified in the news as a regular at the George. Two women were fighting on the dance floor. A flying glass sliced his balding head and left a permanent scar.

Bridie and I have a few drinks sitting at the bar and chatting with the young barkeep. My aunt drinks vodka and Seven, is more comfortable with drinking than my mother is. The conversation moves to gypsies, or *travellers*, in the area.

"The mess they make when they halt somewhere. Car parts and junked washing machines and trash blowing up and down the byway. And who is supposed to clean their mess when they move on to the next halting site? Do you see now they're after blocking backroads and demanding a fee for anyone to get through? Farmers can't get to their own damn fields."

When I was here in 1981 gypsies were called tinkers for their talents fixing holes in tin pots and pans — put a whole new bottom on your wrecked saucepan or sharpen your knives and scissors. In the countryside I saw many gypsy camps — amazing displays of refuse strewn all around where they pulled over their caravans. I met friendly rural gypsies when hitching around the west of Ireland in 1981; I often talked with them by roadside ditches and country crossroads, and they let me take photos of them and their worn carts and caravans and stoic donkeys on the condition that I mail them a copy of the snapshots. But all my film was stolen in Spain, perhaps by gypsies. Cars and vans hitched to small aluminum trailers now instead of the old-fashioned wooden carts and animals I saw then.

I remember tinkers in the city in 1981: young boys sniffing glue from Kleenexes and women handing around a baby to make for more lucrative panhandling: *Pennies for the ba-ba?*

"You're not to use the term 'tinker' anymore," Bridie says, and I suspect the term "gypsy" will die out or be banned as well. Now they're travellers or travelling folk.

"The travellers put on a boxing match a while back — bare-knuckle, mind you — the two thrashing away at each other like lumberjacks. Boy, they're tough fellas." The bare-knuckle boxers represent two traveller families, each with its anointed champion, piles of cash riding on the outcome and fight videos sold.

Travellers are refused service and jobs, and their children kept out of schools. If they put their children in school, other parents pull out their own children. They are accused of stealing anything not nailed down, and of drinking too much and not being able to handle alcohol and causing trouble and pulling out shotguns at rival family funerals. Today there are rumours in the pub of a fight with a gypsy in a nearby town and a shotgun going off in the crowded public market.

The papers mention no such incident. I can't tell what is reality and what is hearsay, but I am reminded of the old Jim Crow laws, reminded of parallels with North America's reservations. Many Europeans are smug about North American race relations and our treatment of aboriginals and blacks, thinking that colonialism and slavery and prejudice had nothing to do with Europe. I clip out an article about a Czech town building a wall around "problematic" Gypsy apartment buildings to "help relations" with other residents. Maybe I'd want a wall too if I lived in Usti nad Labem, but there are some odd ghetto echoes in that article and in that new wall.

In Slovakia skinheads sometimes carry out attacks with baseball bats, and a soldier used a bat to beat a 49-year-old Gypsy woman to death and club some of her eight children.

Irish travellers are not Romany or East European. Their DNA is Irish. Some say they may be remnants of those who hit the road during the Great Hunger — exiles, strangers in their own land. Others say they go back further than that era.

The young bartender says, "When travellers die they burn them up in their own little caravan, like Vikings in their boats."

"Go on with you, you're messing. Burn them up?"

"They do," insists the bartender. "I don't serve travellers. They drink and then fight. Steal and wreck the place. I know they're human. . . . They're human, but they're *different*. They just are. It's their nature. They're terrible. Steal and fight. Time'll come we'll have to serve them. I give them takeout."

Bridie and I waltz into the bar: no problem. A traveller coming in is told to get out the door. They're Irish, but a different pedigree.

A friend, Tamas Dobozy, asked relatives in Hungary why they hate the gypsies. *Because they steal.* Tamas asked a gypsy why he stole. *Because they hate us.*

A young fox does odd circles, confused, spinning in our headlights. Beautiful tail. Huge ears. Rabbits cross the country road.

Hedgerows grow into the road, making it narrower. Man dead who used to cut them back, says Bridie. Another widow. Don't know who'll do them now, she says. I am reminded of my mother's litany: *My husband's dead; all my friends are dead. Even my doctor is dead.*

"I'll take you to another little place before we go home, all right?"

After the rewired roadhouse with the brilliant lights Bridie drives me to a more primitive country pub out in the fields, a few miles uphill, closer to her farm and the coal-miners' church. No big sign, no rows of bulbs across the front, and inside just a simple room with milk crates and 1950s kitchen chairs. I like it immediately. No televisions, no fancy decorations or fake hunting prints, no fancy loos. This is a simple pub, a true local, not yet rewired or reinvented. The pub has a postwar addition, but the original section boasts the same two-and-a-half-foot-thick walls and recessed window frames as Mary Phelan's farmhouse, walls so thick that each window frame forms a wide ledge.

A large local family is drinking there for Month's Mind, a month after the death of their father (yet another widow). All ages in the pub, from children to seniors. I can tell Bridie feels bad that she missed their special Mass (Bridie's Mass yesterday was dedicated to Willie, a year after his death). Margaret the bartender has the same chest cough as the priest in the stone church and Rose in Dublin, the cough I will inherit.

I ask a man next to me what he's drinking, and he tells me a Derry: a pint of Smithwick's ale with a touch of Guinness stout for a head. It is not a Black and Tan. I like it (or as Claudius says, "It likes us well"). The reddish ale is not as thick as the stout, but the stout's boxy taste is at your mouth for the whole pint. The two don't mix; the stout head stays on top of the red all the way down. The Smithwick's is livelier than the dead-flat bitters I've had in

England, and Smithwick's has more colour and body and taste than Budweiser, Harp, Heineken, Carlsberg, etc. — the watery, dull alternatives to stout in Éire.

Drives me around the twist: a centre of world brewing and so many brands taste like pissed-in bathwater. Care about decent beer and you're seen as suspect or weird. Please imagine that you're a wine aficionado and you travel eagerly to France, only to find they ply you with blue Kool-Aid and nothing else while insisting that it's all the same anyway, and that you're just too picky to want anything more than blue Kool-Aid.

Strolling into pubs now, I know what to order. No more staring at the beer pulls, asking stupid questions. Bartenders know what I mean.

Smithwick's with a Guinness head.

Right you are, they say.

I also hear it called "a drop of diesel." I'm no longer just a dumb tourist (well, I still am).

Then one pub refuses to make me the mix.

"We don't mix drinks," says the young waitress. There must be some mistake; it's a simple request. All I want is a drop of diesel. I ask to talk to the manager, a man with wild blond-red curls. He comes roaring out of the hot kitchen, sweat swimming on his meaty forehead, and stands an inch from me with his bloodshot eyes drilling into mine with some hostility.

"*Yes?*"

I feel it's that moment before someone head-butts you, bashes your gob, and you fall to gush your suburban blood upon the filthy floor.

He spits out the words: "We. Don't. Mix. Drinks. Okey-doke?" Then he turns back into the kitchen, leaving me looking at the swinging door covered in marmalade-coloured grease. Okey-doke.

In the country pub on the hill there is a man who looks dead. How else can I say it? I can't take my eyes off him, but I don't want to be caught staring. He looks driven from another century, risen up from the stony earth, from the potato fields, dirt still like fine powder on his rumpled clothes and hollow cheekbones, like dirt dusting a rough vegetable. Black hair and eyebrows and large ears, a compelling wastrel face more Mediterranean or Slavic gypsy than Irish. His coal black eyes glitter, but his eyes don't quite focus; his eyes are not quite with us in this world. I keep staring. He moves carefully, slowly drifts a glass to his mouth, a pipe lifted slow-mo, nods or looks up at the group surrounding him only occasionally, peers only occasionally into our puzzling empire.

My aunt nods, says, "Your man over there, in and out of the hospital. He gets right and then kills himself with drink."

Everyone else looks vaguely "modern" or at least postwar. He's the only one who could have fitted in two hundred years ago. I entertain the notion that he passed out from a killer bottle of poteen in the corner of a forgotten field, evening sky the colour of fine mosses and lichen and oranges, passed out in the weeds and crowfoot herbs of another century and woke up, tested his head and cracked his joints, and made his yawning, wandering way in here for a Month's Mind drink, for a smart Christian drop to warm his chilled, puckered innards. Staring at the past is like staring at an accident. I can't stop looking at this wrinkled wanderer.

In the pub Bridie tells me about my uncle Dermot the cooper visiting my mother in England and jokingly being introduced as a doctor, perhaps because his younger sister was a nurse. An Englishman said, "Hardest hands I've ever felt on a doctor."

Strange dreams at night, ransacking the image banks. I'm sleeping on my aunt's Irish farm, and yet I have a crystal-clear vision of Teresa, my high-school girlfriend more than two decades ago in Canada. In the dream we are rafting on a canal and she has a beautiful cream-complexioned face and many suitors, and I am sick and jealous all over again. My brain stem enjoys taunting me in my old age, keeps mixing drinks. Once more I feel whipsawed back and forth through time.

Chapter Twelve

TRAIN IN VAIN

LARRY, A FAMILY FRIEND, OFFERS US A RIDE to the train station.

"Hope this'll get you there," he says of his little car.

"Anything wrong?"

"Ah now, the wheels turn all raa."

Like my aunt, Larry loves fourth gear, even at five miles per hour. They want to get to fourth as soon as they can, though hardly moving. Larry comes almost to a stop and tries to take a corner still in fourth. Gear down! I want to scream.

We drive into Athy, a pretty country town with a small-scale castle built by the earls of Kildare in the fifteenth century, its tower right over the river, like a toy version of Kilkenny's much larger castle. Athy's weathered stone buildings and black lampposts make me wish I had time to look at its streets and architecture, the Grand Canal (how long would it take to swim on my back to Dublin?), the River Barrow; wish for time to check out how the bartenders pull them in the Leinster Arms or the Emigrant's Pub. My aunt, however, is not much for walking these days, and we have a train to catch.

We stand on the narrow platform and stare along the narrow tracks as if we can will the train into being. My grandparents, leaving the farm for the big city, looked at these same sleepers and iron rails. Iron filings and Dublin our magnet. A group of teenage girls have clearly modelled their look on Alanis Morissette's, a dash of Spice Girls (that's so five minutes ago). The ugly seventies look is big. Many kids wear black Adidas track suits. I feel like an extra in *Trainspotting*. The town was founded in the twelfth century. Once there were monasteries, freckled redhead kings, crooked oak forests.

"Let. Eejit train always bloody LET!" complains a rumpled local.

His skinhead son mentions needing money for some school project.

"Ah, jaysus. Kids today come home from school, need a pound for this, a pound for that. I was lucky to get one p. One p! I had to walk to school barefoot!"

"Ya didn't," says a woman.

"I did."

"Ya didn't."

"There was no money and no waste. No tins of meat for a gobshite cat. We would've skinned and eaten the bloody cat and been happy for it."

The night before we catch the train I become strangely depressed looking at a shoebox of old family photographs in Bridie's living room. In the black-and-white snapshots, mailed to the Irish farm from Bristol and Barrow-Gurney and Plymouth and Oxford, and later mailed to the farm from wintry Canada, my dead English father looks so dashing and agile before the kids, before we came along. Both my mother and my father look so young and grinningly happy with each other. I never saw them look so expressive, so *possessed*. Then they had six kids.

There are no pictures of my grandparents in the box. Photos must not have been common then, especially in a poor part of a poor country. I'd like to see more pictures of my grandmother and grandfather, to know them a bit, get depressed about them.

The train is crowded, so my aunt Bridie and I can't sit together. Bridie, in a seat across the aisle, smiles happily at me, excited that we're heading to the big city. The train picks up speed, turns its hurtling carriages into concentrated noise, into music, *rack-a-dack* its timeless train-track mambo.

I sit with three older men; I look at a paper and eavesdrop surreptitiously, a spy. Much more public banter in Ireland than in England. On my first visit to London I noticed what seems a typically English tendency: as you sit down on the tube you raise your newspaper as a private barrier. You go down and the newspaper shield comes up in one smooth move, and ignore the riots in Brixton, the sinking island. England seemed to be coming to bits in 1981, the papers full of strikes, riots, and mines closed and factories shutting down (you're all redundant now).

That summer I rode the Magic Bus from London through Wales and sailed the night boat (same boat my mother rode fifty years earlier) from Holyhead across to Ireland and caught a double-decker at the port of Dun Laoghaire at about 6 a.m. I climbed to the top of the double-decker with two young New Zealand women I had met on the night crossing. A man uncorked a big bottle of rye and passed it around the passengers. A man in uniform, a conductor or a guard, I don't know, took a swig and handed the bottle along. Boy, howdy, is this a different country from England, I thought. No stiff upper lips hiding behind their papers.

My father liked his newspaper. I like my paper. I have English blood and Irish blood. I love London, and London in the new century is vibrant, on a roll, but something in my divided genes *connects* with Ireland. Ireland is repressed, confused, *seedier*, to use Graham Greene's term, but Ireland is also wilder, looser, less worried about what the next person thinks. England is still England, a nation of shopkeepers and shoplifters, despite the hip chefs and neon B-boy nightclubs and Tony Blair's Cool Britannia rubric.

Bridie smiles. I smile. We have no idea what is in the other's head. A man on the train says, "I never took a drink in my life, but my three sons are making up for it."

I think of my three young boys home in Canada, wonder what they'll be up to in a few years. Can't escape your quiet children, your garrulous pack of uncles.

"Must be desperate for a sober man to listen to three or four drunks."

"Ah sure, Kilkenny used have some good hurlers. Gave everything, and that's a lot! No longer."

I see another red fox in a green field. Cattle, Dorset sheep, Romneys, sleek, silky horses, stud farms, villages. There would have been more sheep a century ago, supplying the wool factories.

People on cellphones: "Hallooh! I'm on the train. I'm grand ya! Roit. Fair enough. Where yous off to tonight? We slagged them something terrible. Kept slagging and slagging them. Brilliant. Give us a shout. See yas."

Hallooh! I'm on the train; hallooh, I'm on the bus, I'll be there soon; hallooh, I'm walking down the street irritating other people wit' me new stolen mobile; hallooh, I'm at the bottom of a canal; hallooh, I'm dying in childbirth; hallooh, grand, I'm after driving all the snakes out of Ireland; hallooh, I'm killing myself with drink in a field; hallooh, I'm tied up in a pile of dead bodies in front of a machine-gun nest; hallooh, Cromwell's after tying me to a rock and the tide is coming in a bit; hallooh, they're pulling me bowels out right now and burning them, okay if I ring you later, right, we're all grand ya, and you?

Pleasant pastoral landscapes zip by like my English grandfather's watercolour scenes. Like my quiet English father I hide behind my paper.

Lady Di on Yacht with Dodi

Portadown Woman Loses Eye to Rubber Bullet

ABBA Musical Set for 1999

Few Mourn Pedophile Priest

I see a strangely compelling article about an East German man who was dead for four years before he was discovered in the attic of a house, a mummified East German still faithfully watching television, *TV Guide* in his lap. There's something perfect about a dead person watching TV, though likely that's not the exact demographic the executives seek.

"I got a hip replacement. Worked on my feet all my life, so I'm out to grass, out to grass. Got the new hip in and played my first eighteen, and moya wasn't I hitting the ball grand! Hitting it grand."

I can tell I've been in Ireland too long because I'm dying to know if these golfers are papist or prod, green or orange.

The train slows and stops, and we are ordered off by men in army-surplus jackets and ski masks. Our pastoral watercolour interrupted, fractured. They must have pulled the emergency cord. They run up the aisles yelling, "OFF! OFF!"

Not all have weapons, but I see one handgun. I don't know who they represent. My Roman holiday. They could be IRA provos or a splinter group like the RIRA (the Real IRA, also known as the Coca-Colas, the real thing) or Continuity IRA or the UDA (Ulster Defence Association) or UVF (Ulster Volunteer Force) or

Johnny "Mad Dog" Adair's UFF (Ulster Freedom Fighters) or the LVF (Loyalist Volunteer Force) or the Apprentice Boys or Orange Volunteers or the Red Hand Defenders — or maybe it's the Women's Coalition or the Legion of Mary or the Catholic Women's League or the local chamber of commerce or the Peep O'Day Boys or the B-Specials or the fifth Beatle or the Molly Maguires or the Wide Streets Commission of 1756 or maybe they're Japanese soldiers who don't know the war's over.

Glass breaks in another car, windows breaking. No one knows what's going on. The golfers are quiet. I carry my small knapsack, one I carried in 1981, and we jostle calmly in the aisle, push to the doors and wait to leap to the ground. It's grassy below, but it's a good jump down. I help my aunt, her skirt out like a parachute, pull something in my back, feel a mix of adrenaline and fear in my stomach.

When all the passengers are off and walking toward some warehouses the masked men start burning the train, including the streamlined diesel-electric engine. You wouldn't think that metal and plastic would burn, but they do burn. The masked men use something, perhaps just gasoline, and the plaid seats where we sat chatting and reading darken, then flame into a storm of smoke and the smell is sickening.

What a waste, I think. This demonstration, this muscle-flexing, brings out the Puritan cheapskate in me. Why are they burning a train? Just to do it? Tradition? What's the fecking point? Who on earth is going to learn anything from this lesson? Who wins? Who is going to be better off? Will Ireland benefit in any way from a smoking train?

"*Let*," I recall for some reason. "Train is always *let*."

"What's that?"

"Nothing."

I suppose it's to show that they can do it if they want, that they run the show: punish the joyriders and dealers, administer six-packs, bomb a market, shoot a rocket at MI6's Secret Service headquarters in London, burn the odd train.

No one is hurt. I didn't get six-packed, didn't get bullets in the elbows, wrists, knees.

"This is just like a movie," someone says.

Christ on a crutch, I hate it when people say that. It's *not* like a movie, it's real life. And movies try to mimic that, mimic what's out in the big world, what's possible. Movies don't make something real. It's the opposite. What is so difficult about that concept?

Modern blue buses take my aunt and me the rest of the way to Dublin. People seem excited, then tired. I want a drink, a lively Smithwick's with a Guinness head.

My grandfather and my aunt's brothers, my dead uncles, used to be young masked men, used to be in the IRA around the time of the civil war. No longer. My same uncles grew to hate the modern IRA, thinking it rotten with Marxists and Libyans and Cubans and Colombian cocaine gangs and moustached bozos waving Mao's Little Red Book.

"You don't bomb innocent people," my uncles declared when they were alive, and my cousins and aunts say it now. "You don't bomb innocent people."

My dear aunt asking me in England: *Well, what could anyone think of the IRA?*

In the Irish newspapers a burning train rates only a tiny paragraph, like my grandfather's drowning. In Canada this would be the event of a lifetime — mystery men hijacking and burning a Canadian train would be front-page news for days. This might attract the dreaded Royal Commission. Here my charred train is part of "another day of violence over Protestant marches," not as important as the swimwear Di dons before she heads up to Paris for dinner with Dodi — Di teasing the reporters, Di bending over at the French beach to show generous cleavage, spilling her breasts to ensure she steals some newspaper space on the day of Camilla's fiftieth birthday party, a modest soiree thrown by some lovable jug-eared chappy named Charles.

7,000 Orangemen in Dark Suits Defy Ban

Blair Condemns "Orchestrated Violence"

Di Gives Jiggle Show in Bikini

Romanians Must Go

No Justice No Train

Boy Saved Up to Neck in Mud

I want a drink. I stop in Slattery's, a northside pub on Capel Street, and a man slurs something at me. I can't understand him — a mushmouth north Dublin accent — can't tell if he's drunk or joking or wants a fight. Part of me wants to keep on trucking, but another part makes me stop and ask, "Say what?"

A woman interprets for me. "He says, 'Did you forget to slap a razor to your face this morning?' Your beard, man; he's talking about your beard."

I'm glad she can translate. Give her a gig at the United Nations. Both fine humans have obviously done a little hard living, that weathered look — you could patch a favourite recliner with their tough skin.

"Cheers," the young bartender says by way of asking what I want. I order a Guinness. "No!" the bartender says to a man moving closer to me. "No!" He points his finger at the man and slowly and emphatically says, "No, no," as if addressing a good dog who is eyeing a slipper. "No. No." They converse in Irish.

It's never explained to me, but I assume that I am being protected from a local wanting to be stood a drink or cadge a smoke or sell Amway.

Standing at the bar, all of us share sections of a Dublin newspaper, and I am drooling over the bands playing: Wilco, Calexico, Lambchop, UB40, Cat Power. The Pogues may get back together. The Stanley Cup is on, but no mention in the papers. The bartender yells to someone down some kind of hatch or dumbwaiter: "Big guy was here, says you owe him twenty punts. Yeah, big guy. Twenty. Joe Kavanagh. Yeah, big guy." A mobile rings: "Hallooh? I'm just chillin'." Just being an ass, I think. All of the Capel Street crowd smoking industrial-strength fags the whole time, flyash flying, thick smoke hugging us like a cleaning lady. The bartender drops a glass and laughs when it smashes.

"By all the saints on the feckin' calendar I'm never drinking again after last night," says the bartender to Interpreter Woman. "Shots and shots and shots! One pint to every ten shots. Never drinking again," the bartender says with an easy wink.

She laughs and teases the smooth-skinned bartender: "Oh, he's bold. The boldest ones come from Donegal — raised on nothing but turnips and drink."

Your man moves an inch toward me. "No! No!" Three men sit beside me on the other side, and all three light up immediately. Why can't they have a smoke on their way over here? I know, let's all wait until we're inside and right beside Mark. Why don't they just quit? You have to expect smoke at a bar, people say. That's like saying you have to expect leprosy. I go to a bar for a drink. Booze. Bar equals drink, bottles, glasses, beer pulls. No one had packs of cigarettes when Shakespeare wanted a quick pint at the Boar's Head. Not one of my relatives smokes — not Sharkey, not Helen, not Padraic, not Rose, not Bridie, not James, not Jean, not Liam, not Seamus, not Mary, not Michael Mee-haul — but I'm always saturated in smoke; the rest of Ireland is compensating.

My friend Interpreter Woman is leaving with the slap-a-razor man, and he drinks up and finishes his eighteenth smoke and borrows cigarettes and retrieves shopping bags and a brand-new guitar amp the bartender had stashed for him behind the bar. He points to the amplifier: "Thought I'd treat meself." The first fooking sentence I've understood.

She says to me before going, "I *hate* Canada — biggest collection of transvestites and lulu headcases per capita, but they won't let you smoke. I hate Canada."

Chapter Thirteen

ARMCHAIR NATION

"OH, THIS COUNTRY'S CHANGED," SAYS ROSE in her kitchen, listening to Joe Duffy's radio show. "Not a day goes by without a stabbing. On Merrion Street they hit a woman in the face and stole her mobile phone. The greed! Prices have gone crazy. People across the road sold, and the new couple stripped out the stairs, walls, everything. They don't even live in it."

Sharkey has put a big addition on the back of his house. Rose has done an addition. Sharkey has a mobile phone. Rose has a mobile. The radio is loud and the smoke detector keeps shrieking as Rose fries me some nice back bacon. She waves a tea towel and the shrieking stops, then it starts up again.

"We used to go to the seashore in the south. Now they all have to fly to the Continent or even the Caribbean. One car, two cars, three cars if they have a teenager. Young couples starting out have to buy a little place fifty miles out and get up at five to avoid the rush. And the highway jammed. Sure they never see their kids all day, drop them off somewhere in the dark, pick them up in the dark. Oh, this country's changed."

A man from the country in Dublin for a match at Croke Park, the big stadium.

"Watch your car, mister?" asks a streetkid hoping for a little protection money.

"No," says the man, not taken in by city slickers. "I've got a Rottweiler inside." The man walks toward the stadium.

The kid pauses. "Does he put out fires?"

The man turns back and pays the kid.

This is the price (No money down!) of jumping into the pool, jumping into the new world so fast, of racing from thatched roofs and peat to real-estate scandals, from cow chips to silicon chips, rolling from rosaries to mobile phones (Easy payments!).

But would they go back to how it was, to the good old days before it was *thing*? Doubtful. Besides, you can't put toothpaste back in the tube, can't force the genie back in the bottle. And most don't want to.

Hello, tiny old man mumbling to yourself on the commuter train.

I thought him touched in the head (*teched*), but now I spy his rosary — the man is praying, working the beads, mumbling, and occasionally covering his face. This would have been a common sight in the pious old Ireland, Holy Ireland, but in the new Ireland he's an oddity picked up on our jaded yet sensitive urban radar — the insane guy on our train.

Praying Man is well dressed, but he seems to be shrinking into his garb, his sleeves a little long on his houndstooth tweeds. Very dapper, though, a perfect tiny gentleman: beautiful brushed flat-brimmed hat, large grey eyebrows like an owl's, small hands with no rings, impeccable cuffs, polished black shoes, and in front of him his rosary beads and whispering glossal consonants in the air.

His lips move in prayer and a Ballymena man is sentenced to seventeen years for beating a woman and gluing her lips together.

Her lips are not moving in prayer. He kept the young woman's body for a while, then took a trip with his estranged wife to the seaside, burying the body in a shallow grave at Broughshane. The papers don't say if the estranged wife enjoyed the trip to the seaside, if it reignited the spark in their marriage. The man had lured the woman, just released from hospital, with a promise of heroin at his house. That sounds like fun.

Neighbours heard noises but thought it was an animal whimpering. I wonder if that's when he got out the glue, to keep her quiet so he could get some shut-eye while she suffocated.

Few of us praying now, but every train boasts a smooching couple glued to each other's lively lips. Like the small man praying, it is a display both private and public, both common and rare. I envy them. Every train in the world possesses a pissed-off young man a little on the short side and trying hard to look ghetto tough. Every train rocks its boisterous kids and frazzled mothers. Every train a middle-aged woman wearing those giant plastic eyeglass frames; every train a pimply kid with a sci-fi book; and every train a woman with a sad secret, staring out the window. Why do I always like the sad ones?

Smile, though your heart is breaking. The Spanish chambermaid sings while doing our hotel beds, while changing the tables from breakfast to lunch. She wears black tights and an untucked black shirt, her thick hair held behind her neck in a loose ponytail. She sings and then the visiting rugby team stands and applauds. She is embarrassed, tells me she doesn't sing as much as she used to.

"I hate the weather here. I'm going to Whistler to teach snowboarding," she says when she finds I'm Canadian. "I fell in love with a Polish man I met in Ireland. I don't know if he can get into Canada. Don't travel and fall in love. Too many problems. Find someone in your own little town."

In the 1980s disposable income here was half of that in Canada. A decade later disposable income is higher than in Canada. A shortage of nurses, Help Wanted signs, hiring in Newfoundland and Spain and Romania to staff hotels and restaurants.

Trendy restaurants full and churches empty. In the late nineties there are no indications of change or a crash, and Ireland's economy outperforms the English economy, but I can't see this boom going on forever. EU payments will stop soon, though. Twenty-eight billion dollars. And there has to be a ripple effect from American high-tech companies that are hemorrhaging, cutting jobs, selling office furniture, folding their tents. In 2002 Irish newspapers are full of talk of a downturn and layoffs, and students I speak with express fears they won't be hired after they graduate, but real-estate prices are still climbing into the heavens and you can't get builders — all busy. Perhaps the worm is turning this moment.

Everyone in Dublin asks proudly, "Hasn't it changed?!" I hear the phrase "Celtic Tiger" more times than I care to remember. The late nineties IT boom has people sounding like Texans, although they still have the lovely Dublin accent.

"Hasn't it changed?"

"Utterly," I say, but no one gets the 1916 Yeats allusion. Bespectacled W. B. Yeats seems quaint and innocent and myopic against this backdrop of pharmaceuticals and disco dreck and californication monster-house renovations.

We drive to see if we can find the canal where our grandfather Michael drowned, and we drive to the graveyard to see how many bodies are tipped in the narrow grave on Finglas Road. No one is sure how many bodies are there, and the others are curious once I bring it up. Five bodies inside the German car: Sharkey is our obliging chauffeur, driving Rose, Bridie, myself to our history lessons, and Sharkey's little boy has come along for the ride.

While driving to Glasnevin Cemetery, Sharkey points into

a dim stretch of row housing, developments built when they dynamited slums in the oldest parts of Dublin and forced the slum-dwellers out of the central city.

"Used to be a nice little valley. Some bad parts in that neighbourhood now. Batons always out when we're in Finglas. Hats and bats, we call it. Riots every weekend. No time for community work. They just march us in, expect us to solve everything," complains Sharkey. "Can't get to the root of the bloody problem that way. They just send us in with batons to crack a few heads of the local boyos. Solves nothing." We drive a bit more.

"Still," Sharkey allows, in a lighter voice, "they enjoy it and we enjoy it." A hint of a grin now as he drives.

Sharkey makes me laugh. I can't imagine his brother, Padraic, bopping shitrats on the head and talking of both sides enjoying it.

Rose and Bridie decide our generation is much worse than their era, all this swearing and naughty jokes and drinking and carrying on. "Why, nowadays everything's *thing*."

Sharkey disagrees. "It's not *thing*. Remember Dad's friend Ginger Smith? Drove a lorry for Guinness, and he was a thirty-pint man. Ginger Smith drank a skinful at every pub where he delivered stout. We'd be sacked now. If we did that on the job now, we'd be sacked."

We stop at a police checkpoint. The men stare in. It's marching season in Drumacree and the Bog, marching season in the north, fife and drum, the bowler hats out of *Clockwork Orange*, and they're expecting trouble. Bombs are going off again, trains hijacked and burned, business vans hijacked for roadblocks and the passenger compartments in flames and oily smoke. Beat the drum and sing "The Sash My Father Wore," sing "Land of Hope and Glory."

This summer weekend the Royal Ulster Constabulary (no Catholics on that force) fired 1,600 plastic bullets into the festive crowd and 691 gasoline bombs were returned, as is polite, as is meet. What lucky bureacrat's task is it to tally the number of Molotov cocktails, measuring out your life in coffee spoons and petrol bombs. While travelling, I noticed that airports in England and Ireland were tense: "Please Do Not Leave Luggage Unattended." As I pulled out more and more cash (Europe is expensive), bank machines asked me in neutral terms to report any untended package. In Dublin and the south, though, this mayhem to the north seems very distant, invisible, in another country, beyond the pale.

"Heard the north is very pretty," my aunts say.

"Do you want to go with me?" I ask.

"Ah no, I don't have time."

An hour by train and Rose and Bridie have never once been there. Northern Ireland is the North Pole.

Sharkey the policeman nods at the uniformed policemen standing around us in the road and they wave us through. Sharkey is wearing a bright red golf shirt, jeans, and workboots. I wonder if the gardái have some secret signal for each other.

Two of Sharkey's cars have been stolen: one car burnt, one car stripped.

"Because you're a garda?" I ask.

Sharkey shrugs, noncommittal.

He drives a luxurious moulded German car, steering wheel on the right side. Over and over I walk up to the passenger door and find a steering wheel. I can't map this reversal in my head. Sharkey lets me do it, laughs at my confusion. My cousins are pilots in a wraparound cockpit now, better cars than mine. When we park, Sharkey winds a big blue bike chain around the steering wheel and steering column. Lots of crime in the new, improved Ireland.

"That chain stop anything?"

"Feck no, just looks like it does."

This is another change in Ireland: fewer cars or apartments

were available when I was here two decades ago. Padraic and Sharkey had to borrow their dad's tiny Toyota. First they'd say to me, "Mark, we're going to Howth for a pint. Care to come along?"

Is the pope Polish?

Then they'd yell, "Mom! Mark wants to go out. Can we borrow the car?"

Ordinarily their father might not have given them permission, so they used their foreign cousin as an excuse. A car then, even in the 1980s, was more of a rare luxury.

Now we enter wide elevated highways, Celtic autobahns, and I see fewer shady lanes and hedgerows. Car sales are up. Buckets of European Union money for roads, infrastructure, marketing (to market, to market, fetch us a pig). More money, more freedoms, more articles on stress, and more break-ins and jump-overs and the big new roads fill up, bumper to bumper by the Liffey or the roads out to Malahide (Hardening of the arteries, wrote the coroner).

Unbelievable amounts of crime from just a few addicts, Sharkey tells me. One man, they held a syringe to his neck and marched him to his ATM to get his money. The heroin problem is growing, whole areas now stunned on junk. Kids grow up with it, with no parents basically, porch light on but nobody home, light pours into a vein, buy an envelope, buy a verb, no fecking rules, and neighbours down the row all the same.

They don't even get high after a while, Sharkey says, but they have to keep shooting or be sick as a dog. Some junkies quit just so they can crank up again later and have the high once more, get off like they did at first. Nostalgia for the good old days.

Crime Spokesman Fends off Crazed Car Thief
Fine Gael's justice spokesman fended off an attack by a crazed drug addict who broke into his Mercedes. The

County Mayo deputy, whose brief includes crime and security issues, described how the incident brought home to him the reality of crime in Dublin and what people have to deal with every day in the capital.

"I challenged him about being in my car. He produced a screwdriver and told me he would use it."

The young man became enraged when he noticed he was being followed and attacked the Mercedes.

"He started kicking in the front grille. He was a tough young man. The gardaí were on the scene in minutes, but he had gone."

Sharkey tells me that addicts picked up for questioning are allowed a solicitor and a doctor.

"If it's a good doctor he gives me their methadone to hold while I'm asking them questions. Pour out a bit of their meth," he says, holding up his thumb and fingers to tilt an imaginary vial, "and they start to talk, they start *grassing*; they'll tell you anything. Of course, you can't believe most of what they say. They'll say anything."

With paramilitaries on either side there is no equivalent of methadone to let them withdraw. What is the incentive for a paramilitary to go straight, to flip burgers or turn bolts in the new order? An addiction, like with Sharkey's junkies.

Some players are going to prefer the old fractiousness — touts and turf wars, extortion money, the juice, your AR-15 or 9mm pistol putting the fear of God in some sinner or rival — prefer that to pushing the lawnmower or washing the family car (Oh, honey, I got that cheese you like).

Meth is not going to cut it for some of the hard men; eco-tourism and the service sector and the Good Friday Accord are going to be a hard sell to the hard men. They've travelled a long way from my grandfather's IRA or the Ulster Volunteers.

Once you've boosted the Ballsbridge bank or booted up a few points of junk or shot out a few kneecaps to prove some obscure, feverish point — well, sir, it's then tough just to hand over the stockpiled arsenal of Semtex and Redeye missiles and Robar SR90 sniper rifles and travel back and join the armchair nation of wee well-behaved widows waiting patiently for the television talking heads to tell them who's been bad and who's been good.

Sharkey works at the airport, intercepting illegal aliens, who are arriving in larger and larger numbers. He gets free trips escorting aliens back to Amsterdam, Paris, New York, and other cities, which sounds like a bit of all right. Many aliens are a little duskier than the pale Irish, coming from countries like Somalia, Mauritania, Nigeria, Senegal, and Zaire. Some illegals are from Algeria, some from Eastern Europe — say the Kurdish Kalnramanmaras region, Turkey, Romania, Bosnia — and some are maybe Czech or Slovak gypsies, or Roma. They pay thousands of pounds for the chance to play "Danny Boy" on a tin whistle; they want our Botox and pashminas.

It's gone way up, says Sharkey, from one or two hundred cases a year to that many in a week or two, a thousand aliens a month. The *Irish Independent* lists notable scams the way other papers list ships visiting a port. The so-called Lagos Cycling Club: all their paperwork forged, they were found by immigration officers to be chancers (I love a journalist who employs the word "chancers"). The fake Romanian choir going to a Sligo choral festival, the Vietnamese students who disappear from their desks, the fake film production crew from India (150 visas), the Asian men granted visas to visit factories or buy machinery or attend horse auctions and last seen taking a taxi to the north.

An upsurge in clandestine human movement and human trafficking, especially since the breakup of the Soviet Union: brave migrants looking for new worlds but steered into sweatshops, joe jobs, or the sex trade, steered into the backrooms or the back of the truck with no air or pushed out in the dazzling, terrible desert, where the sun moulds you into a dessicated mummy — *Walk north that way, and you'll find the road. Trust us. We'll be back soon with jugs of water to slake your thirst.*

Bright sunshine, the truck driver hears moaning, pounding from his containerful of Canadian furniture. Turkey, Bosnia, Milan, Cologne, Belgium, rough seas crossing and dock in Rosslare, then a truck driving in Wexford. What a long, strange trip it's been just to die of anoxia in Ireland; lack of oxygen to the brain, say the post-mortems. Pay £5,000 to suffocate. Multiply that by thousands. The eight dead include two boys, aged four and nine, and a ten-year-old girl.

Sharkey complains that the aliens are lured by shady agents (like Mexico's Coyotes and China's Snakeheads) and rampant Internet stories of free hotel rooms, steady dole payments, and Ireland's booming economy (there's that Celtic Tiger again, and its mink capes and ostrich overnight bags!).

A container opened in the port of Dublin holds three boys from Albania, and no parents with them. There is a public uproar and backlash over this alien invasion.

"All of them seem to be driving cars, and all pregnant with two or three kids."

"They're very aggressive."

"These foreign girls can't clean."

"So many you'd t'ink this was Beirut."

There are less-than-charitable letters to the Dublin papers about nig-nogs taking Irish money, benefits, health plans, housing, taking advantage of us, taking poor, innocent Ireland for a ride.

"It's a huge problem." Sharkey the policeman, his thumb in the dyke, decries the aliens pouring in, crowds of people put up in hotels for ages, put on the dole the whole time — the system can't take it, and why should we pay for that? I don't get free money, he says; I have to work (though my cousin does get free rides and meals and decent hotels when flying them back to someone else's jurisdiction on a fast-track deportation agreement).

"Sharkey is a racist!" says his brother, getting mad. Unlike Sharkey, Padraic the liberal cousin is agog at the open prejudice of his fellow Dubliners, easy-going Padraic suddenly livid ("They should be *ashamed*!"), almost spitting his words at me in a furious embarrassment. Perhaps he knows something personal about prejudice.

This Irish umbrage at immigrants approaches black humour in light of Irish history and the diaspora. Is there some irony in a country sending out millions of starving immigrants in coffin ships and later carping about those who turn up begging at its own door?

"We immigrated to America, and we had to work hard."

"They don't keep their gardens up."

"Why don't they stay in Nigeria?"

Ireland's Nigerian-born Monopoly champion, Ekumdayo Badmus, has changed his surname to O'Badmus to sound more Irish. He will bring two squares of turf to the World Championships so he will always have a piece of Ireland under his feet.

"It's all Asians and Nigerians and Romanians in town now," says Rose. "More of them than English," she says. "World changing, and it's not for the better." I find it interesting that she calls the Irish English.

Some migrants pay a fortune to get ferried here, only to be turned about and lose their money and shoved back to some other country, some other lonely frontier or overcrowded detention camp by the sea. One crooked agent plunked a group of African refugees on a boat from England to Ireland but told them they were sailing to Canada, to my distant country (talk about your basic journey without maps).

This is not entirely surprising. Mexican migrants I spoke with in the Baja and southern California were not intimate with schoolhouse maps or geography or driving distances. In dim, narrow bars we tried to converse and drew each other cocktail-napkin maps of where we hailed from, and for some migrants Los Angeles was way up the coast and San Francisco might as well be Siberia. They had little idea of the whereabouts of Seattle or Vancouver or the rest of Canada, yet illegals show up regularly in Idaho and Alberta for farmwork, nosing their way into amazingly nuanced backroad treks up the lovely spine of the continent and back down with a few dollars to take home to the village.

My great-aunts and great-uncles were emigrants, my aunts and uncles were emigrants, my parents were emigrants, my cousins were emigrants, uprooting for work, for broader oppor-tunities and strange shores, for dark soil and a solemn Oldsmobile in the dappled shady lane and a house where they're not always kicking down the door.

Sharkey is against aliens and against travellers and bleeding hearts who want to serve them.

"You serve one traveller and (Sharkey makes a two-note whistle to indicate the speed of events, *swoo-it*) you get a swarm of them, and they steal from you and they fight and wreck the place. You can't serve them. You can't. Give them a house to live in, and it's a wreck; strip all the copper to sell. Fix up the house, and it happens again."

He says, "Most hotels don't want traveller weddings. Sorry, all booked up that day," mimicking a phone to his ear. "There was a big wedding party out in Howth, travellers passing forged money at the hotel bar. The hotel calls the local police detachment: What should we do? Kick them out, and they might wreck the whole place.

"The policeman says keep serving them.

"Hotel manager says, 'But it's costing me money!'

"'Do you want our help or not? Keep serving them and mark down who gave you which notes, how much, etc.'

"The Howth detachment calls up the task force in Dublin for a van of guards; this is when I was still on the task force," says Sharkey. "So we head over. I took a few to the station, and I had great craic with them; I like them, great fun, but if I had a place I wouldn't serve them. And they all rat on each other. Think they'd be tight," Sharkey shows two fingers wrapped together, "but they're not."

"'You'd be the main man doing the forging, right?'

"'No, it's him. Look under his bed.'

"'No it's him,' says the other. 'Check between the seats of his van.'

"I search the van and find a huge pile of forged notes right where the guy said.

"Up in front of the judge and solicitor: 'Was the van locked?'

"'No.'

"'Then anyone could have come and put a pile of money there in an open van.'

"Right, that happens every day, someone putting money *into* a van rather than taking it out of a van.

"'Case dismissed,' the judge says.

"Lawsuits now if they're not served," says Sharkey. "Book a wedding and they sue if they're told no, call up the solicitor; it's a new scam now. They're amazing. They'll go to a big new business park, say Microsoft or Sony, and camp in the parking lot. Now, the business doesn't want the knackers there, but it takes months to go through a solicitor and the courts, so your man from Sony goes outside and asks them how much money to move on. Another new scam.

"And I'll come in here and Rose is watching some bleeding-heart program on the telly. 'Oh, they have it hard, I tell you,' she says, a tear in her eye." Sharkey mimics a tear rolling down his cheek. "And I say, Look!" He points at an imaginary TV. "Look, that's the knacker I collared passing piles of counterfeit money, or that's the guy who robbed that farm in the west.

"They always have some nun sitting with them. 'Now I talked with them,' the nun says, 'and they told me they didn't do this.'

"If there's a big traveller funeral the guards have to keep the sides separate — old feuds they have — and we search the graveyard beforehand for hidden weapons. People were shot at a previous funeral — pull out shotguns," Sharkey pretends to aim a gun, "at the graveside and blast away."

Chapter Fourteen

Ladies Watch
Your Purses

We drive in the narrow stone entrance. I like graveyards, these gated communities, these upside-down-cake cities, and Glasnevin is an impressive graveyard.

"Dublin's Famous Necropolis," says the brochure. Black-and-grey stone and carved faces as far as you can see — more than one million citizens waiting for us in their dead village. Stone walls lifted up, stone lintels laid, stone balanced everywhere in a miniature Connemara. No golden bough or elk moving through a sunlit mountain meadow; no pine needle paths; no silk spider-webs shaking in tight golden light.

A high Norman tower with a pointed cap dominates the spooky marble crypts and mondo grey crucifixes with Jesus (slightly cross-eyed) hanging sadly on them, the lichen-crowded crosses and aloof stone archbishops and polished cardinals lying on their backs, staring with regret at the roods and roofs of their gothic mausoleums and monuments. The stone holy men wear the same rueful expression as the Prufrock men drinking their pints in jowly Jurassic Park, all seeing the same things in front of them, the same things in all our tiny heads.

Sharkey's little boy, Jack, climbs gleefully over these giant prone bishops. Their white stone arms are folded; at feet and head they are tended by wincing angels. Padraic says the son, Jack, made Sharkey a new man. My two aunts, sharing a bright umbrella, stroll past Celtic crosses and limestone sarcophagi.

All the rebels and patriots who are anyone are buried here by the old monastery, which survived the Vikings. This is where the martyrs meet. I go looking, a tourist.

Charles Parnell, the Chief, the uncrowned king of Ireland, hounded to an early grave after being named in an 1890 divorce suit. The movie *Death Wish* played here in 1981, and I used the theatre marquee in a photo: the big red letters DEATH visible behind Parnell's statue.

Jeremiah O'Donovan Rossa, a.k.a. Dynamite Rossa, whom Patrick Pearce called "the unrepentant Fenian," believed in taking the war to England, jailed and banished, subject of a come-all-ye song mentioned in the James Joyce story "Araby" and an inspiration for the 1916 Easter Rising.

Daniel O'Connell, the Great Liberator, his imposing caped statue over the broad street and bridge named after him, suppos-edly father of many children born on the wrong side of the blanket; his body in a vault here, but his heart cut out to travel to Rome, where he wanted to die.

Maud Gonne, a radical writer and actress, educated in France, a nationalist, an influence on Yeats, and married to a 1916 martyr.

Countess Markievicz, born in Buckingham Gate, born to the Anglo-Irish Ascendancy, yet she joined the Irish Citizen Army, taking up arms in Easter 1916, jailed over and over, sentenced to death by firing squad, but like de Valera's, her execution was commuted. The Rebel Countess, the first woman elected to the British Parliament.

Sir Roger Casement brought in German arms by boat and submarine, was foiled and, after his lascivious diary was leaked to turn opinion against him, hanged.

A monument to the dead of Easter 1916 seems to eroticize the uprising with its glowing half-naked statues of a lovely woman embracing a handsome young man lying across her (*Lady, shall I lie in your lap?*).

Famine dead and cholera victims and dipso writers and local wits with Liffey fever. The stern old Taoiseach Eamon de Valera is lying here, as is his colleague and enemy Michael Collins, the General, the Big Fellow, with a big hole in his head he needed like a hole in the head. Flowers and statues and pictures fall over the skin-pale slab of Michael Collins's grave, as if it's a Hollywood sidewalk or the Lizard King's Paris tomb. Because of Neil Jordan's high-profile movie with Julia Roberts and Liam Neeson, General Collins has become more of an international media star, a *personality*, though Collins has always been a celebrity here. Perhaps the largest funeral ever in Dublin, yet my grandfather chose to avoid the event.

And my grandfather, the drowned man, is lying here somewhere, waiting for us to divine his plot. If he's like me, he's wondering what all the fuss is about Julia Roberts.

It takes some searching, but we find our narrow grave. My aunts place flowers: tiger lilies and daisies. I have nothing: should I have brought a pint of plain? The modest tombstone states that this sunken grave contains Michael Lyons, Mary Lyons, and their children Cathleen, Michael, and Jean. Five of us in the German car; five relatives hidden in this tiny plot. The Glasnevin paperwork spells the girls' names Kathleen and Jane. This reminds me of Irish clocks: I've yet to see two that agree. Did your man chisel the wrong names? Did Michael have funeral insurance or did Guinness pay for his stone? The Coopers' Society? The coopers and pallbearers stop after my grandfather's funeral for a drink in Kavanagh's, the pub by the cemetery known as the Gravediggers.

Michael drowned in 1922 and his wife, Mary, died in 1957 (my brother Martin was born prematurely just after Mary died, his birth prompted when a telephone operator read my mother the death telegram without warning). The civil war petered out in 1923.

Mary Doyle Lyons waited thirty-five years a widow, raising the brood, running the Island Hotel, making butter and raising cattle and turkeys and chickens in the summer, haunting quayside auctions and quayside churches and marches and political meetings and riots and the Guinness clinic and the massive graveyard where she buried her husband and three of her children.

Michael Kennedy Lyons waited a long time too. Fell down in the canal's empty, beautiful water and was pulled out by men and laid down by men in the claustrophobic beetled earth, a valley converted to the dead, his tiny grave opening and closing, opens and closes like an eye, iron spade clinking a stone, another still body and another body and boots stepping again in this soil full of bones and spades probing their blind way (Where are you?), and gravediggers going once more to the Gravediggers for a pint after their bent work. Michael's modest grave getting more and more crowded — our dead ones must be held tight in the soil on their way to China. The word "cooper" comes from cup or to confine. Here the cooper is confined.

Is anything left of their bodies, their good clothes? A buckled shoe? His daughter there, his son named for him, another smiling daughter, and finally his wife — spades and boots and my tiny doll-like aunts and uncles and my grandparents in black falling down on each other in the Irish earth with no knowledge of me or mine and then left alone in their villa for eight decades until one of these nasal, twanging foreigners arrives to prompt a rare visit graveside, to find them waiting in the slumbering numbers and afternoon light. My strange pleasure. A million here, but this corner is mine.

Near us is a young girl and her mother. "Is her soul down there?" the girl asks.

"Well no, I don't think so."

"Is her head down there?"

"Well, yes."

"Her feet?"

"Yes."

"Her arms?"

The mother starts to cry. "She's there."

Dermot, the eldest son, is buried here too, but not in the family grave. His mother, Mary, died of hardening of the arteries, as did Dermot. Narrow grave, narrow arteries, closing the scarlet inside passages like blocking a tunnel. Who closed first, hardened faster? Perhaps it was something else entirely and that was an easy cause of death for a jaded doctor to scrawl on a death certificate.

Now you can be a little more specific. Now you can die of SIDS or AIDS, crash your BMW or SUV, get pinned beneath your ATV, caught by a silhouette with an Uzi or .45 or AK-47 or AR-15 or Koch SPG, take a seat on Flight 101 or 111, die of a virus sliding into your bloodstream or a plane into a building like an axe into a birthday cake or a jumbo jet falling to the bottom of the watery sound. Now you can fall into H, fall into E, fall into expensive convulsions on the sidewalk in front of a trendy night-club, or just fade out with sleek remote in hand, watching Homer and Mr. Burns from within the sanguine cockpit of your genuine Naugahyde easy chair — TV on, but nobody home.

So much more to choose from now (Hasn't it changed!) in Ireland, in the world. The illusion of choice, though — some-times dead is dead (*none, I think, do there embrace*). Everyone in Glasnevin dead under a rood, another theme park bristling in the troubled blood. The inhabitants are too bloody quiet, anti-social. Why don't they rise up from the ould sod and blather something witty about their own checkpoints, their discoveries, their hidden intrigues? (We do *embrace* down here; we neck and snog and on our mobiles order in homebrew poteen and two-for-one pepperoni pizza!) Do the dead here meet their weasel-eyed enemies in the afterlife? Their lovely loved ones? Are they troubled or content? Enquiring minds want to know. We've come so far, bellied up to the bar, using up all our feeble lines of credit to be here with the deceased, the Irish shades, the millions in the necropolis and the five bits of bones that mean something.

I'll never die, and I'll tell you why. My arteries are soft and supple because I favour aloe vera and Palmolive enemas, I drink extra-virgin Oil of Olay by the hour, my Romanian personal trainer smacks me upside the head with celebrity placentas, and well-adjusted peasants smear my body (stately, plump) with seaweed handpicked by legal leprechauns from a sandy strand below Buck Mulligan's Martello Tower Amusement Park and Shooting Gallery. And because my grandfather Michael was a master cooper I am allowed, when in Dublin, to bathe naked in giant vats of creamy Guinness porter, singing "Remember Boy, You're Irish" in an untutored tenor while swimming and splashing with naked, athletic chestnut-haired women from the west who murmur only sweet Gaelic in my innocent ear and can't keep their hands off my limbs and private parts and for some sweet reason are devoted to me and me only, and when all of us are all sated in all respects then the contents of my Guinness vats are piped out to the free world and beyond the back. And it's naked me and the naked, sumptuous Gaeltacht colleens that influence the distinctive colour and taste and fabled mouthfeel so valued in the fake Irish pubs around the world.

And how is it, pet?

Oh, it's loovely, just loovely.

A pint of plain is your only man.

Slàinte!

My grandparents' gravestone asks, "JESUS MERCY MARY HELP" and under that the letters IHS, a Greek abbreviation for Jesus that I remember seeing on church crosses when I was an altar boy. The wood for the coffin was cut and hammered around the corner from their house; hear the man working a saw for you while you're laid out on a door in the living room and neighbours drop in for a bite and a gargle. All of them dead now.

The gravestone carved on Thomas Street, a stone's throw from Guinness and my mother's old neighbourhood by the river. Thomas Street, where you can buy heroin now. Guinness stout and heroin battle over microbranding and market share.

Many Glasnevin tombstones are kicked over. I see a loser peeking in the iron fence rails and a sign: "Ladies Watch Your Purses." A Dublin man was murdered here in a recent robbery, and he died sprawled over his wife's grave (*not a day goes by without a stabbing*). Padraic doesn't come to the family graves. He flies to Spain to live, live it up. In 1981 my mother knew she wouldn't see her brother again. I won't see Padraic ever again.

The 1922 newspaper blames the Grand Canal and an old funeral card states Ashtown, but we can't find it, lost and irritated outside of Dublin, driving lush, rainy countryside, estates that belong to Guinness outside of Dublin, lost and finally asking in at a canoe-and-kayak club on the pretty River Liffey.

A man holding a kayak says, "Ashtown is on the *Royal* Canal."

"Can't be," I argue stupidly, a stupid tourist.

"I know north Dublin like the back of my hand," Kayak Man says to me with admirable patience. "Especially the water. It's on the Royal."

Kayak Man finds a map and shows me.

Sharkey nods, says he knows the way there. It's very frustrating to be on a wild goose chase, maddening to be searching the wrong canal (and now I realize that I was staring at the Royal Canal when I fled up the Dublin docks and sat in the Funnel Bar). It turns out that Kayak Man's grandfather also worked for Guinness, on the docks. He too was Catholic, but he was hired after serving in the Great War.

"Most drownings are at the lock," Kayak Man tells me. "Four drowned in the canal a few years ago — their car went off the road beside it and in. The canals are still dangerous: the water is very cold, and few people in this nation know how to swim — the weather here doesn't get warm enough for that long. People drown in the canals every summer."

I can't get over the newspaper saying the Grand Canal, the paper sending me to the wrong canal, feeling foolish, mad at driving in circles and looking in the wrong places, and I neglect to ask Kayak Man why most drownings are at the lock.

The Angler's Rest in the dreamlike afternoon: a lovely country pub where we stop for a break while searching for Ashtown, searching for the Royal Canal. Fishing gear and gorgeous Paul Henry landscapes hang on the pub's walls, one work similar to a

Henry painting my mother has had forever. I stared at that painting as a child — stared at four long thatched cottages on a muddy
road under a dark mountain, and in the high clouds I saw George
Washington's profile and behind his a woman's face. I assume my
mother's cloudy Connemara landscape is a print because Paul
Henry originals are worth a fortune. A grateful or smitten patient
gave it to my mother when she was a wartime nurse.

We drink outside on a narrow porch where we can see
Sharkey's little boy sleeping in the carseat. When the child
wakes up, Sharkey gallops to grab him so he doesn't think we've
deserted him, and then, to my surprise, we don't leave, but
instead all troop inside the bar and take a table by the fire. Liquor
laws concerning children in pubs are more relaxed than what I'm
used to growing up in Canada.

The bartender says, "My cousins immigrated to Toronto in
the 1950s; never heard from them again." They evaporated like
an old tenement, like my grandparents' old furniture.

"My mother immigrated to Canada in 1952."

"Ah, then, she'll know them," the bartender decides.

We zigzag pleasant leafy backroads, double back the way we
came earlier, bearing north by northwest. There is a misty rain,
but white light bounces off the pearly cloud cover. We cross a
small bridge, and beside us a lockhouse and forbidding black
gates held in deep stone walls that drop down into water. It's a
narrow construct, long strands of dried rushes or seaweed glued
on the black gates. We've found the Royal Canal; we've found
Lock #11 on the Royal Canal.

Later that evening, after the canal, we stop at a seaside pub, then
walk upstairs to a pasta place for dinner. Sharkey knows all the
locals and all the owners from when he walked the beat out this
way. Says they used to drop in after a shift and throw their police
hats on the table and drink until four a.m. with the doors locked,

give a bartender or staff a ride home. Says if they did it now they'd be reported and lose their jobs. Knew everyone before, a quieter town then.

"Horse walks into an Irish pub. Your man says, 'Why the long face?'"

"What's the difference between a redhead and a terrorist? You can negotiate with a terrorist."

After a few drinks my aunts are in stitches and staggering. They're hilarious, like giggling schoolgirls. It takes very little to set them off, for them to have a grand evening. I admire this. Too bad Padraic is not with us. Leaving the pasta place my aunts take some time negotiating a narrow, rickety stairway. Some young thing waits irritably at the bottom of the stairs with her eyes to the side and up, world-weary at seventeen, disgusted with anyone who is not seventeen.

My aunts once young. "Marty came back home for a visit, in an American uniform, and Josie was wearing a fur coat. All of us went for a drink at a place just across the Liffey. We had maybe two drinks, and I've never been so drunk. Oh, we were laughing and falling over. I don't what that bartender gave us. He must have slipped something in our drinks or given us Red Biddy. Maybe he thought we were ladies of the night with a Yankee soldier, fur coats and thing, and gave us Red Biddy. Oh, we were laughing; we couldn't stop. Later, when we got home, Bridie was in tears on the floor crying, 'I want my Willie! I want my Willie!'"

As we drive, Sharkey complains that the gardái in the Gaeltacht, the Gaelic-speaking areas in the west, are paid 12 per cent more and have far less trouble than their counterparts in the cities, who deal with knives and dirty needles and broken bottles and ganglords and IRA bank robbers.

"The whole Gaelic thing is a racket," he says. "Farmers in the west get grants for sheep up a mountain; they borrow neighbours' herds and get paid by the head."

"Not any more," protests his mother, Rose.

"They did."

"They got on to them now."

"They get grants to keep up their stone walls. Eligible every three years, so they kick them over every three years."

"Sharkey, they don't!"

"They do!"

"You're a terror, so." They enjoy his teasing, his irreverent jokes, the whiff of scandal in his talk.

"On a golf tour in Ireland, Tiger Woods drives his BMW into a petrol station in the west. Two tees fall out of his car.

"'Now, what are you after dropping?' asks the attendant.

"'Tees,' says Tiger Woods. 'You put your balls on them when you're driving.'

"'Feckin' Jaysus, now don't the lads at BMW think of everything!'"

On a Dublin wall spraypainted graffiti: "NIGGERS OUT!"

Over top of that a new message: "RACIST WANKERS OUT!"

I think, That could be my two cousins at work.

Sharkey is a bit of a redneck, but I have more fun with him and my older aunts than I do with Padraic, the swinging single. They take me out, guide me around in ways that Padraic does not.

Bridie complains to me of loud foreign students crowding our suburban train. "They come here to learn English and all yabbering in Spanish."

Somehow the O. J. Simpson trial comes up, and Bridie says to me with a sly smile, "Your man must've been hungry to bite an ear off."

"Uh, I think that's Mike Tyson."

She stares at me through her thick glasses as if I'm always splitting hairs. And I am always splitting hairs, slicing and dicing, nitpicking, a walking monument to specialization.

One night I study photos in Tim Pat Coogan's *The Irish Civil War*, take a child's magnifying glass to photos of Dublin street battles and photos of the two kinds of armoured cars the Brits gave to the Free State Army (some were quickly captured by the Republicans, so both sides had them). One is the Rolls-Royce Whippet, a low-slung, cigar-shaped jalopy with a squat conning tower and a slit for a Vickers water-cooled machine gun. Another is the Lancia — bulkier, more like an armour-plated truck, an iron box on wheels. Both factions proud of their machines, their dangerous new toys. With a kid's plastic magnifying glass, I try to decipher two looping sentences I notice chalked in white on their armoured panels:

For Goodness Sake Aim Straight

We Have No Time for Trucers

These flinty soldiers want a fight, fight to the end, no surrender, want to aim true and kill their fellow countrymen up the street, up in the Block, the wrecked tea shops and fortress hotels with holes smashed through bedroom walls so the men aren't pinned down, so snipers can make fast leaps between hotel rooms and halls and flit building to building. Poring over the photos I notice the familiar name Ashtown stencilled in neat white block letters on the blunt iron hood of a Lancia armoured car.

What I think of as the Ashtown Lancia is parked on the street to protect the gun crews blasting away at the stone walls of the Four Courts in late June 1922, machine-gunning and shelling the garrison inside Gandon's domed creation. Field guns dug into the road by Merchant's Quay, on Winetavern Street, Bridgefoot Street, the south side of the river.

My grandfather Michael might have nipped down the quays for a quick peek, to join the curious crowd watching the war down the brick street from his house. Michael could have easily read the name Ashtown on the armoured car, not knowing he was reading the name of the lock where, in a few weeks, he would sink his head into the green water. Perhaps the name on the iron plate gave him an idea: *Haven't been out that way for a while. Should go for a stroll out along the old canal, get away from all this bloody Collins business.*

If he was on the Republican side he must have been sickened to see men he knew burn up in the Four Courts, men dying just downriver from his front door. Even if he was neutral. And a large, neutral IRA faction didn't want to be pulled into the mess.

A siege down his street and downriver by the Block, parts of town cut off, streets empty, families evacuated or families trapped in smoke and noise and shells and snipers, shops ruined, armoured cars handing out bread, windows shot out or scissored into shards, bullet holes in bricks, bricks ground into powder, timbers askew, cisterns shot out and leaking into the floors below, bullets in baby cribs, walls gone in 1916 repaired and now gone again, ground zero, the centre of the new war across the river, across the water, the war starts here, though the war will end for him soon in the water at Ashtown.

IRA men across the river from Michael, the sewers their escape plan. My thoughts drift to the tunnel under my grand-father's house, a tunnel under the river. Did it connect with the sewers or travel to another cellar? Blocked off now.

My mother remembers a closed-up chamber or wine cellar in the basement. The tunnel could be recent, from 1916 and the Tan Wars that followed, but I suspect it is much older than that, having served some utilitarian purpose or been a remnant of earlier uprisings, from 1798 or 1803 or 1848. The many doomed Fenian forays against British rule, always too few weapons or allies or no plan and too many loose tongues wagging for money or revenge or betrayal.

Wolfe Tone caught and slitting his own throat in prison and taking eight days to die; young Robert Emmett caught and hanged close by on Thomas Street, the shopping street, his head cut off and held up for spectators; the King's Own Scottish Borderers looking for rifles unloaded from a yacht in Howth harbour by Ireland's Eye; Sir Roger Casement caught consorting with the German submarine U-19 and hanged in scandal after his homosexual Black Diaries were deliberately leaked. Did Roger drop by the George for a pint? The rebels beheaded, slack bodies; the dead rebels transformed into martyrs, into memory, into throaty ballads sung in my mother's gaunt house on the murky river.

Chapter Fifteen

A Secret Gunman

IN THE MIDDLE OF MY VISIT PADRAIC LEAVES for Spain with plans to rent a red convertible there and seduce an acquaintance I met at the Long Hall pub — just postponing the inevitable, Padraic says. His friends are taking bets on his chances. I prefer to not know the details, feel conservative and reactionary and prudish. He apologizes for leaving and claims he didn't know exactly when I was going to be here.

I did leave a message with Rose.

Didn't get the message, he says. Dates weren't clear, he says. Sorry.

I was looking forward to seeing him the most, but now my favourite cousin is always in a rush somewhere, always in a crowd. I have longer conversations with bartenders, have longer conversations with strangers.

I return to the National Library and notice that Michael Collins was shot dead in an ambush at Beal na Blath, in the hills near Macroom. Macroom is where I went with Bernadette and

Padraic and his girlfriend to a rock fest in 1981: Elvis Costello (good Irish name that) and the Undertones, from Derry, and some other bands. Collins's armoured car and machine gun didn't help him outside Macroom. I slept in a tent with an Irish woman, no idea where I was.

At the outdoor concert I posed as a music journalist from Canada and was allowed through a hole in a hedge and admitted to a muddy pen right in front of the stage, where, with my Russian camera, I took fast pictures of Costello and the Attractions while studying the grey sky above for beer cans lobbed high by ersatz punks in the audience behind us. The ersatz Irish punks didn't care for rock writers, didn't know I was faking it too. All of us faking it.

They were talented at lobbing cans up high so they arced down like shells onto our heads (*my aim is true*). It hurt if you got beaned. I'd look way up, snap a quick picture of Costello and his frenetic band zipping through "Oliver's Army" and "Less Than Zero" and "I Don't Want to Go to Chelsea," look up again for incoming, crank off another picture, Costello surprising me with a post-punk double chin, his bass player in a cobalt blue vest, angry at the crowd and running the band, driving the show. A phony war with beer cans. They had rage, had the range.

In the real 1922 war a secret gunman has the range, pulls a trigger, kills Michael Collins on a hillside, a roadside, the trigger finger on a rifle leading to the death of my grandfather the day of Collins's funeral. Our family lore associates the two deaths, the two Michaels. I believe it was a .303 shell. Collins at the height of his power. The exit wound huge, part of Collins's head gone; the convoy lost for hours on backroads, driving in circles in enemy territory (though Collins was from that part of Ireland) while Michael bleeds in their arms (their efforts to rescue him failed), dies in their arms (my mind flashes to poor Jackie and JFK's smashed head in her lap, and the confused motorcade speeding up to nowhere).

Some accounts say the triggerman was sorry when he heard he'd killed Collins, the Big Fellah, the General, the son of a seventh son of a seventh son. No one was ever charged. It might have been a fluke shot, the last shot of the skirmish. Others insist it was an English secret service sniper who deliberately nailed him. After all, hadn't Collins killed any number of English intelligence men? Collins had made it a personal war for many, a very twentieth-century war. Collins chose direct action rather than some doomed symbolic stand — Michael Collins shunning fuzzy martyrdom and becoming a martyr.

The mysterious triggerman in the hills hit more than the Big Man's pink hummingbird brain, more than the commander-in-chief, the shooter connected to more than Hollywood fame and Irish hagiography. The triggerman left my grandmother a widow with ten children to raise on her own. Kathleen with the lovely oval face, who died at three; and Dermot, the eldest son, who smiled as a baby and played violin and the pipes and worked hard and was a lovely singer but *hooshed* away his wife's hand on his deathbed; and Martin, my favourite uncle with a big nose, who in family lore slept through the Black and Tans dragging Dermot out of the same bed; and young Michael, who fell in the Dog Pond in Phoenix Park wearing his good clothes and was afraid to come home with his good clothes wet and got pneumonia and died as a boy (keep your feet dry, you'll never die); and Josephine, who's in a nursing home in Philly and met her husband, George, an electrician for the railroad, in her mother's boarding house, and Jo thought she had a face to stop a clock and her husband the electrician didn't want to leave Ireland and cried at the boat and drank unhappily in America; and May, who had a lovely voice and played piano and died in Philly not long after she started losing her balance; and Kay, my spitfire mother, named after the dead eldest daughter, Kay who jumps on an old Model T in a white dress to hog the limelight in a photo, her alone on the hood, the rest of the crowd in the front seat and rumbleseat; and Brendan, my mother's favourite brother, who was athletic and sang IRA songs when he was young and hated the IRA when he was older, who married the very lovely Rose and followed de Valera all his life, liked Dev and died soon after my first visit and I'm glad I met him; and Jean, who died at age six, perhaps of rheumatic fever, leaking heart valves, bedridden, serious doctors and nurses stomping up and down the many stairs; and Bridget the baby, my funny, feisty aunt in the country, who step-danced and also met her husband in her mother's tall, narrow boarding house over the river and now lives down on the farm and has a touch of vertigo and says she forgets things.

After her husband's drowning, my grandmother had to convert her big pre-Georgian pre-something brick home into a boarding house, the Island Hotel (Board and Residence. Every Comfort. Terms Moderate), just two doors down from the building in James Joyce's story "The Dead," the house where Joyce's aunts had their annual dance and dinner, the same house in John Huston's movie version of that gathering in *The Dead*, Huston's final movie before he became one of the dead. My uncle Marty was excited to see the movie but disappointed it didn't feature more outside shots; he wanted to see his old block, his old home.

One morning I take a long walk along the river to Usher's Island, down the walled quays, past the many bridges — Ha'penny Bridge, Bloody Bridge, Queen Maeve Bridge — to see the dire places once more, see if they've fallen down yet. Usher's Island, where my grandparents lived, where my mother was born

— not an island but an old street lining the River Liffey and named after the family of Archbishop Ussher, founding scholar of Trinity.

My mother says she thinks her house was a children's hospital in the 1700s, an upper-class gentleman's residence in the 1800s, then an iron merchant's, then classed a tenement. My mother says one door inside the house had the word "office" lettered on its glazed glass. The area's decline accelerated in the 1950s and 1960s. The buildings look austere from the outside, big boxes jammed against each other in a row hard against the sidewalk. In "The Dead," Joyce describes a "dark gaunt house on Usher's Island," where his great aunts rented the large upper rooms from the corn factor on the main floor. The buildings resemble warehouses more than homes, but not so long ago they were elegant and spacious, a world of gaslit pantries and drawing rooms with chandeliers and pianos and beeswax on the floor and waltzing skirts and hired help run off their feet. You'd never guess it now.

The Joyce house is boarded up when I walk past, ugly corrugated metal masking what was a beautiful Georgian entrance, fanlight still visible, second-floor shutters crippled on their pintles and moving in the wind, jimmied open by squatters living rough. Broken bottles and tinnies and trash heaps out front where Nora Barnacle and James Joyce strolled, where my mother played with a doll on the walk.

Strolling the quays another time to catch a train west I saw workers in hardhats cleaning up "The Dead" house. I told them I was happy to see them because the place had been such a mess.

Still is, they said, laughing.

Rubble everywhere, but the bones of a beautiful house. The door is open for the workers, so I can see inside, see the famous staircase where Nora and James descended into the snow general over Ireland, the stairs where Nora hears the ballad's piano chords and hoarse voice singing, where she remembers her dead suitor in the west. Distant music and a woman on a staircase — your brain caught, remembering a lost lover.

I was hoping the house would be restored by my next visit to the block, but several years later it is still a shambles.

The houses used to be three or four storeys, but the top storeys have been sheared off to take away weight and prevent collapse — the houses have been decapitated, and now circles of barbed wire stretch up atop and around the backside, attempting to keep trespassers from jumping roof to roof as the IRA and IRB lads did eighty years before. Where rebels from the country windmilled and jumped two storeys higher is now thin air, no rooftop up there for their feet, lonely silhouettes pinned against the sky four storeys up, ghosts with nowhere to land.

To save money when they first married, Rose and Brendan lived in the big place on Usher's Island. Rose didn't appreciate her mother-in-law, Mary, snooping through their things when they were out.

"I'd bought a beautiful cake and left it in our room. 'My Brendan doesn't like store-bought cake,' she told me. Well."

All the old photos show Rose smiling and affectionately grasping her mother-in-law's arm, but Rose tells me they had to move away before they'd planned to, had to find their own little place. Her daughter says Rose didn't like Mary at all; Rose is too tactful to tell me.

In her car Bridie sternly defends her mother, Mary: "She was amazing, the things she did. You don't listen to everything Rose says. She *dreams* things."

Travelling in a car you pass Usher's Island without a glance at the doorways or windows, trying to make the green light, trying to get out of the city. The street is gruesome now, a colourless world where giant lorries and trailers shake the small sidewalk and crack the house foundations. A yellow-and-green Dublin Corporation lorry looks hallucinatory, so bright against the grey, drab planes, as if a cartoonist had time to colour only a single item in the entire panel. The year my mother was born in this house they were singing a popular song: "Ireland Must Be Heaven, for My Mother Came from There." This little part of my mother's Ireland is no longer heaven.

James Joyce and Nora Barnacle walked out the Georgian doorway and turned right, walking past my grandmother's house, Joyce and Nora looking for a horse-drawn cab on the snowy quays. Red lamps glowing and the big Four Courts domed tower glowering down on them as they stepped toward the bridge at Winetavern Street hoping for the sound of hoofs. My mother liked the Guinness wagons with their huge, shaggy horses. On the plane an Englishman from Hertfordshire says Guinness still has its heavy horses. The narrow roadway squeezed along the quays wasn't made for a new century's monster trucks and traffic jams. It's unpleasant to walk in the lorries' constant roar and acrid wind of Eurodollars, which will either doom or save this old block.

I think of a photo of my mother, Kay, and her young friends clowning around on an ancient open car in front of the house — the road is so noisy now, you cannot converse, but no traffic is visible in the old photograph, no monster trucks and speeding buses shaking their world. In the old photo everyone looks relaxed, laughing. People promenaded along the quiet quays. Kids played on these steps and cats rolled about. Just down the block the wharf and long brick warehouses and adjacent roadway were filled with Guinness stevedores and draymen, a workplace bristling with winches and cranes, steeves and jackscrews and braided hemp ropes, so there must have been no through traffic on this side of the river. Now it's a major route out of a gridlock town.

My uncle Marty comes back home for a visit from America, wants to see again his childhood school and his old house. Is it a happy walk? Sore old feet hurting, his grand house on Usher's Island wrecked, the top cut off, the family house burnt and humiliated.

"I'd say he got a shock," says Bridie.

Marty has to sit and rest in Adam and Eve's church, stunned. The coins had changed, the street gone to rack and ruin, his home unrecognizable where once he'd been a kid with thick glasses and a big grin, a kid playing jokes on his sisters while his mother troubled her lovely piano.

He doesn't make it to his old school. Took the starch out of him a bit, agree my aunts.

James Joyce's aunts had the same last name, Lyons, as my mother's family. I like to amuse myself with the possibility of being related to Sunny Jim. My favourite uncle, who may or may not have been gay, took music lessons at James Joyce's aunts' house, but he made a face at the teacher and was kicked out. The merry widow next door fancied him. Everyone danced. I can't dance. Everyone played instruments or sang. I can't sing or play.

The Usher's Island house is not far from the train station (Heuston Station now, named after a martyr of 1916; Kingsbridge was the British name). "Too close," complains my mother. "Lads would come and stay there and my mother didn't charge them. Stay years or a night. No apartments then." The house is almost next door to the giant Guinness Brewery, with its old brick chimneys and walls and tunnels and whiskey towers and plumes of steam and the smell of malt in the neighbourhood and the old signs and beer coasters: "Guinness Is Good for You."

Guinness, the modern corporation with a folksy image — the corporation that is unkind to small breweries in Ireland (Guinness is *not* good for them) and exports fake Irish culture just to sell more and more units of its dark porter and the other brands it controls, to keep expanding every year because those are the orders from the offices above and the bottom line.

Guinness is not really Irish. It is a multinational company now with global marketing plans. The Guinness family lost control of their own business after some in-fighting and slick corporate finagling. The term "boycott" originated in the west of Ireland. Some American pubs now boycott Guinness for its sins.

My aunt Bridie says a job with Guinness was thought of as money, dead or alive, because of its pensions for widows.

Guinness Brewery was on the side of the Eton and the Castle, but the cooper's house on Usher's Island was a safe house for rebels. Lorries of uniformed men in the street, Black and Tans banging at the door, and my grandmother putting on her act ("Ah, you're after waking all my poor babies, and me a poor widow"), wondering who had informed on the safe house, who was in the pay of the Castle, who was grassing.

My Irish side of the family has racetrack luck with dates: my mother born right in the middle of the doomed 1916 Easter Rising, born April 26, British artillery crashing Georgian slate, bullets lodging in stone walls and bodies, Sackville Street knee-deep in rubble and the post office destroyed, the martyrs shot and my mother's tiny head pushing out of the womb, peeking around, criticizing, and a few more martyrs shot, and my grandmother putting on the poor mouth to buy time for her friends and sons and strangers to climb the big wooden chair upstairs and out the skylight and running over the tenement roofs.

First they run from the Brits and Black and Tans, then after Collins signed the Anglo-Irish treaty, they run from the Irish, run from their own, run from Michael Collins, the Big Fellah, who now has the very artillery that once fired at him in the General Post Office. Churchill gave him the English guns, and Collins pointed the eighteen-pounders at his old friends. Who could have foreseen this while taking cover in the GPO and getting blasted in 1916? Collins, who became so good at killing British spies — who, in pragmatically taking out his enemies instead of making a doomed dogmatic stand as a martyr, invented a new kind of hit-and-run urban warfare — is now made to turn on some of his own, find what it's like to kill his old friends. Unfortunately, some of the boyos are only too happy to kill old friends.

My family split, as Ireland did, as the army did, as the river splits the city. Some relatives in the country liked Michael Collins and the treaty, but my grandfather and grandmother's family in the city followed de Valera, who was anti-treaty, who seems a bit of a pompous ass, though he eventually rose to Taoiseach, or prime minister, and was also president, holding power in different offices for about five decades. My grandfather didn't live long enough to see this, but he did know that Collins was shot dead in the hills in a valley of blossoms and brought by steamer from Cork to Dublin, brought across the water. Michael Collins's assassination was fresh news to my grandfather, a visceral shock and not a tattered, sun-faded clipping, not on a library scroll.

Half of Ireland swarming Dublin for the parade for the famous corpse being planted in the ground, a deliberate propaganda exercise as well as a state funeral, winding through all of town and cameras recording it, a silent movie made to show the populace what the Republicans had done to their Irish hero. Soldiers in uniforms and cartridge belts walk; priests in cassocks and rosaries walk.

Downtown Dublin statues black with people climbing for a vantage point, and my grandfather Michael Lyons moves the opposite way (as I would shy away), travels out into the country for a tram ride or the electric railway, a fresh mouthful of strawberries, a pint or two of Old Peculiar, a good long walk and an impulsive swim in the canal. The last acts of a happily grumpy man.

My two Michaels. Collins and Lyons. The famous death and the obscure death linked in August 1922.

Chapter Sixteen

The Canal

IN SHARKEY'S GERMAN CAR WE HAVE TRACKED down the obscure death, found the canal and Lock #11's clogged weeds and rushes, the lockhouse and black gates. Such a beautiful spot, lush, verdant, its danger masked like Ireland's: much beauty and a small chance of danger.

We walk the quiet banks, stand thinking in the mist and light's diffuse lens. The sky white and the banks green. This stretch of canal so peaceful, innocent. I look in and see my reflection. Should I climb in?

On the other bank trees hang over the calm water, reminding me of pre-Raphaelite renditions of Ophelia drowning: soft rushes, mist-muted greens, ethereal and unearthly, shadows of birds on leaves and water like small hands passing. The locks and docks and towpaths and canals dug at great expense and almost immediately made obsolete by railways.

At the side of the canal I imagine Michael leaving his bowler hat on the shore, his shoes dusty from walking the roads, he and his friends singing "A Kiss in the Dark" and "Water Boy," sweat at the small of his back, a hot sunny day for a stroll, and cooling down a grand idea, laughing at the cold-water shock.

All the way in, boys! Last one in buys the next round!

His moustache wet in the cool, murky water, this pointless canal engineered into the heart of the heart of the country, perhaps a wide barge barging from the lock, a barge heaped with peat for Dublin hearths in wet winter or a Guinness barge stacked with his own barrels (his eye going to study them), a high tarry hull at his face, trying to move away and the boat's wake rises over his thinning scalp, the boat pushing past and his friends

on the other side of the barge can't see. And blast it all to hell, where's Michael?

Or the black gates under the lockhouse creak open and pour water, fast current stirring the rushes (drownings always by the locks), a surge of water changing the depth, and Michael, my grandfather, moves and goes under, slick footing gone and fine kettle of fish he can't swim, arms out but nothing under him, trying to keep his mouth up and failing, realizing he is in trouble, and his sputtering grief at the thought of their grief if he can't get out of this balls-up, thinking of his wife in a long swaying skirt, moving room to room, past the piano, beeswax polish on the hardwood, kettle on the gas glimmer (watch out for the Glimmer Man lurking!), her stiff lace curtains she's so careful with, his toughened cooper's hand on her, the children reading library books or drawing together on the big landing on the stairs, where the light is good, then one girl, the six-year-old, my mother, coming down the stairs of #11 Usher's Island toward the River Liffey, and my grandfather a glimmer below Lock #11, thinking, This is a mess, bloody stupid, not a good time for this, not at all. They'll expect him at work tomorrow, nine kids, he is not ready for this. *Is this how it is, then?* Is there time to think, to be embarrassed, disgusted, sorry?

The funeral procession for General Collins marches in the sun, passes the ruined GPO, the post office where Collins was wounded and captured six years earlier — six long years — lines of priests shuffling past in long black cassocks, dirges playing, Ireland in mourning, ninety slow minutes to snake past any point, the body carried, the holy water, uniformed soldiers burnt by the sun.

In the bright water under the sun the body carried, puzzled, ninety slow seconds in drowning, needing oxygen in the lungs, the blood, *pain*, puzzled brain giving order after order, reflexes and ritual, songbirds swooping the canal, carbon dioxide, strange underwater murmurs, pops and cracks, cymbals, pressure on the heart.

Michael's brain remembers his father swimming outside Kilkenny, rushes and ruined castles, fish and insects, sunlight refracting in cold water, white dory skimming past black castle walls, Jesus Mercy Mary Help, can't go now, I just want to walk home, in that big door off the road, the children reading on the stairs by the window, milk delivered twice a day, the dark piano anchoring a safe world, world's sky shutting down darker as if going under trees, light shrinking around a kerosene lantern.

His body falling away from the tall people on the narrow shore under their feet, shore stretching overhead like a middle sky, his pocket watch left on shore ticking in a pocket, hands moving, spooky eels slinking away and back again, blood in your loud heart, blood shunting to your heart and brain, noise in your ears like wild steam shooting through the Cask Cleaning Shed, keep your mouth closed, watch-works ticking, feet kicking, arms pushing mud, finally forced to pry open your mouth for air, for something, to shout, to protest, to climb out laughing with your muscles and smash that tiny ticking pocket watch and walk home singing, but air bursts out of your mouth, exploding bubbles and light in a halo, and heavy canal water flows in to fill your lungs like sacks and the head goes lower and no more singing "Waltzing Matilda" or "Ain't We Got Fun" or rebel songs in the gaslit drawing room and never again in your mouth Mary's cold butter and tasty homemade soda bread and wild strawberries and never again a seaside tram to Howth's pier and mended nets and Ireland's Eye.

Did anyone bring his hat home? His jacket and watch? Who has it now? Most families have something. We do not.

Barges and narrowboats float, tight oak barrels float, but my grandfather drifts two or three feet under the water, head down in a slow dive with eels in the green distances and bird-flittering canal shadows, moving with the current, waterlogged, a vigorous boy from the hilly landlocked farm, a physical man, good with an adze and a hammer, muscles gone, exhausted, hypercarbic, hard muscles dying in agony in a place of beauty, thirty seconds on the watch, three minutes, pain lessening and his eyes open to the new green world, a farmer's son staring out.

His face staring out of the rare photos, a good-natured man with mischievous eyes, our family face, my face at a 747 window, a Dash-8, a 767, a man my age, like me a man who enjoyed walking with his young sons and became a man walking the bottom of the Royal Canal by Lock #11, a man swimming alone in green microfilm in a Dublin library eighty years later (their efforts to rescue him failed).

I feel that *my* efforts have failed, but I have seen my grandfather's birthplace, his cottage on the stony hillside farm at Johnswell, and I've seen Kilkenny's tiny black lanes and tall stone towers; I've walked his gritty Dublin neighbourhood and sniffed the Guinness malt and the River Liffey at his ruined front door, and I've stood at the Royal Canal, looking down the green depths where he went under below the lock, the only one in the family to go looking. I have seen what I think of as the four corners of my grandfather's shortened life, and I've been to his grave in Glasnevin and we left some flowers and we thought our thoughts and then we go back to live with the living.

Chapter Seventeen

WINKLE-PICKER BLUES

HOW QUICKLY A FAMILY BRANCH VEERS into different galaxies.
Demobbed in Plymouth. After the war, my mother and father had
three blond children in Oxford. They want more children; my
father the convert became more Catholic than the Catholics.
Housing scarce, food rationed, can't get furniture, old sheets
dyed green for curtains. I was the first child born after they immi-
grate to western Canada, after they cross the water. A lovely
crossing, but Dad seasick anyway. We're strangers now to our
relatives. What if I had been born crying under the golden spires
of Oxford? How different would I be? What name, what job,
what family would be mine? How much of my blood is Irish?
How much is Norman or Viking raider, a ruddy snake in the
woodpile? How much is the random green breast of the New
World that weaned me, that nourished my private version of the
family face?

I keep walking by the house at number 11 as if it will tell me
something. No one else does. I visit it every time I'm here, as if
it's a grave, a face I want to know. In Dublin's National Library I

find the city directories from 1850 to 1973 fascinating, like seeing time-lapse photography of my mother's block: buildings go up and fall down, poor become rich become poor, horses become trucks, men in bowler hats run toward a distant bridge, a distillery becomes a funeral home, a gentleman's house becomes an engineer's office becomes an iron merchant's becomes a tenement house.

In 1850 John Carey, Esquire, lived at 11 Usher's Island. He must have known of the tunnel if it was an old one. Because of the river, the address numbers run in sequence on just one side of the street: 10 is beside 11. George Pim, Esquire, owner of a number of well-known Dublin stores, owned numbers 15, 16, and 17. (Number 15 is "The Dead" house.) Number 18 was a Ladies' School and number 22 an apothecary. There was a corn factor and Patrick Lane's pub on the corner, at Watling Street. An odd mix, but the yearly taxes charged indicate a good address, as does the fact that Mr. Pim (Esquire) lived there.

In 1902 at number 15 I see Mrs. Callanan and Mrs. Lyons, James Joyce's aunts. In 1911 they are gone, replaced by a forage contractor and seed merchant. No more dancing the quadrille upstairs at Christmas, no more pier glass and lessons in deportment.

Next door to my mother's place, number 10 is listed as "Ruins"; it's where my mother played as a child, thinking it their yard, and where they kept animals. Decades later number 10 becomes Wm. Woolfson, Waste Merchant. I assume this is a polite term for a junkyard, a rag and bone man. In 1950 the block is still full and seems healthy. In 1957 number 14 is vacant. By 1973, numbers 3, 4, 6, and 7 are listed as demolished, as are 18 to 24. The Ladies' School demolished, eleven houses or buildings lost on one block. Number 14, however, has come back to life as a sausage casings business. My mother's house is Island Motors in 1972 and vacant in 1973, pinpointing for me the time of the fire.

Number 12, the house next door, is home in 1950 to Class and Sons, Wholesale Clothing, Island Manufacturing, and O'Regan's Ladies Coats and Costume. Number 15, "The Dead" house, is forage and coal. In 1957, number 12 is Class Clothing (is the father dead or the sons?) and Carlyle Upholstery. Number 15 is now a corn merchant, Mr. Fagan moving over one door from 14. Did he get a better deal on the rent at "The Dead" house? I am giddy in the library reading the years, reading the block. I love this.

Number 11, the family house, a gentleman's house, a children's hospital, a home, a boarding house, a car lot, vacant, then a scooter shop. The Island Hotel (Every Comfort. Terms Moderate) has become Scooter Island, with pictures of the Jam, Quadrophenia, and other mod icons and mechanics in boiler suits and a roof over the backyard like a rusty airplane hangar and the Guinness smell hanging in the neighbourhood air. I could have lived in this universe.

In the late 1970s I listened on vinyl to the Jam and their version of England, studying record covers and *New Music Express* as if there was an exam. The mod and ska scene was huge in Ireland and England when I was over in 1981, but now it seems as quaint and mannered as a Georgian minuet — the studied parkas and pouting and the scooters and red Rickenbacker guitars and sharp shoes, gleaming winkle-pickers on your feet.

The owner or leaseholder's son is friendly and shows me around; Mark shows me what he can inside the shell of his scooter shop, what was once my mother's house.

"A few years ago two little old ladies came around saying they lived here once." That would have been Bridie and my mother seeing their sad old house.

"After the fire in the 1970s we found a tunnel in the basement that went under the river." Rose says there was a train tunnel under Phoenix Park. Now the city is digging a giant tunnel from the port so trucks can avoid the city. So much work.

"Tunnels all over Dublin," says Mark. "This one was made of old-fashioned tiles so thick they couldn't dent them with a sledgehammer. Tried to smash them and couldn't, then just sealed it up."

The tiles remind me of 17 Mile House, a pub on Vancouver Island from the 1800s — tiles this deep so the spiked boots the old-time loggers wore wouldn't destroy the floor of the road-house bar. After the fire at my mother's house the tunnel opening was walled up again and the basement filled with cement. There is no basement now, no giant brick stove, no scullery sink, no old boy sleeping in his subterranean room (unless he didn't get up); what was open is closed. British barracks over on the other side; my grandmother sold the British milk while running a Republican safe house.

"Here, I'll take you inside the next house," says Mark. "Much better preserved."

It's an automobile upholstery business. The woman running the show is surprisingly shirty, doesn't want me poking around her workplace, but I beg her for just a minute (while wanting to tell her to *fook right off*); I plead and I promise not to go upstairs, not to disturb anyone. It's a business now — often the main floors were in these buildings — but it still looks like a house inside, and that allows me to understand the scale of the old Georgian rooms and stairways, the foot-square beams and giant carved and turned banisters, ornate newels, high windows and doorways and ceilings, glass fanlights and leaded transoms, woodwork and Italian plaster of fronds and birds over a canal. It's all wasted now but at least surviving in a form at this address, a glimpse of what was beautiful, what was before the fire, what was standing here by the river when my mother's house threw a shadow in 1722, in 1822, in 1922, a house hard by the farmland and parks right across the chartered river and brewery barges going to sea and for a while an address attractive enough for the leading Dublin merchant of the time.

Full moon on the river, the moon lighting my home on the other side of the world and lighting the water here and the stone walls with their curved capstones, and on the other bank of the River Liffey the former British barracks staring. The glossy black iron of Crimean cannons and the Irish martyrs beheaded, their bodies hidden by the British in haunted Croppies Field, and that tunnel from the house basement and going under the river toward the British side. My grandmother had a pony and trap to take milk and salted butter to the barracks. Milking cows and churning butter by hand, and no refrigeration for any of it. There were several farms nearby even a few decades ago: a farm by the barracks and a farm where Guinness now has a giant truck parking lot. This river street was both a centre of town and the edge.

At number 9, next door to my mother's house, was the Mendicity Institution ("Bettering Mendicants"), a poorhouse and bathhouse built almost two centuries ago to house and employ beggars. Dublin was full of miserable, half-naked beggars in the streets and at the docks. If you entered a shop, you'd be surrounded by clochards and ragged wretches on your way out, as they knew you had money on your person. Inside the Mendicity beggars were kept busy with lacemaking, spinning, netting, making and mending clothes, picking oakum, pounding oyster shells, and street-sweeping. Children could become apprentices under the control of the Lord Mayor, a make-work program to get the panhandlers off the cobbled streets and out of the gentry's hair and eyesight, though many of the gentry left after the Act of Union in 1801, which abolished the Irish Parliament and gutted parts of the city.

"I was scared of the place when I was a girl." My mother

remembers old men living in the spooky Mendicity. "We had to help serve in the dining room there at Christmas. The kids used to dare each other to ride their bikes inside the stone walls."

"The caretaker let me in to pick daisies," says Bridie. "He let only me in. No one else."

Mendicity Institution, 9, Usher's Island — Instituted 1818
Patron, His Excellency the Lord Lieutenant
President, The Right Honourable Lord Mayor
Secretary, Robert Maxwell Purcell, Esquire, Lincoln
Chamber, Lincoln Place

This institution provides food and shelter for the poor and destitute and the return of destitute persons to their homes. It is open for all classes of poor, want being the only passport requisite for admission.

Now it's a modern health-care unit, but around the block you can still see the old-fashioned name carved into the fortified back of the building, letters visible dripping black down grey walls — like statues bleeding. Barbed wire up top worthy of a prison, and every window and door barred or shuttered or clad in iron or bricked as if deep in a war (it is a siege, but the enemy is inside the gates).

Sailor's Home
Alm's House
Night Asylum for the Houseless Poor

Dublin's version of gentrification creeps close up the river, teases, but it's not yet here. My grandmother didn't own number 11; it must have been a lease, though Rose and Bridie aren't sure.

"Michael and Mary, they didn't own it," James, the country boy in a Mercedes, tells me, "but they didn't publicize the fact."

"After she died there was enough to bury her and not much else," say Rose and Bridie. "And valuables were missing: table-cloths, a bed high with blankets, silverware, trunks of linen, books, things like that."

My mother says she had a trunk of books there from before the war and has no idea what happened to it.

Where are Mary's sideboards and mantle clocks, I wonder, the gilt-framed pictures, rugs, the heavy drapes, lamps, and candelabra? Perhaps someone cleaned her out in her old age. Did she have Alzheimer's? It's obviously in the family tree. Like Marty and Jo: not all there at the end. All the households Mary set up, all the auctions, all the children and friends and tenants from the country, the dairy cows, a horse, a car, and little seems left of it all, little left but barbed wire high above ugly walls.

Bridie suspects a hired woman. "She stole a watch from me. I know she did it."

Mark the Mod Scooter Guy tells me that his father, in England now, rented the yard from my grandmother in 1947 for a spot to work on cars. Island Motors, I assume, from what I saw in the Thom's directory. So Mark's father knew my grandmother late in her life while she was still in the house, then he took over the whole place after her death and was there for the fire in the early 1970s. I wonder if there were still tenants in bedrooms, a deep fryer or gas or rags, or if it was a suspicious fire (insurance?) or a neighbourhood kid having a bit of fun.

The kitchen-scullery was down in the stone basement, as that was cooler for cooking and damp, and because there was a real fear of fire in old buildings, old cities, structures packed tightly against each other all the way down the blocks, trying to hold each other up.

"Laws, like houses, lean on one another," states Edmund

Burke in 1765, in "A Tract on the Popery Laws." These houses were standing when he wrote, but I don't know how much longer they will keep leaning without help.

A second woman working in the upholstery office tells me she remembers the sign for the Island Hotel being up when she started at the job, but the sign is gone now. She's trying to be friendly after the grumpy display by her boss. From an old photo I know a sign hung out over the sidewalk, and the name was also stencilled on the fanlight glass. That fanlight melted like a stolen car. The second woman's attempt to make me happy does make me happy.

Padraic and Sharkey's older brother, Liam, comes over to Rose's for Sunday dinner. "I remember going to visit our grandmother's house." A duty he didn't care for. Liam and I walk and talk in a big park near Rose's house, a sunny Sunday, though there is also hail riding the crisp air and I have finally caught the ubiquitous cold and feel feverish and light-headed and depressed.

"It smelled. The house smelled like an old person's house," Liam says. "You know how it is as a kid. I didn't like going there."

Walking off our meal in the park named after a saint, Liam and I stumble on a burnt car from Saturday night.

"Now, we haven't had one of these for a while."

Joyriders carved up soccer fields and smashed over young trees, finally crashing the stolen car into a larger trunk, bending the tree over at an odd angle, scorching the tree and what was left of the car when the joyriders torched it while the owner slept. A weird misshapen sight: glass blown out and paint gone streaky, long melted lines on metal like stars in their silent speedways, a grey Jackson Pollock, seats and steering wheel and dash evaporated except for skinny metal parts. The hood is up and all the rubber hoses have burnt into nothing. The windshield is on the grass, shattered, but it has held together as one webbed piece. And the owner looks out his window: Could've sworn I parked the car there last night.

A little kid kicks the charred car.

"Now don't!" yells his mother. He keeps kicking, exhilarated. "Stop."

"One more kick," the boy says.

On the soccer pitch a coach shouts hoarsely at his young players. "Push up, push up, get in there, put your foot in it!"

This car's corpse reminds me of the burnt cars around Sheriff Street in 1981, a tough area past Connolly train station, an area I wandered after being warned to stay out. A burnt car both fascinates and offends my naive eye. Here they are perhaps more inured to it than I am, though citizens walking in the park grumble about crime and young punks.

"Someone might have been hurt!" says a woman.

"Well, it'd be self-inflicted," says a man, mad at the vandalism. This ruined grove was a plantation of brand-new beeches and ash, cypress and eucalyptus — a millennium arboretum.

"No police around," says the man. "They're useless. If ye want a stable society, you have to keep the thumb down. Have to keep the thumb down."

Washrooms and change rooms in the park are wrecked. We stare at the car's remains as if it's an art installation. A magpie watches the humans from atop a goalpost. Rose hates magpies because they punch holes in her milk cartons after the milkman leaves them at her door.

"The guards don't care," the man says. "Where are the guards?"

Sharkey is just one block over. He runs in this park. He cares, but people like to destroy, people like to burn things, see flames lift in the dark, like the kid who wants to kick the car, pulled by impulse and desire. Cheap and cheerful, as my mother would say.

Liam didn't enjoy visits to his grandmother Mary — driving to a dark house in a bad part of town; damp, abandoned buildings with an ancient hemmed-in river gurgling below them — but I envy him because he caught a corner of the Old World, an old person's musty house, a boy lectured not to touch the lace curtains by an old person who, like my mother, does not want to play with grandchildren, was not always charming, was grouchy. Like Uncle Marty. Like Brendan. Like me. Sometimes grouchy is the logical reaction to this world.

"I was thrilled to be up from Bridie's farm and right in the big city." James says, "I remember staring out the front windows at the river and all the people and cars passing the house." James was told that my grandmother Mary had a friend visiting, and two women waved to Michael from that same window when he left on his last walk, two happy women watching his figure recede toward Phoenix Park and the bridge to the afterlife.

So many children's voices in the house over three centuries, music and meals and shrieks, but 11 Usher's Island becomes an old person's house, a closeted smell in a child's nose, old pictures covered in dust. Another coffin finds its way out in 1957. Number 11 becomes no person's house, a handyman mechanic, a business, a bottom-feeder; becomes history, rust, a fire, an echo in a Joyce story; becomes "The Dead," my shrine; becomes Island Scooter; becomes Mr. Gearbox Mr. Clutch. I can live with that.

The next generation happy to move into smaller places farther out of town — houses with tiny halls and stairways and no dining rooms and no pianos and no secret tunnels under the river and no room to swing a cat — but these are their own, and the houses are new with grass and geraniums and fresh air and no vermin colonies boiling out of the wallpaper and no animal gangs fighting with chains and knives and butcher hooks on the quays and bridges and no pawnshops and no more Black and Tans and no ancient stigma of this block or that block and new must be good and no more smell of malt and hops in your nose and no more river rats in the scary scullery when your mother says she forgot her cigarettes and be a dear and no more Usher's Island link to James Joyce and "The Dead."

At the James Joyce Centre on the northside, I meet James Joyce's white-haired nephew, Ken Monaghan. "We go for years without anyone asking about Usher's Island," he says, seeming excited, interested in the family link, picking out books for me in the library up the creaking stairs, bringing me an annotated version of the story "The Dead" ("This one regrettably out of print now"). He seats me at a big wooden table, fire crackling in the hearth (spring and summer slow to start in Ireland). He climbs a ladder to look up Usher's Island in the 1850 city directory (what if he falls and it's my fault?), and he explains to me the figures and taxes listed. I'm hanging out with Sunny Jim's nephew (I bet the great man himself would not be so friendly), but I play it cool.

My relatives in 1981 told me not to read James Joyce. That's not Ireland! Smut. Has it all wrong. The Joyce house at number 15 boarded up, trashed, patrolled by squatters and me and ghosts from "The Dead," and Bloom's house is gone too, but for the door saved for a museum, and it's the suburbs we're in now, south of Clontarf and Buru's battleground, west of Rome, west of ruckus, and ritual is vapour, is exhaust from passing trucks, a murder of scooters.

Chapter Eighteen

WHITE HORSES, BLUE LIGHT

THE PRETTY WOMAN AT THE GUINNESS CORPORATION desk is extremely polite, but she insists they have no record of my grandfather or my uncles or cousins working there. To Guinness they don't exist.

I protest, "But my aunt is on a Guinness pension this moment!" Surely they have records if they're paying a pension to an employee's widow.

"Well, I can't be explaining everything now, can I?"

I love Éire and will return as soon as I can afford it. I am addicted to Ireland. I drink more Guinness with each trip here. But I do not love the Guinness Corporation.

At Rose's kitchen table, over black tea, my city aunt and my country aunt complain that kids today watch too much TV and get no exercise.

"'Ah sure, next generation won't need legs,' Brendan always said. Driven here and there and sit around. We cycled and walked everywhere."

"I ran miles to the Model School to save the streetcar fare!"

"Didn't I cycle from Dublin to the farm?"

"Used to cycle all the way to Carlow for a dance and cycle back again after. God, when I think about it."

"Didn't Marty and Dermot and Brendan walk for miles in the country with Father?"

"He'd give them a penny, and they filled their caps with apples at the orchard. Marty was a great one for walking. Next generation won't need legs."

"That's what Brendan said. 'Next generation won't need legs.'"

"Driving everywhere now or watching the silly telly! Too much TV — kids get *thing*."

"So you feel like a walk?" I ask my aunts after another huge supper.

"Ah, no. A show coming up on the telly. That awful one, King Rat, was shot in the Maze Prison. They had weapons *inside* the prison, now I ask you. How, I don't know, and didn't they crawl across the roof and shoot him in the prison yard?"

Men on the roofs again, I think, reminded of the workers at the library, of rebels running over top my mother's house seventy-five years ago. Snipers, drive-bys, retaliations, Libyan rocket launchers, Kalashnikov assault rifles, Semtex and fertilizer.

The British newscaster is black. "He's a nice-looking man," says Bridie to Rose.

King Rat, a Protestant extremist, killed in prison by an IRA sniper — an impressive feat, certainly doesn't happen very often in Canada — but you know that because of this sniper some innocent Catholic will soon be shot in a pub or waiting for a bus. A secret gunman.

You started it.

No, you started it.

"You go out if you like," my aunts say.

Also on the telly is the tastiest scandal of the summer: a former prime minister, Charles Haughey, is being investigated. A great one has dirtied his bib. Haughey, nicknamed the Boss, Il Duce, has somehow purchased — or been given, or innocently come across — an island in the west, an impressive seagoing yacht, a stud farm, lush houses, huge champagne and Guinness parties, and interest in downtown high-rises.

"And on a civil servant's salary!" says Rose. "Before Charley, the Taoiseach lived in an ordinary house. But not Charley! Oh, no. And Dunne, the big boy, giving him envelopes of cash on the golf course. And seeing that woman for years! Who'd want to kiss him? I don't know what's happening to the world; it's *thing*." A Dublin official is arrested at the airport lugging suitcases of cash. The ex-PM agrees to pay over one million dollars in back taxes on "gifts" given to him. An MP is locked up by the tribunal for contempt. The tribunal grinds on, a tribute to missing files and creative accounting, to a dead accountant.

It's scoundrel time, vultures circling, but it is also business as usual. Journalists knew for decades that there was a fiddle but didn't dare write the story before, muzzled by Ireland's dicey libel laws.

"That Charley, he's a chancer," says Bridie, laughing at the television. "Look at those fools breaking an ankle to shake hands with Charley! Oh, he's a chancer," she says. "If he wriggles out of this one, he's Houdini." There is a fear that he will wriggle out. "More lives than a cat, that one."

"You go out if you like."

I go out, cross the tracks past the graffiti and glass. The local is a dump, a kip. A man with red hair is smoking and fuming about rich Americans buying up authentic Irish pubs and shipping them piece by bloody piece overseas. Sure, didn't they send one lock, stock, and barrel to Budapest? They didn't. They did. Go away. And another pub to Siberia, wasn't it?

I think, No one is going to buy this crapola pub and ship it across the globe. Ireland is not going to lose this pub.

"Now, I wouldn't be too comfortable going into that pub," Sharkey told me. "A few tough families, and I'd have dealt with them when I was on the task force. They might not be too happy to see me walking in. Dealt with the parents, their kids, and now a new lot coming up the same way." Sharkey's not missing anything by avoiding this local.

This is my last night in Ireland. Tomorrow I fly back to England for another stay there, then back home to Canada, zooming the polar route once more with the other passive passengers. I can't relax, don't want to be blasé about travel. I don't know when I'll be back here in Ireland. My younger brother used to tease my mother, calling out, "Mom, there's a special on Ireland," my brother just making it up, and Mom'd come running *every time*, wiping her hands on a tea towel.

Now I'm the same as my mother, thrilled when I flip channels at home and stumble on a PBS special (I don't care for all the Celtic mysticism malarkey) that takes its cameras inside my favourite pub in Dingle on St. Bridget's Day, likely my favourite pub in the universe.

I don't want to watch this country like a special. My last night in this crazy theme park and I want to be out doing something real, anything, but I can't bear to stay in a kip by myself just for the sake of staying in an Irish pub.

Outside, the light is blue. Huge white horses thunder past in the lane like hallucinations, streetkids from the projects and terraced rows racing their old jades, their hammer-headed mounts, their inner-city polo ponies. I admire the simple audacity of the streetkids to actually keep and race giant horses in the middle of the city; I admire their snot-nosed get-up-and-go, though Sharkey says they don't know anything about horses, pick them up for next to nothing at the Smithfield Market and kill them racing and racing, sides heaving, foaming; they kill the poor beasts.

"Ah jeez, they t'ink they're cow-byes and Injuns," says an older woman in cat's-eye glasses, making me laugh. She watches the kids ride their white horses in dusk, down toward the perfumed canal.

I carry a tin of cold beer back to the semi-detached house and stare at the big colour telly with my aunts in Dublin. All my relatives spend their evenings watching crime shows, detective shows. Their light is blue if you're looking from outside. I am watching TV with my uncle and aunt in north London; watching TV in a seaside cottage in Essex, coin-ops in the airport, on the 767 streaking home over Iceland and Hudson Bay; watching TV with my widowed spitfire mother in Canada, with my cousins in Philly and Jersey and Holland Park and Madrid, with my unborn students on the West Coast and the East Coast, with my children, with the mummified East German, with the nineteenth-century man from the stony fields who sends himself stupid, who kills himself with drink.

I am watching TV with dead people and with people I haven't met yet, every soul and clone on the crowded blue planet gazing at the same TV, killing our evenings one by one, putting in our time watching the same gruesome shows out of England or America and the show's a mystery, it's something about murder, something about loss.

Part Two

Interviews with
My Sainted Mother When She
Was Speaking to Me Once More
and Before She Lost Her Mind in
the Wilds of Hollywood,
So to Speak

The sanitary and mechanical age we are now entering makes up for the mercy it grants to our sense of smell by the ferocity with which it assails our sense of hearing. As usual, what we call "progress" is the exchange of one nuisance for another nuisance.
— HAVELOCK ELLIS

Why should we do anything for posterity; what has posterity ever done for us?
— SIR BOYLE ROCHE

Chapter Nineteen

Interviews with My Sainted Mother

In the 1930s, when I was sixteen or so, I motored with my mother, Mary, all around the whole coastline of Ireland — Cork, Killarney, Kerry, Bunratty Castle, Galway, Mayo, the Sligo mountains, Donegal — just the two of us, two women driving by ourselves around the country in the Depression, but no one thought anything of it. Not as many cars as now, but there were cars, epecially in the summer. Had to find gas at shops or pubs, that kind of thing. Not like in Dublin.

I was new to driving, and my mother insisted we get out at every single church to pray; she didn't know if she'd ever get home alive. Got out at every church. I went into the churches at first, but after a while I said, "You go in and say a prayer for me." She didn't much like that (*laughs*).

The car might have been a Model T; I think there was only one kind of car available back then. For driving I had a sun visor (very fashionable), which I wore on my head like a gambler's cap. It was a fine-looking Ford — soft leather seats, chrome everywhere — and you could open up the car's front

windscreen to let air in. A Baby Ford, we called it. Perhaps it wasn't a Model T.

My mother was no longer the glamour girl she had been, but she was still stylish at that time. She liked her hats, just like me. After the war you'd never know she was the same person; she just suddenly got old. She had a hard time of it. A hard worker. She was bed-ridden later in life, wasn't all quite there, and Brendan had to drop by and collect the rent from the boarders or else she'd neglect it.

My mother could do anything she put her mind to, and she could have made oodles of money, but she was too generous when she had any. A widow with all those kids and she didn't always charge people room and board if she got to know them at all — made us cross — and if she had money she gave it away. She could make money, but she couldn't keep it. Give it to you if she had any. My mother, Mary, and an older, handsome man from Cork were an item for a while. We kids knew of him. Then he went to America.

Imagine being a widow on your own with all those kids and all those boarders. I get tired just thinking about it. Sometimes she'd send us down to her mother's farm to get some peace. Also, my brother Michael had breathing problems as a boy, and he'd be sent down for the air. Then, when they'd had enough at the farm, they'd send us back to the city to have some peace. Both her parents were from around Wolfhill. Her father dug wells and installed pumps, worked in England a lot.

Our boarders had their rooms up on the third floor. That floor's gone now. Ten young men, usually from the country. Lorry drivers, bus drivers, cement workers, factory men, accountants, electricians, politicians, IRA, farmers, railway men, draymen, every class of people, from all ends of the country — Sligo, Mayo, Tipperary, the Swan, Johnswell, Kilkenny. All grand. Had to be nice or Mother. . . . There were no apartments in Dublin then, you see; they weren't common. Sometimes we had overnight guests too. They all behaved. My mother made sure of that. The men were *nicer* then, not like now. Josie and Bridie both met their husbands in that house.

One man who stayed at number 11 did well in politics down the country. When he campaigned he rode a bike with two signs: "Here Comes Oliver J." on the front of his bike, and "There Goes Oliver J." on the back. It was simple, but it worked well. His son followed him into office and just lost his seat in that last election.

The men ate separately, had their own sitting for a meal in a dining room on the third floor. We didn't have a dumbwaiter — we were the dumbwaiter! Up and down those stairs. Up and down. We had three families in at one point and an old girl to help out in the house. An old boy lived for years in a little room down in the cellar. I think he was a teacher. He used to dress up as a nigger minstrel. Wouldn't be allowed now — seen as racist. It's too bad. I wonder what happened to him? Dead now, all dead except me.

We had to polish the stairs, and then you'd fall down the polished stairs. No wonder my back is so bad. Floor wax and Zebra grate polish. We had wooden floors, but we scrubbed them every day, you see, and they didn't look that nice after a time, so my mother covered the wood with linoleum. My mother did laundry on Blue Monday, a wringer washer and hang sheets on posts out each window. Come home and the house looked like a sailing ship.

A big front door and a small space between it and our inner door. We never locked the doors. Once now Bridie saw a woman's hand in the front entrance — there was a little bell on the door to announce guests — someone darting in to the thing, our coat rack, and didn't she run off with someone's good winter coat. Bridie saw her and told an adult in the house what happened, and then Bridie ran right outside, you see, followed the woman to a pawn office down the quays. Couldn't find a guard, so Bridie ran back home and they called the guards. They found the coat, and they picked up the woman. The poor woman must have been desperate: starving or after drink.

Guinness boats went by every day on the river, like motor launches, the crewmen at the wheel looking very smart in their caps and dark navy sweaters. Their steam funnels folded down to slip under the low bridges. The schooners or bigger ships couldn't get by the bridges. All big trucks now. No more boats or horses. Meat used to come by horse and wagon, and a man sold hot potatoes off a cart. Ice came by wagon too, but we didn't have an icebox. Our milkman came by every day with his horse and

GUINNESS BARGES ON THE LIFFEY

wagon — maybe twice a day if it was warm out, I'm not sure. He had a yoke on his shoulders to balance the four-gallon cans. He'd pour milk out of a big dented dairy can into your pitchers. Buy what you need and store it in a shady spot, what we called a safe, with netting or gauze to keep the flies out. No fridges then. Not even ice, no icebox. It must have been hard, having to buy food every day, buying and cooking and feeding a big family and a gang of hungry men in a boarding house.

A man went around selling dead rabbits hung on a stick over his shoulder, an apron wrapped around to keep his coat clean. Leighton's mother in Oxford would buy a rabbit and skin it and sell the skin for six p. Christmas Eve she'd make a rabbit-and-steak pie.

Nearly every morning we had homegrown eggs and lovely back bacon. Not like the streaky bacon in Canada. Or toast with scrambled eggs on it. Or bowls of hot porridge with cream and brown sugar. We ate carrots, cabbage, turnips, potatoes, ham, goose, roast beef. Fish on Fridays. Had our own geese and chickens and turkeys and cows, right in the city. We never had juice or pop; we had water or milk or tea. Fruit was rare, but we had oranges and apples at times. We had cake, hard sugar cookies, bread with jam or marmalade, maybe bread toasted at night over the gas stove or fire, but no sandwiches; sandwiches weren't common until later. Sometimes we had special loaves with a high back, like a chair with no legs — a turnover loaf, I think we called them, crust all around. My mother had thick brown bread, and I envied anyone who had soft white bread. Now I like good brown bread. We'd walk to Kennedy, the bread people, and buy six loaves at a time to carry home. Bridie and I'd sing: "Kennedy bread, kill a man dead, especially a man with a baldie head."

The kitchen was in the basement, a big scullery sink down there in a sideroom and a table and a giant brick stove from way back that burnt wood or coal, though coal became scarce because of a fight with England. The stove had a water heater on it. A gas stove was put in later. When there was a shortage of gas you weren't supposed to turn it on; times of day when it was low. There was still a glimmer that you could use to heat tea, but it was supposed to be dangerous and the Glimmer man skulked about to make sure no one was using the gas. Down in the basement there were rooms closed up, like wine cellars or coal bins, but all bricked up, you know, like that story by Poe. They said they found a tunnel later; maybe that's where it was. I never knew anything about a tunnel.

I hated having to go down there at night; I was terrified of rats. My mother'd say to me, "Oh, I left my cigarettes downstairs. Be a dear and nip down and fetch them for me, would you? There's a good girl." No lights, and I was sure big river rats were crawling all over the dark stairs and basement floor and ready to leap on my ankles or face.

My mother's doctor made her take up smoking to ease her

nerves after my father died and my brother Michael died, and then she couldn't stop, smoked until she died. Cigarettes were rationed during the war, but my mother would go to the shop and say, "I'm here for my cigarettes," as if all was normal, and she'd get them. If she was down the country at her mother's farm and ran out, she'd have to come back to Dublin to get her cigarettes. She smoked Wills' Gold Flake (*Gold Flakes Satisfy!*). The poor smoked Woodbines, Wills' Wild Woodbine, made right in Dublin and half the price of Players Navy Cut. I never smoked, though. Never.

My mother had a picture of Michael Collins, but she didn't follow him; she followed de Valera and Fianna Fáil, the Warriors of Ireland, as did most of the family. Bridie was the only one to vote Fine Gael, the Tribe of Gaels. She got brainwashed down in the Swan. My mother was in everything — parades and arguments and marches and fights — I had too much damn politics in that house, enough to last me a lifetime.

When I was young we had an outhouse in the yard, down off the kitchen, then later a bathroom was built on the second floor. Before that we washed up in the kitchen or out in the yard. A lot of people didn't have plumbing; they gave themselves a lick and a promise and went to a bathhouse once in a while. We had cats and dogs, but we never bought them food. No electricity in the Dublin house until the 1930s. A German company came around and put electricity in, ran a thick wire you could see going from the switch to the ceiling. Giant spools of wire they had. One light to a room.

When I was very young I believed in the banshee, but not when I was older — the adults liked to frighten us with their stories.

I'm afraid of water and swimming at the lake, and I think it's because my father drowned. It's odd that he drowned because my father could find water, had a gift, could dowse with a stick or a wand, you know, if someone needed a well. He could find the water and then he drowned.

I don't think my father went out to the pub much. He wasn't a drinker, I never saw it around the house. Once my mother went to America visiting and she drank some poteen there someone had made in a still, and when she got back home she made a vat of her own poteen down in the basement. That's the stuff can blind you. Now if people were visiting you'd order from the pub and an old boy brought around corked bottles of stout in a basket. Ryan's Pub was close. I hated the old boy who had that pub. Counter as tall as me and him looking over at me. Tried to fondle me — they had that business back then; that's not new. Made me mad. I'd spit at him. That old boy picked the wrong one to fondle. I'd spit at him.

If a visitor offered us a coin we had to say, "No, thank you," at first, just to be polite. The odd one actually believed us, and we wouldn't get the coin (*laughs*). If we got a chocolate bar, we thought we were in heaven.

The tram was a penny one way. Trams up to the north quays and trams out to Phoenix Park, what they called Fiendish Park. With all the kids, sometimes there wasn't money for the tram. Long walk to my school from our house, all the way down the quays to O'Connell and up past the Pro-Cathedral. If my mother gave us money for the tram and a movie, we might walk and save the penny for candy. Penny dreadfuls, we called the movies there were then: cowboy movies, serials, cliff-hangers. They'd end the reel with the hero in a terrible predicament. It was exciting — oh, they'll never get out of that, impossible — then we'd go back next week and it'd be changed just slightly, wasn't as bad a fix, and they'd find a way out. We worried about catching fleas or lice in the crowd or off the old seats. Penny dreadfuls.

I went to a very big school on the north side, the Model School, at least ten classes for every grade. I went as far as grade nine. Only two girls went on to university: one was a brain and the other a publican's daughter. No sports for girls; sports were just for the boys. I never got the strap in school, but my brothers did. They went to a Christian Brothers school across the river.

My hardest subject was Gaelic (my husband, Leighton, took Latin in school in England). I loved my arithmetic teacher. I loved to read, and visitors brought us books. I used to read in the stairwell, where there was light from a big window in the landing. "The quality of mercy is not strain'd, but it droppeth as the gentle rain from heaven upon the place beneath." I used to know all that speech.

We were all great readers. A lady in a neighbourhood shop signed library cards for anyone who wanted one. She could've been on the hook for missing books, but she would sign cards for any kid in the neighbourhood — she wanted us to read. After I was out of school I worked for the Irish Sweepstakes. My poor brother Marty — all his life buying his Sweeps ticket and his lottery, and he never won a thing. Even if he did win he'd never get back all that he put in.

My best friend was Kayo; we were great friends. I introduced her to her husband, and I'd stay with her every visit. We both went to London for nursing at Putney General Hospital. Kayo was very bright. She and her husband had a store in Putney after the war.

I had to leave Ireland. Kayo left, Marty left, Jo left, May left, Jennie left, Kitty left, Leo left. Now this new generation, I think no one has to leave.

In nursing school there was no pay until third or fourth year, plus we had to buy three uniforms. I was eighteen or nineteen in London; we had great fun and lots of beaus. We were in the west end, by Baker Street — posh, men in silk hats. If we were out late we had to climb back in a window — once, sneaking in late, I knocked a big black phone off a table by the window and Jesus, Mary, Joseph, the blessed thing made such a crash, and I ran down the hall in the dark and hid in my room. They didn't know who caused the commotion.

During the Blitz there were bombs down everywhere, smoke up in the air like a forest fire. The German bombers came flying right up the river; at first you could see them, pretty as you please. From the eighth floor I watched Madame Tussaud's Wax Museum burn on the next block. During the raids I didn't want to go down in the basement of the hospital with everyone else — all those gas lines, pipes, scalding water — that made me nervous. I preferred to stay up above, ride down with the top floor if it went tumbling in.

In the underground you had bunk beds five or six high, families changing out of their clothes and getting ready to sleep as if the platform was their bedroom, and trains still running and passengers getting off and on. Almost like a stage with an audience. People talking, singing, playing cards, wind blowing up the tunnels as a train came closer, some of the bombs close. It was no library, I tell you, and we'd wait for all the noise to die down a bit and try to get some sleep. It sounds strange, but the war was fun at times. I didn't mind the tube shelters and the bunks; I was young and single. Couldn't do it now. Now I get nervous, have to have the doors locked and curtains drawn, keep thinking someone's looking in at me.

In London the eastside docks were hit the most. We all lost someone, but those London Cockneys were something. They'd make it to work at the hospital in the morning and call out, "Got bombed out again last night, luv!" God, they were tough.

Leighton's twin brother died in the war. I never met him.

Leighton and I were married in a Catholic church in London, St. James Square, a very foggy day in December, pea-soup fog, people couldn't find the church. Mixed marriages weren't allowed before the war, but the war was on and we were both over twenty-one and they couldn't stop us. Our hotel was one pound, one shilling; now it'd be three hundred pounds. There was no Mass because Leighton wasn't Catholic. The priest asked if the ring was gold, and Leighton thought he asked if Leighton had a cold. I think the priest was about to sprinkle holy water on the ring. Have a cold? No. I genuflected and Leighton almost tripped over me. Ah, we laughed afterward.

In Dublin my parish was High Street, but our church was Arran Quay, St. Paul's. Mass every twenty minutes and the churches were full then. Everyone went. I never missed Mass in my life, but now that I'm in here . . . Have I had my tablets yet? This damn leg. I don't get out much in this place. Some of the men here piled up the picnic tables outside and made it over the fence. Next time I'm in Dublin I'll see a good doctor.

There was a very good pharmacist near us in Dublin — Mushatt's, they were Jewish, very kind. Anything wrong, no one went to the doctor, they went to see them. Locals from the neighbourhood went and people from all over Dublin. They had all sorts of cures and concoctions, made their preparations themselves. Go to Mushatt's. It was very popular. Just a tiny place. There were little shops all around the neighbourhood: cheese in one shop, a pork butcher in another shop, a shop that mended umbrellas (imagine that), a salt shop just for salt, a victualler, canned sardines, condensed milk, tobacco, Brimstone matches, hardware, a bootmaker, a chemist, a draper, fancy goods, a wool merchant at number 9, tea at number 12, coal two doors down at number 15. A distillery at number 17 became a horse dealer, then that became Medlar and Claffey's funeral establishment. The Maypole for butterboxes and huge blocks of cheese they'd slice with those wire cheese cutters. My mother made butter too, put little patterns on the edge or shaped it. The Mill for bulk oats, and Halligan's bakery on the corner of Usher's Island and Watling — they were there forever. For one penny Bridie and I would get beautiful gurcakes, big and square - chestercakes, we called them too, like a pudding inside with just a light crust — they were very filling. Berry pies for pennies. There was a chip shop on the opposite bank. And we'd always say, "Go to the market on Moore Street to get your nose educated": no refrigeration, meat and fish laid out on shambles, manure in the street from the horses and wagons, and flies walking over everything. Get your nose educated.

My mother picked up beautiful furniture at the auction rooms for next to nothing. We had a huge dining-room set — hutch and buffet and big table and chairs — chiffoniers and mirrors, pictures and paintings, a few rugs. No, we didn't have armoires, we had closets. I think the main rooms had nice chandeliers; they might have been gaslights. A big fireplace in the dining room. Coal fireplaces in every room, paraffin-oil lamps. Black-and-white tile in the front hall, beautiful black-and-white ceramic tiles in the deep window wells, and iron railings and steps up in

front of the house. All ruined now, a wreck. A shame, because it was a beautiful house.

I was famous for giving my mother backtalk: I'd say something smart and run off fast as I can. If she hit me, I wouldn't let her see me cry.

Oh, I was *mad* at my mother one time. The piano fell over on us — I don't know what we had done to it, but it fell over and we were trying to hold it up — and she was shrieking about her hundred-quid piano, a lot of money in those days. Oh, she loved the damn thing.

"Mind my hundred-pound piano! Mind my hundred-pound piano!" Falling on us, and she cared more about her precious piano (*laughs*). I fell to the floor when the operator told me she was gone. I was pregnant, big as a house with Martin. Telephone rang, and the woman read out the telegram that my mother was dead. I didn't even know she was sick. Martin came out prematurely and was in the incubator; we didn't know if he'd survive, and they all prayed for him at St. John's. Tiny as a kitten and now he's big as life, tallest in the family. If he was bad I'd call him Paddy. I'd say, "Where's Martin gone? No, you're not Martin, you're Paddy. You tell Martin to come back."

My mother did a good job with all of us, did a lot, a hard worker. She could do anything she put herself to. My mother could have been rich, but if she had anything she gave it to you. She got me a scooter when I was six — must have been just four months before my father drowned. I fell to the floor when the operator said my mother was dead.

Part Three

Put the Moan on Ya

To have an opinion about Ireland, one must begin by getting at the truth; and where is it to be had in the country?
— WILLIAM MAKEPEACE THACKERAY,
The Irish Sketch Book

And so every anecdote in Northern Ireland has to come accompanied by its refutation.
— WILL SELF

Chapter Twenty

MR. GEARBOX

IN THE YEAR OF OUR LORD 1999. Light like porridge pours past our lowering plane and onto the Irish Sea and the pretty land along the water, a frigid, grudging spring yielding a frigid, grudging light. Flying into Dublin once more. Every airport bar between here and Canada is full of Germans with fishing rods, and I appear to be not dating Courtney Love. If I can just arrive, can just crawl to my aunt's house in Ennafort.

A wet cold winter we had of it in Canada, and a very hard winter for my aunt Rose in Dublin since her son Padraic died. My favourite cousin stepped politely into a coma after Christmas, and Aunt Rose caught pneumonia and a big black dog attacked her leg and her leg it gave up a tendon. The dog mauled her on the street just around the corner from her own house, and she made it back to her door but couldn't manage the stairs with her torn leg, thought it was broken.

Her carefree, cosmopolitan son's liver destroyed by a tainted hep C transfusion courtesy of the Dublin hospital. *This won't hurt a bit.* Handing out diseases, as long as you've paid up the plan.

A hard winter. No more golf for Rose. Sharkey came over and helped his mother make it up the stairs.

I lean my tired face on a window in a British Midlands plane. The stewardess in her little fold-down seat looks ready to cry, perhaps reconsidering her career choice, and I'm a flying zombie.

Snow fell last night on the Irish coast, dropping on the soft hills and spooky Wicklow mountains. Snow is so romantic, except when it isn't. There's a snowstorm at the end of "The Dead." I'm expropriating the story, making it mine as a squatter might in a Georgian house a door or two from my mother's ruined house on the Liffey. My mother's old house, barely erect in its latest humiliating devolution, has now gone from Island Hotel to Island Motors to Scooter Island to a Mr. Gearbox Mr. Clutch, somewhere down there if you could follow the River Liffey up along the quays. My mother's maiden name the same as Joyce's aunt two doors down. Scholars say Joyce's collection *Dubliners* was about paralysis, but isn't it clear he mostly wrote about me?

I can't find my mother's house on the seagull quays — it's too far away and around a corner — but from the old plane a startling view of the smoking Irish Sea and coastline: ships I'll never know and harbours and snowy fields falling into the sea, and snow on Dalkey and Dun Laoghaire, snow on Clontarf and Howth, and day and night the sooty orange train rushing and pushing past Ireland's Eye to Belfast and Derry, and snowy hills curving like big arms and snowy breasts nuzzling Dublin Bay, surreal snowy breasts dwarfing the city (*only if my love was lying by me*), and soon I'll be walking those cold cobblestones and bricks.

From the air I can't make out individual streets, can't find my mother's tenement house, but I can make out the Royal Canal creeping west in bad weather from Dublin City, can see the useless eighteenth-century locks and canal that pulled down my grandfather Michael in the green, green water the moment they placed General Michael Collins's bullet-shattered head in the green ground at Glasnevin, and I didn't think of this before, but who, I wonder, who climbed the steps with the jet-black iron rails to my grandfather's high house on Usher's Island, my grandmother's house, my mother's house, who hammered the brass on the big door to tell them that your father and husband and breadwinner is dead as a doornail and may the good Lord preserve ye. My mother in her eighties still remembers the wailing and gnashing of teeth in the house after that knock at the door.

And now my cousin Padraic is dead too, but it's not 1922, so there's no back-story or historical romance, no war and no myths; Padraic's dead just because the hospital that was to help him instead destroyed his liver (the likes of that liver we'll not see again). As I feared, Padraic was HIV positive, but he kept himself in good health. After Christmas he checked himself into the hospital because a platelet count was down, but unfortunately he was given a transfusion of blood contaminated with hep C. Hep C and a lowered immune system is not a good combo, a secret gunman in his blood, a single-stranded RNA virus destroying his liver and sailing him into a very fast coma. Hep C lawsuits stopped this years ago in Canada but it still goes on in Dublin. Padraic awoke once, smiled and told his sister and others that he loved them, and fell back into his coma.

What are your reasons for entering our fair country? I'm back in Ireland, chasing two corpses now and arguing with ghosts. My usual obsessions and lack of clear motives. I want to compare the Ireland living in my head with the real one under my running shoes.

I'm not looking for my roots and I'm not tracing my ancestry or family tree — I just want to see what I see, a bit more each trip, take a drink with my aunts and cousins, go to pubs, ramble around the country. I fly back when there's a chance and the cash or a credit card for airfare. Ireland is my magnet (What are your reasons for entering my memory?).

And this time I want to ride the cross-country train to the west of Ireland; cycle Dingle peninsula again; tope a pint or two in Tralee, Dunquin, Brandon Bay, Limerick, Galway, Westport; stand at the wildflower cliffs; climb the loose quartz of Croagh Patrick up into the clouds, a wallflower pilgrimage retracing random steps I took when I was younger (*let us compare mythologies*), a lifetime ago when I met and lost the woman at the stone dock.

If only like a crab you could go backwards, interview the dead, walk with them, swim with them. Sharkey the policeman tells me you never get rid of the smell of a decomposing body. Sharkey uses Vicks VapoRub, goes swimming in a chlorine pool, stands in scalding showers, gets blind drunk on black stout, and that nuance of a corpse still way up at the top of his nose and he can't rid himself of that tinge. A different smell from sewage or excrement or other powerfully bad smells. You smell the dead; they stay with you.

It's always women, Sharkey says. Milk bottles or newspapers not picked up at the door, no answer, have to go in. Open a window and recoil. They're often in the bathroom, Sharkey says. Maybe they wake up, don't feel well, gravitate to the loo.

My cousin forces a door or window and finds them. Always women. A man dies, and a woman's there taking care of him. A woman dies alone.

Silently, my cousin and I think about our aging aunts, our mothers, that day down the road and whether we'll be the one who forces the door, the one who finds them in the loo.

The couple next to me on the plane flying in are very friendly, talkative, but I can't form sentences, try to hide my jet-lag face against the glass. They are flying to a friend's funeral in Ireland

and seem rather pleased, though they complain that they put the body in the ground too fast in Ireland.

Barely time for us to book a ticket, they both say. They wait longer in England, you know.

The woman tells me that someone offered her a seat on the small airport bus.

"Am I that old now?" she asks me. "It sneaks up on you," she tells me, and I like her.

Their friend is dead and I am dead, not fit to bring guts to a bear, and she feels young still, wants to explain what it's like, how sneaky it is.

My mother remembers the Glasnevin gravediggers and the bumpy wagon ride and the wagon wheels black and the glass bier heaped with white flowers and two men in tall black hats holding the reins formally and two black horses with black plumes and the sound of their hoofs on the streets. Crowds of other coopers and men from Guinness, a cooper assigned to each family child, and she remembers a cooper holding hands with her and the dirt thrown on her father's body and it meant nothing to her then but now she's in her eighties on another continent and no more horses with black plumes and we come in jets and my mother keeps telling me of dirt dropping on her father's body and she dwells on it more now than she did as a little girl in the warm summer of 1922.

I'm three months too late for Padraic's funeral. No one told me. We wouldn't have known in Canada for years if I hadn't called. Sharkey apologized, said he looked for my number in Padraic's effects but couldn't find it. Can't blame my aunt: she had things on her mind. And perhaps easier for older relatives to *not* explain things they'd rather not explain.

Padraic and I e-mailed a few times over the past two years, then in the spring I let him know I was flying there again, but there was no answer. I was e-mailing a dead man. I phoned my aunt Rose and got a shock. I wanted to laugh for some reason, because it seemed so unbelievable.

"I'm sorry to say we buried Padraic after Christmas," said Rose bravely on the phone, though later I found they didn't bury him.

Too late, no matter what. This morning I flew into Heathrow early, a tail wind from Canada, disembarked, breezed customs, and eagerly ran miles to gate 80 for a 10:50 to Dublin.

Yes! I was so happy, making it to an earlier flight; the passengers all just boarded, and they have seats and I have a ticket.

They say yes, then look at my ticket and say no. This is for a later flight.

So?

Security concerns. My luggage must travel with me.

I plead with the man at the gate (the plane lifts off without me), then plead at counter after counter. There are several flights I can get on — I see them listed on the board: *Dublin, Dublin, Dublin*, where now everyone has bags of money and a new Mercedes Benz, a new Fiat or Lexus or Land Rover. But they won't let me go. I beg, I grovel, I just want to get to my aunt's and sleep. Toss me on a stupid plane! If this was Vancouver to Victoria, they'd say, "Sure, jump on board." Not here. They say I have to wait four or five hours. They worry I'm the mad bomber of Canada.

The Beatles' tune in my head: *I'm so tired.* Trying to stay awake I walk outside for air, exhausted in exhaust and black British taxis, buses, and pushing past zebra crossings and concrete ramps and tunnels and glass flyovers and tour groups with heaps of suitcases and backpacks and awkwardly flailing skis almost taking my eye out, my exhausted eye. I'm in London and I don't care ("When a man is tired of London, he's tired of life," said Samuel Johnson). I give up on fresh air, fresh exhaust, turn back inside the airport limbo, where I must collapse. But what can you do when there is nowhere to collapse?

I walk the wretched airport (abandon hope, all ye) where a tuna sandwich costs you thirteen dollars, tea tastes like clay. Why can't I embrace and love this world, and permit it its brute casserole and moronic languages? Just need some sleep and I'll be a good little boy again. Our gruesome obligation to sweetness and light.

I need to move, do something, decide to push deep into the city on the tube, quaff a pint or two of the real stuff in a real London pub, and then turn right back around to unreal Heathrow and catch my flight to Ireland. Still have hours; I'll be okay.

I fall into the airport underground's shunting crowds of post-Asians and post-Anglo-Saxon yobs and blokes bound for Hammersmith and Cockfosters and the Department of Departments, Ealing shopgirls reeling past cricket pitches and bramble ditches and graffiti and Chiswick and council flats and Wren crypts and tombs and magpies and meatpies and *punters agonistes*, humanity hot against the tonsil roar of other blunt trains, blurred citizens yoked and flung in opposing directions in a groaning world that must defeat silence.

On the commuter train I close my eyes, hand on my small pack, exhausted, just close my eyes a minute, fall asleep with the rocking, lovely sleep, to dream I am on a Chunnel train to France, to *gay Paree*, and I have somehow slept through all of London's stops, stayed on the train too long. In my dream a dark train, a tunnel under the straining gin-coloured sea, and people are staring at me.

"I have to go to Dublin!" I shout.

I wake in a train in a dark tunnel, people staring at me in squares of anti-light. Did I just *shout*? That dehydrated panic of half-consciousness, of moving and not knowing where. Am I under the Channel? *I have to go to Dublin at 3:15.*

An older man in a cloth cap slides over, smiling: "Ah sure,

Sunny Jim. Don't we all miss the ould sod. Dublin moya, get your nose educated in Moore Street!"

"I mean I want to go to Dublin rather than Paris."

The man exhales loudly. "Well, jaysus, that's all right for some."

A man says with a French accent, "It's Pay-ree, not your mangled version." (All of Europe contributed to Kurtz's making.)

First they won't let me on a plane, now I'm going to miss my fucking flight. Maybe the airport robot is blowing up my backpack this minute.

A woman says, "This train is going into London."

"Oh, thank god," I say.

"Thought it was bloody Dublin you wanted!" the man in the cap exclaims.

"I have to turn around."

Several people make cuckoo sounds, fingers circling at their temples, not caring whether I notice. We stop.

"Mind the gap," says the tape-recorded voice.

"Might as well be talking to the wall," says the older man.

It's not the first time he's been disappointed. He reminds me of my uncles.

"I'm from Canada," I explain.

"Mind the gap," says the voice.

"Is Canada still there now?"

I'm in Dublin, asking for stamps in a tiny side-street post office. (At the Dublin airport armoured cars were picking up and delivering money. Coming in from the airport you see Mercedes after Mercedes — twenty years ago I didn't see a single Mercedes in the whole country.)

"We don't hear anything about Canada," says the postal clerk. "Now a few years ago you had a fight with Spain over fish. I knew a sixty-five-year-old woman, lived here in Dublin for thirty years but had a Canadian passport. They threw her in jail in Tenerife because she had a Canadian passport. Sixty-five years old and never done anything wrong, never so much as drank out of a dirty tea cup, and five days in a Spanish prison. Well, I hope you make it up."

Ireland always in the news. Canada never in the news. No news is good news.

In my aunt's neighbourhood I say hi to passersby, branding myself a knobhead North American. Memo to self: I've got to try something else. *Hello, top of the morning, g'day, good afternoon, hark, forsooth*. I try to stop employing the word but can't. Locals reply, "Are ya?" meaning, "How are you?" Or maybe they're closet existentialists.

Sunday noon: restless and walk to get the Sunday *Irish Times* for me and the Sunday *Independent* for my aunt Rose.

I cross over the tracks, bronze church bells chiming, walk a neighbourhood path between bleak cinderblock walls decorated with barbed wire, metal spikes, broken glass, garbage, and sooty evidence of a fire lit last night against someone's garden wall. If it can burn it will be burned, if it can be wrecked it will be wrecked. This is the ugly future, I think pessimistically. Spray-painted names in raging colour: Fingo, Brano, Nixer, Derzer, Toss, Dayvo, and Harmo, the last perhaps an abbreviation of Harmonstown.

Then on this wonky warehouse street I sneeze, and a man pacing toward me smiles and exclaims in a loud voice, "GOD" — dramatic pause — "BLESS YA!" He cheers me immensely; your man makes me glad I sneezed, glad I'm back in Ireland and caught another Irish cold. "GOD . . . BLESS YA!"

Chapter Twenty-one

LARF AND SING AND
ROTTEN FLUTHERY-EYED DRUNK

MUST GET TO THE WEST, BUT BEFORE I do I ring up Declan to arrange a pub crawl in Dublin.

You don't know me, but . . .

I'll take you around, he offers.

My sister met him once in Edmonton; she gives me a phone number, tells me he owns several pubs in Dublin. Do I want to meet a Dublin publican? Does the pope smoke dope? I don't know him from Adam but want to look him up, have a drink, quiz him about beer and Irish microbreweries and brew pubs.

Now, why on earth would you want to meet someone like that? asks my mother.

Sometimes I wonder if me dear old mother knows me at all.

I ask for Declan in Hogan's, a popular spot on George Street, not far from Padraic's gay bar, the George. At night Hogan's is packed and loud and jungle-sweaty, but this afternoon it's a quiet, airy chapel. The less-than-friendly barman points down the bar.

Declan hides in a crowd that attends him, hides behind

fashionably tiny glasses, unkempt short, spiky hair. In a band photo he'd be the vague guy in the back, the disposable drummer, but in real life he's a player in high-priced downtown Dublin. Declan opens mad trendy clubs and pubs and restaurants and sells them off, hoping the string keeps going, hoping the Celtic Tiger keeps roaring. He deals with the banker for millions of Irish pounds. Has the knack of creating a place people want to be seen in, a new address for attractive and charming sycophants and piss artists and wannabes who will drop buckets of money because, like Hillary's Everest, it is there. This is just part of his talent. Part two: he puts his latest Everest on the market, cashes in, and starts another one. I soon realize he has far more on the go than the pub or two I thought originally. It's good of him to show a stranger around his town; he even offers me a ride in his own plane. I believe Declan was flying through Vancouver and Edmonton for reasons of romance when he met my sister and ended up at her kitchen table — a "friend of a friend" deal.

How much of the empire, I wonder aloud, is yours and how much belongs to the bank?

He laughs at this absurd question. Doesn't matter, he implies; there's always money to be had. And it's true: wheelbarrows of money to be had in Ireland now; real estate higher every time I'm here, despite my prediction that it can't last forever.

The Temple Bar area was run-down and slated for the wrecking ball, for a big new bus station, but now it has become Party Central. Declan says he, with others, owned the original Temple Bar, the one you see on tourist postcards. His group renovated the pub on the cheap.

"We made it look bit older." An authentic shebeen, as in *not* authentic. The sign outside reads "Est. 1840." "We made that up." The Temple Bar area becomes trendy and lucrative, the place to be seen. U2 hangs out here, has a studio, a hotel. Everyone and his dog hangs out, sitting on the curbs with backpacks even though other side streets are more interesting. Declan's bunch sells the bar for a tidy profit. Buy cheap, sell dear, live in the balance, live well on the difference, the gap (mind the gap).

"The corporation tells the next owners they must preserve the bar décor just as it is because the building is historically significant, is on the Heritage List." Behind his little glasses, Declan is bemused telling me this.

You can't trust anyone in Ireland, I joke.

You're right. He laughs.

The streets are crooked on our pub crawl; the streets lie, twist, and it seems lying is the norm in Ireland's land of saints. Blarney is a bit of a cottage industry, a sly game — tell a good one, confuse a tourist, keep a straight face and tell fibs. I will take a lesson from this, learn from the masters. Like William Faulkner: no duty to truth, beholden to no one. Like council members and politicos with their brown envelopes and Cayman accounts. Like me trying to recreate the old days: the house, the deaths, the gossamer myths.

Declan slouches into traffic on Exchequer Street without looking. He's cool; he's the guy at the auction who barely nods. He grew up in a southside house built by Guinness, has come up a step or two.

"Here's a good one." Great pubs: the Old Stand, where Michael Collins used to drink; the International Bar in smoky light and no hands on the clocks; the Palace and Mulligan's (Dublin journalists go to one of these, can't remember which — who cares); and Messrs. Maguires, one of the few making their own beer and the doormen look like the Krays. We jump the crowded line to get a table and some good wings at Pravda, Declan's Russian-themed establishment on the north side of Ha'penny Bridge.

In Mulligan's, Declan takes tea from older bartenders in V-necked sweaters who gingerly insult us, a privilege of age and the institution.

"Can I buy you a beer?"

"Stopped my drinking days," Declan says. He complains of drunken English stag parties coming to Dublin. The stag parties move like loud private armies, like soccer hooligans ("Do we get kicked out of a place or do we get kicked out of a place!" "So a blowjob is out of the question?"). Chant and yell and larf and sing and rotten fluthery-eyed drunk on porter and whiskey. Males in mobs and their always exemplary behaviour.

"They take over a place. English always been good at that," allows Declan dryly. Declan not too bad himself at taking over. Then selling — a step ahead of the game, a gamble it will keep booming.

Declan says, "Guinness controls all the taps. Look. That's a Guinness tap. It looks like a variety — Miller, Bud Lite, Harp — but Guinness distributes those brands; Guinness makes money on all of them. The publicans and vintners in the city are a tight lot." He crosses two fingers. "They do what they want. It's very difficult for new brands or microbreweries to break in. Guinness has a stranglehold."

The bartender in the country pub told me that if they try to carry an independent cider or beer, a big rep shows up and offers a new cooler or fridge if they get rid of the independent. Hard for a ma-and-pa operation to say no; easier to stay with the status quo.

Guinness pushes 10 million pints a day, 116 units a second. This may seem blasphemy to aficionados of Guinness stout, but there is better brew in Victoria or Montreal or Halifax or Seattle or Portland (either coast). I'm used to dark wheat beer and light wheat beer, oatmeal stout, brown ale, amber ale, special bitter,

Bavarian lager, dark lager, raspberry wheat ale, cream ale, Scotch ale, India Pale Ale, even hemp ale. A golden age in brewing, but not in Ireland.

I am staggered that anyone in Ireland wants faceless, tasteless American-style beer. "Who would come to Ireland and want *Bud Lite*?" I ask.

Sharkey's wife, Helen, says softly, "I don't mind Bud Lite when I go out with the girls."

"Well, sure, that sounds all right," I reply, struggling to pull my foot from my big mouth.

Some beautiful pubs in central Dublin, but a good number are so bloody packed you cannot climb in to them to get paloothered. And this is April and May. What of July and August? What good is a good bar if you can't actually get near the bar without a neutron bomb?

There are pressed-tin ceilings and snugs and Victorian etched glass and stained glass's bent crimson light like a church and bevelled whiskey mirrors, heavy and ancient, and ornate oak and zinc bars and glittering shelves of liquor and giant chiselled doors under Georgian fanlights and joists and jambs and mahogany walls and wainscotting the shade of blood-red ale.

"Are you web-enabled?"

"Sorry, haven't had my medication."

"Want some?"

"No, it's coming."

There are also scouser drunks full as the last bus and spilling weak pints and waving a quid and cellphone bozos (Hold on, I've a call on my other ear) and sharp Gordie Howe elbows in the smoke and bleary eyes and tourists who must convince themselves the craic is good and no food after eight and cries of "World class!" amid trendy designer labels and doltish disco and tattoos and stinking jacks and shite beer like Harp or Miller (they should change the sign on the iron railway bridge to "Carlsberg

— Probably the Worst Lager in the World") and by the river, rivers of beer and more vomit per capita and shall I tell ya a good wan about the Celtic Tiger?

"My growth instruments cratered."

"Yet a true martini is 1/4 ounce dry."

Ireland's changed a wee bit since my first trip two decades back. They've had a decorator in.

All of the pubs are renovating and expanding, since the number of Dublin licences is limited — establishments knocking out walls and taking over neighbouring spaces. The lowest, grottiest dive is now extremely valuable simply because it has a pre-existing licence, like taxi permits, like salmon-boat licences in British Columbia, like a licence to print money. A shortage of pubs in a way, though there seem to be so many. James Joyce wondered if you could cross Dublin without passing a pub. Now the question: can you cross without seeing a fake pub?

Make your man an offer, do a quick reno of the old joint, deep-six the seedy non-trendoid, non-demographic clientele. Where do these men go now? You're not allowed to be old any more. Market forces force you out the door — supply and demand, colour schemes, key demographics. You're not in with the in-crowd, so money talks and you walk, Pops.

Money talks and Ireland talks, chats on a fookin' mobile all day. Something odd has happened to me: I was young and Ireland was old, but now Ireland is new and I am old; we've done some weird gymnastic flip. I've become Uncle Marty complaining about the world going to hell in a handbasket.

"Hi, I'm single and my friend is *really* single."

"Have to have tits to get hired. Which I have."

The pubs are packed in soot grey April and the great stone churches are empty, slowly closing their gaunt oak doors. The stag partiers will move on to be separated from their traveller's cheques in the slow light of Iceland, in the volcanoes and igneous trance clubs of Iceland (settled by Vikings and their Irish slaves); the party will move on when Ireland loses its ingot glow, when the market makes a wee little correction or information tech goes in the toilet.

"You want to show some leg on the poster, you need a bit of sex."

"But it's about a fookin' hunchback!"

"But he has a *crush* on her!"

My Irish cousins have found lucrative white-collar jobs, streamlined German cars, hoppy Dutch beer, swish French doors, low-cut Brazilian jeans, ergonomic white kitchens, and black Japanese stereos and stacks of CDs teetering in their new homes. Once the Irish worried about the little people and hellfire. Now they fret about neurotoxins and Microsoft stock options and feng shui.

In this beautiful green country, statues of saints once wore away at the feet from being kissed. Will the strange new statues wear out as well?

No one, fixed Ireland has ever existed, but we believe there must have been — we crave a benchmark to compare — a true Ireland, a pure, untainted Ireland, a mythical Ireland, a dreamscape Ireland, an ur-Éire.

Chapter Twenty-two

SCROATS AND CORNERBOYS

WOULD THERE BE AS MUCH FOUL LANGUAGE where you come from?
Our crowded train passes rows of identical chimney pots, identical windows, identical doors. Women ask me: Now, do you have to lock the doors where you come from?

I love the Dublin accent, love the way they say the word "drugs." Would droogs be as much of a problem where you are?

Central Criminal Court was told that Mr. D. was shot dead after being tortured for hours because 40,000 Ecstasy tablets exported from Amsterdam went missing. The accused said the rip occurred when a man had a gun put to his head at a northside pub and was ordered to drop the bag. The people who owned the drugs were not a bit happy.

Tara Street Station platform, where a country woman complains to her daughter about how dirty Dublin is — grime and garbage and big empty beer tins rattling all over the steel rail and cross ties and the trains are running late and we're going to catch our death in this freezing weather. Never come into Dublin again if I can help it, says she.

A curly-haired man talks excitedly to a bald man on the platform: "Shall I tell ya a good wan? Something on at the Cock Tavern, and don't I come in and he thought I was Jeremy, and he pipes up. 'Do you know what a gobshite is?' says he. I go up to him head to head: 'Yeah, I do, and I'm looking at a real old one right now!'"

The DART train to Howth is cancelled because of a lack of drivers. Not all of us are keeping up with the roaring economy. The cock crows and the train is cancelled at Tara Street, so I nip down for a glass at Kennedy's while I wait, a less than polished drinking hole that. Once someone like Declan is done with it, will doubtless be much posher the next time I'm through town. If we're really, really lucky it'll have a "theme," though we'll pay through the nose for the privilege.

> Two boys broke into the crypt of the 800-year-old
> St. Michan's Church after reading an article in the *News
> of the World* about possible treasures buried on the church
> grounds. The younger of the two played football with the
> skull of a baby's corpse, taken from a coffin marked E. Hall,
> died 1838, aged four months. A fire was set at the back of
> the vault. The court was told the accused come from a
> dysfunctional family.

An elderly man barricades himself in his tiny home with metal doors, barred inside. Kids keep breaking in, his golden years and the little shit rats won't leave him be, so he makes a fortress. The firefighters can't get in either and he burns to death. Kids take the DART train out from the city and do break-ins. They trot along the track with stolen goods. My cousin Sharkey has strung four separate barbed-wire fences on the slope below his house and above the railbed. Weeds up over the fences now — no man's land, weeds hiding the barbs.

"They'd never get through the wire," Sharkey says.

His neighbour asks him to do the same for his place next door. Factories along the train track boast odd wire silhouettes, their outside drainpipes wrapped in barbed wire so the new animal gangs can't climb them, a stark empire of cinderblocks and razor wire, an invisible tong war with the offspring of what the court terms dysfunction, the covetous, the accused.

Over a dark pint my cousin the policeman talks of busting knackers and sending them to jail, and then at home he reads of judges and top politicians and dignitaries all getting away with whatever they want, and even if they're charged they never face a chance of jail. Sharkey seems bothered by this more than last time I was here; it seems to weigh on him. There is crime and then there is crime.

Solon, circa 600 B.C., knew some of this: "Laws are the spider's web which, if anything small falls into them, they ensnare it, but large things break through and escape."

The newspapers and radio talk shows are full of bagmen and kickbacks, cash in plastic shopping bags on the golf course, blank cheques and bank accounts in the Cayman Islands, the Isle of Man, the Channel Islands, silent partners and fictitious companies, rezoning votes and shady real estate, private estates, private lives, private islands and yachts, suspicious stables and stud farms, beef tribunals, slush funds, mad money, Dunne's grocery money, gifts, enchanted objects.

One top dog, spent almost $20,000 US of the country's money to drape his wrinkled shoulders in French monogrammed shirts. And that's just scratching the surface of what went on, still goes on — the old habits hard to kick cold turkey, the old Adam game of politics (a metaphor in your mouth and a bribe in your pocket).

At Sunday dinner my cousins and aunts argue furiously, enjoyably, especially Rose and her eldest son, but we know that the top mandarins won't be punished, other than by the pile of legal fees they'll pay to their friends' law firms (I think of *Bleak House*'s case Jarndyce vs. Jarndyce, but also a Sligo law firm called Argue and Phibbs).

"It was a fiddle!"

"It was not a fiddle!"

"Now, Mother, that judge resigned only because there was a *perception* of corruption. Judges are not all corrupt; they only interpret the law."

"Well, he landed on his feet. Got a new appointment soon enough. And Bertie's kept all the same gang around him. Jobs for the boys." Bertie Ahern is the new PM.

"No evidence we're any more corrupt than the rest of Europe."

"Didn't Bertie sign all the blank cheques for Charlie? That Charlie's a scoundrel, a chancer!"

"Ah, he's no worse than the rest."

Did the great Charles Haughey, I wonder, gaze upon a green light at the end of the dock? Did he have a Daisy Buchanan to splash tears of joy upon his rubies and tigers and his rich, many-coloured heap of linen and silk shirts?

When retiring, Mr. Haughey quoted *Othello*: "I have done the state some service." This was before the charges, the scandals, before the endless tribunals that found the state had done *him* some service. It struck me as an odd choice at the time, for in the tragedy it is the speech of a great man fallen, a man arrested by the state, a man who has destroyed what he had; it is a sentence spoken moments before suicide (*And smote him, thus*).

Dubliners just laugh at the daily revelations and comment cynically.

"He's so crooked he has to screw his socks on."

"No politicians are saints."

Rose says, "I don't trust them Fianna Fáil; I'm voting PD to keep an eye on them."

"All politicians are thieving swine."

"Well, they're the swiniest," says Sharkey.

"And all along, didn't I say he was?" says Aunt Rose. "Now, didn't I?"

"Jack Lynch wrecked this country. Haughey saved it."

"Lynch! Haughey! Are you joking? Haughey doubled the debt! Are you off your trolley, man? He bought that election." And they're off on another round.

I rarely see this kind of sharp engagement with politics in my relatives in Canada or London or Philadelphia. It's fun to watch. The fractious political scandals in Dublin are ongoing public theatre, a chaotic spectator sport like the coverage of the Habs in Montreal, like the endless trial in *Bleak House*. The Irish are cynical yet more involved; they take it personally. A small island, so there is less distance; politics are close to bone.

Money fluttering in the air, including three billion dollars from Brussels and the EU. But, as in most places, the money's not for everyone's pocket or secret bank account; the cash doesn't always trickle down. Dutch Reagan can't remember what happened to that idea. Mountjoy Prison: my cousin Sharkey says that all the people he puts into Mountjoy's crowbar hotel hail from the same three postal codes. Maybe five parishes, Sharkey says; just five parishes in the entire country populate the prisons, populate the joy.

What am I doing? Sharkey wonders. The poor knackers and scroats and cornerboys are born into it, their parish postal code

— no education or training, no jobs or income — they don't have a chance from the get-go, he tells me. They don't get an island or a yacht or a brass ring on the merry-go-round.

Not all of them are poor, though. A middle-class neighbourhood kid gone to junk knocks on Sharkey's door.

"I know you're on the task force. Tell 'em I'm clean. Tell 'em I'm clean."

This kid's uncle was a policeman who'd been shot dead, a famous case in Dublin, a well-known name. The kid lands in hot water, the police ask for his name.

"You related to Fitz?"

"Yeah, he's my uncle."

The police let the kid off with a stern warning. Keeps getting off because of his name. His antics get worse and worse (drugs send you stupid) — break-ins, heroin, jump-overs (leaping counters to rob cash) — and more and more caps of heroin a badly kept secret altering his skin and eyes, the poisoned glen.

He comes to Sharkey's door just down the quiet street. "Tell 'em I'm clean."

"Strung out all to bits," says Sharkey. "Like that guy from Thin Lizzy. Telling everyone he's using nothing and shooting up between his toes. He's dead now.

"I see Shane McGowan of the Pogues coming through the airport. Worse each time. Comes off on the Tarmac with no shoes on his feet, wandering the airport in socks doing the Shane shuffle, doesn't know where the fuck he is. His man there supposed to help him is just helping him spend his money; his man fucked off somewhere. Shane wanders to the airport bar, hunched over like he's passed out. People trot up for autographs. Shane! *Arr*, he says. Can't make out a word he says. He's come back from the dead several times. A shame — he wrote some great songs."

Aunt Rose worries that Sharkey the policeman is a bad influence on me.

"I'm sure that poor man's exhausted keeping up with Sharkey!" I hear her saying, when in fact I am happy to go out for all those pints, happy to stay up late and actually talk. Rose blames Sharkey for wrecking my health when I catch a cold. I alternate chills and fever, but I try to keep my symptoms a secret. I suppose I hate to expose a design flaw or seem a bearer of contagion.

I saw Brendan Behan vomit on the pub floor in mid-sentence and take up the sentence where he left it in the air in the yellow room. Wait, you never clapped eyes on bleeding Brendan Behan (a drinker with a writing problem). Suddenly wonder, Who has my grandmother's polished piano? It must be in a house around town. Someone who got it for a song. Perhaps it was pawned or stolen with the silver when she was infirm. Can't just vanish; can't be kindling. And I can't believe I'll never see my cousin Padraic again.

The old Dublin hospital where Padraic was working on an architectural project closed for the day of his funeral. Rose and Sharkey show me the newspaper advertisement stating that they are closing in memory of Padraic: *We have lost a friend of strength and dignity.*

Chapter Twenty-three

STATION TO STATION
(THE WEST IS THE BEST)

EVERYONE HAS WALKED THIS RAILWAY STATION's chessboard tiles, made moves in the calm chaos of this platform, alighted a car above these forged steel tracks and switches. All my blood relatives knew this platform; Michael Collins paced here, worries in his head. De Valera knew this station, as did every fevered, famous rebel or martyr or informer or supergrass in the Castle's pay — people squeezing through this portal, my mother leaving the country for Victoria Station in London, never having been there, moving off the map into nursing and then the Royal Navy and returning occasionally to show off her trendy, weird 1940s hats.

My aunt Bridie says my mother loved her hats, protected her hats like babies on the trip home, and she took butter back to wartime Britain. Thriving black market in tea, tobacco, and butter during the war and well after the war, part of the reason my parents sailed for Canada.

"Scrape it on and scrape it off," they joked in my father's family house in Oxford, trying to be thrifty with butter for hot toast. Grandpa demanded he be given the butter and everyone else could have margarine. Granny said, "Yes, dear," but did the opposite, and he never knew, the grumpy old boy thought he had the real stuff. My Irish grandmother sold her own butter for a few extra coins. Tea was expensive, coal rare. I have whatever I want. I line up inside the Italianate station, buy a ticket to ride with my credit card. It's exciting and rote.

I'm taking the train west, sliding across the whole country's waist, the middle of her favours. It took me ten days to drive across Canada, longer to hitchhike. In Ireland you surf coast to coast in four hours, and it would be faster without all the train's milk-run stops. How many Irelands could you fit inside Canada? Be nice to have just one. Get Guinness to arrange it on eBay, ship us the country by parcel post. Men fall asleep as soon as the train moves out of the railyards; they've done the trip a few times. Big ruddy faces, one man ready to have a heart attack, snorting and fitful, troubled windpipes trying to keep him going.

I barely remember taking the train west twenty years ago. I must have been nervous, on my own, no idea what to expect, where I'd stay. The wild west, the weird west, the lonesome west, where men outnumber women and women leave, and where I'd almost immediately fall in love with a Dingle woman standing on a stone dock staring at her familiar sea while I stared at her and tried not to fall down the steep winding path in the windy cliffs and resolved, I must talk to her.

Long hair, a wool jumper or pullover, her bare neck and lovely skin in the wet air, light in our eyes, blue-and-green Maritime light around our heads, and light like a mile of milk overtop the vague distances to the ghost villages on emptied islands offshore, triangular islands laced with surf and no boat today to the Blaskets, the ancient monastic islands, safe from Vikings, safe from me, never got to the islands, never touched her skin, never saw her naked hip. The old woman at the pub keeping us apart, but we stood in the perfumed seawind talking as her hair blew about us.

On the ridge rare songbirds blown off course from North America, songbirds pulled in the jet stream 5,000 kilometres to the spot where she stands before me.

I ran like the clappers when I heard someone shout up the hill that they'd seen the wee fella. We got some magnificent views when he came out to feed on blackthorn berries.

Pedalling a bike to the western edge of Fortress Europe and songbirds from America seeing a lighthouse and looking for land and the wind off the sea touching her lovely skin and I could see her nipples pressing her sweater, but I never touched her skin. Images from 1981 like inmates in my head.

"Be sure to pick up a bottle of juice or some snacks for the train," Sharkey advised me this time around. At a quayside store not far from my mother's old house I see rows of skin mags. Decades ago a shopkeeper would have been attacked for displaying tits and ass in colour; my grandmother, a parish priest, a guard walking the neighbourhood — someone would have put a stop to it. Where did that presence go, that threat, that power? Was it an illusion? Where did that Ireland evaporate to? How did tits and ass win?

The train twenty years ago took me first to Killarney, deep in the southwest.

"You must see the Ring of Kerry," everyone told me in 1981. Sunny and warm, and a very pretty locale, but I left Killarney almost immediately — it was too crowded, full tour buses of all the other people on the planet who had been told they must see the Ring of Kerry.

I also left Killarney because I was embarrassed in a pub. I took a corner table by a leafy window, ordered a pint and ploughman's, then noticed that someone had left a package on the bench. I carried it to the bar.

"Found this at my table. Hope it isn't a bomb." The bartender did not like my moronic joke. I didn't even like it. Wrong thing to say. I was young and stupid. I finished my pint quickly, watching the irked publican pointing me out to others, the eejit tourist.

Face burning, I moved my feet, fled the pub, fled Killarney and headed north — Tralee, Dingle, the Seven Hogs, Spanish Point, Hag's Head, Galway, the Aran Islands, Connemara, the Twelve Pins, Westport, Devil's Head — places less crowded, guessing and following my nose, following the wrinkled, coloured map up the unknown coast, riding clunker rental bikes around the lanes and white sandy strands of each green peninsula wreathed in sun and mist, not knowing where I was going, loads of time, my life a pancake up in the air.

Chapter Twenty-four

DOING A CROMWELL IN THE BOG

DRINKING SNACK-CART TEA, WE CROSS THE WATER, cross the Shannon River at Athlone, our train suspended out over the broad silver-green river, now more than halfway across Ireland.

"This is where we say the west begins," says a pie-faced, curly-haired man, looking very much like the actor Gene Wilder. You know that somewhere in the woodpile they have a common ancestor.

My tea cups and maps are spread over the blue table I have to myself on the train: on the map my eyes cross the country and the realization that I lose too much time in cities. Dublin is great fun, a trap I love, but it's not really Ireland; it's like New York vis-à-vis the rest of the USA.

The Shannon River moving fast under our moving train is a striking scene: wide churning water and spinnakers flapping in the sun and masts clinking and boats bumping below Athlone's aged granite bridges and quays and soft light on pleasing stone buildings and nestled down in the riverbed mud are cannonballs from William of Orange and revolvers from 1922. Athlone was a crossroads, an important city in Ireland's civil war. Ambushes, rail lines torn up, bombs, houses burning — the Irish mauled one another, ate one another, doing a Cromwell to themselves.

My train passes huge wet bogs where turf is dug out for fuel, giant trenches cut down into the ground or peat pulled out of cliffs, a murky pool of water collected at the base. Stacked bricks of peat dry in the rain. How does anything dry in this climate? Some long rectangular heaps of peat are hidden under black plastic to keep away the showers, let the water seep out.

Rose tells me of buying turf in a blizzard when they ran out of coal. "Ah, didn't they sell us wet peat." If it's wet it weighs more and they can charge more than it's worth. "There I was, trying desperately to start a fire with newspaper and twigs and splinters of wood, try to dry it a bit, but the wet peat wouldn't catch, and we were freezing." Her cold babies crying and Rose crying too, out of frustration.

"And it's free," says a cheerful American woman's voice on the train.

"Ah now, it's a lot of hard work," corrects an older Irish woman. There is much trash strewn along the rail line and about the countryside, and I can see an upside-down car far out in the blanket bog, bogged down in the bog, likely stolen by joyriders, for stealing cars is now a popular pastime for the energetic youngsters.

In Noel Leonard's pub on Watling Street, right by Usher's Island, a man told me a car story: "My car was stolen and burnt, so I get a new car and this time put in a brilliant alarm system, cost hundreds of pounds. Well, didn't they steal the fecking alarm system!" We all laughed. Maybe his was the burnt car I saw in the park named after a saint.

My cousin Feargal in Westport lost a dog running out in the bogs. It might have fallen down a boghole. The dog ran off and never returned. Ireland used to be covered by trees, wind moving through oak, beech, ash, yew, birch, elm, pine, hazel, herds of deer shifting, wild boars under flocks of falcons and kites and eagles. Gone like Feargal's dog. The felled timber fed ravenous local demands and lucrative markets in England and the Continent — masts, ships, barns, barrels.

I take in the nude land, the stone and muck. That ancient forests thrived here seems impossible, perhaps a lesson for those, like me, vaguely amused by dreadlocked, bongo-beating tree-huggers. No oak forests now, though they still wrench giant petrified trees out of the bogs. I saw petrified trees that had been dug out inland of Roonah Quay — wild and dark shapes lined up on the ground, limbs tar-black and gnarled — and saw prehistoric elk antlers, wide as a room.

Locals and archeologists dig up Iron Age hamlets that the bog crept over in a giant carpet. Walk over someone else's village every day and not know it's down there like a bungalow basement. Irish ploughmen turn up golden bowls, gold necklaces and collars, bronze trumpets. I stare out at the weird land and suddenly want to know if there are coyotes hiding in Ireland. Never hear them mentioned. I know there were once packs of wolves, primal wild dogs after you or your dear aunt's leg. Were there black bears? Wildcats? You don't run across them in the mythology.

On this holy mountain St. Patrick rassled a bar and drove the snakes and reptilian Hollywood agents as far as Dublin. From this tiny bay St. Brendan sailed — well before Columbus, mind you — sailed to the New World in a little leather bark and didn't he call his dear ould mam every day on his mobile.

The train is emptier as we move west into the stone walls. Lambs run from our train and calves kick up their heels as we pass, as we get more water for our tea (sometimes pronounced *tay*, like the French). Tea seems so ingrained now, so Irish, yet it was rarer in Ireland a century or two back.

"Ah, we're getting nearer now." Pie-face Man's charming accent.

The names along the lovely milk run: Kildare, Tullamore, Clara, Athlone, Roscommon, Castlerea, Ballyhaunis, Claremorris, Manulla Junction, Castlebar, and Westport, where I'm getting off, the end of the line at Clew Bay.

Rose says Mayo was always the direst part of the country, says they prayed to God to look out for poor Mayo. Mayo God bless us, says my mother. Children's graveyards hidden in stones and sedge and wildflowers, graves marked on old ordinance maps — perhaps babies who died before baptism. As a child I imagined these babies floating, was told they were in limbo. Famine and fever victims must have scattered into houses and hills and ditches and fields where families fell and never got up, generations swerving into their own morbid limbo. Why do I assume, when I see these victims starving in the west that exists inside my lamplit skull, that these were all good gentle folk? Some might have been, like me, complete jerks. I follow the milk run on my map, realize I love this side of Ireland — more pious and savage, moving you between centuries in seconds.

St. Patick's big mountain becomes visible in the vapours: Croagh Patrick, the Reek, Ireland's Sinai, a volcano shape rising over saints and stolen cars and torn bleeding feet on the ancient pilgrimage up the loose rocks of the peak. A landscape I do remember, expecting the beautiful triangular mountain before it is visible, knowing where to look. Padraic and Bernadette, my Dublin sweetheart, waiting for me in 1981 as I travelled up from the south to meet them and was late, lingering on the Aran Islands' scary cliffs and shining beaches. I didn't arrive in Westport until Saturday, instead of Friday night, and Bernadette was mad at me, was hurt that I was late to meet her.

The track curves this way and that way, and St. Patrick's sacred mountain changes position, hides in the walls of clouds, sneaks out for a walk, shoulder feints, shifts behind you; the purple mountain steps back into the room. Pilgrims like ants climbing it this minute, climbing it constantly since pre-Christian times, since pre-history, pilgrims climbing the Reek for more than 5,000 years, and Saturday I'm going to be another, going to climb to the summit with Feargal. If I can. In the year 1113, thirty pilgrims seeking an indulgence or a vision died on the peak, poor devils zapped by a lightning storm that hit them at night high on a dark mountain, trapped, nowhere to hide on the open rock up in the clouds, buzzing worlds lit and black again, air humming and glowing and you pray and crawl and dig fingernails into white stone and white light and white bodies and wait until dawn to see who is alive, some penitents killed without a mark on them. This was March 17. No green beer here. Just the fearsome sea to the west, dead on a mountain at the known world's edge, *ubi nemo ultra erat*: beyond which no man dwelt. Not everyone got this far. The Romans never got near this height, near this edge.

"Ah, we're getting nearer now," Pie-face Man says aloud in the train, like a pleasant priest to his faithful flock. Westport is the end of the line. Suddenly I'm nervous about seeing my cousin Nora and her husband, Feargal, in Westport after two decades. Nora is Sharkey and Padraic's oldest sister, grew up in Dublin but living in the west thirty years. Will I know them by sight? What if we are cooped up and can't stand each other?

Chapter Twenty-five

BLACK COW

ON THE WESTPORT STATION PLATFORM I PICK OUT Feargal and Nora immediately and am relieved.

Feargal is tall and soft-spoken, volunteers with a local mountain rescue, pulling rookie climbers off mini-Matterhorns and combing windkanter ridges for dead bodies. He is quiet, sometimes seems ascetic as a monk, but surprises me, turning on the siren and flasher as we drive home in his big white mountain rescue 4 x 4.

"Look how the big trucks just pull right over for us!" he says happily as we scoot by. He's not sure yet how to switch the white monster to 4 x 4, but he knows how to work the flashers and siren. Their house is a few miles out of town, a large cottage right on the sea, with views of water and islands and the mountain we'll climb.

Nora is a social worker, works with travellers in the area, is very hospitable while happily telling you how depressed she gets. Nora asks me questions about writing each visit, wants to start writing.

Well, just start, I say. I am not much help.

Westport is on Clew Bay, where Grace O'Malley, the storied pirate queen of Connaught, had her hideout. It's a pretty town, laid out by tidy Anglo gentry on a small, slightly altered river, the Carrowbeg, that moves politely to the sea. Yet the town does not seem a false ornament. Mobile phones and Mercedes are noticeably less evident in the west. Why am I happier if the locals seem poorer? Does that make them more colourful, worth more points in a tourist inventory or Super 8 home movie? Perhaps it does. But I think I resent cells and trophy cars no matter where I wander.

In Nora's cottage a letter to the editor in the Westport paper catches my eye: it suggests that etiquette for cellphones should be the same as for picking your nose: *Please do it in private*.

Here in the west, as in Dublin and at my aunt's farm by Kilkenny, the new generation flings about in taxis, scarfs up oysters and lobster, buys boxes of yellow Italian stiletto heels and name-brand bags with string handles and pastel perfect sweaters (*For Raoul!*), and sips Slippery Nipple shooters and crantinis, money pouring from Hermès purses (canvas coated with Brazilian tree sap) while my mother and my aunts, who grew up darning lumpy socks and saving bits of twine and wet coal, are horrified at such extravagance.

My father travelled Italy and England and Ireland the year before he died, and he enjoyed Westport, talked happily about it later, the scarlet bay and glowing sky and quaint streets and shops painted brightly, the locals friendly to him in a pub, wanting to know who he is, where he's from, locals keeping watch at the window for my mother and her sister, who are shopping the radiating streets (Ah, here they are now), and my reticent father used to England's social distance. He loves it, tickled to be part of the gang. My father back from the colonies for a visit, not knowing it's his last, not knowing he is carrying cancer in him like a fetus, and my cousin Padraic at the health club with his HIV hidden (Ah, we're getting nearer now) and the owner chatting at the treadmill while making plans to abscond with his friends' wallets. Letters and codes and secret somethings smuggled in all of us, a prize concealed in a box of Cracker Jacks.

Putting the moan on ya: At a restaurant where our obliging waiter runs down the cobbled street to carry up my pints from a neighbouring pub, Nora and Feargal's German friends complain and complain, lamenting about their lot in life. Feargal listens politely over dinner but is very quiet on the drive home in the dark.

"Anything wrong, Feargal?" Nora asks.

"Ah, they put the moan on me."

I'm reminded of Declan of Temple Bar fame snapping at me in the International or the Old Stand, snapping at me to let a pint settle properly before touching it. "If you had any patience on ya," he said. The Gaelic sentence construction like a ghost informing English conversation, the old-fashioned bartender in an old-fashioned sweater grumbling about having to make Declan tea (Tea! Tea! Why don't you go to the bloody Shelbourne) but making a pot eventually and laughing.

I sleep in until after noon, sleep twelve hours, waking with no idea what time it is or how long I've slept. Happens to everyone the first morning in her cottage, Nora tells me. Would you care for some tea? The radio is on, talk radio. Nora gives me tea and juice and zinc and vitamin C and bakes fresh Irish bread in her cottage by the sea and drops the new loaf on the floor in front of her guest.

"Better throw that away," she says.

"I'll eat it."

Sharkey, when younger, drove fledgling girlfriends out to Westport to meet his older sister, Nora.

"They thought you must be dead serious about them if they're meeting the sister," he explained in Dublin. "Back then there was no shagging unless they thought you were dead serious. Now everyone shags at the drop of a hat."

Four in a car consuming giant jugs of cider, pilgrims getting locked while driving cross-country and hoping to have a little action at the cottage in the west, Sharkey using his older sister to help him get lucky in more straitlaced days when it was rarer to get unbuttoned. My favourite eighteenth-century suicide note: "All this buttoning and unbuttoning."

Feargal and Nora used to run a B & B in their house, but they sold it and now work as resident caretakers for a demented, driven absentee landlord. In Dublin, Sharkey and Rose kept telling me funny stories about this "crazy American," but now I find that he's actually from England and spends most of the year in Los Angeles, in a gated house in the hills. So the new landlord, the new boss, is both English and American, as is fitting.

Here in Ireland the man hates the locals.

"He won't buy groceries or supplies in town; he even ships in his own lightbulbs from Los Angeles, with Weetabix as packing material, and then over the summer he eats the Weetabix for breakfast."

Their landlord has fought two lawsuits with locals and won both. More to come. The rich landlord is supposed to be getting away from the Los Angeles rat race, California's fortress mentality, is supposed to be relaxing, but he gallops task to task, *runs* everywhere while barking orders, and he brings the fortress with him, nailing up No Trespassing signs and suing Paddy and Molly Malone and erecting new, improved fences and gates and supervising the bulldozers in their landscaping and earth-moving projects, everything a battle, fighting the wild elements, fighting the ocean's booming winter tides and whipping gales, fighting his enemies, fighting his blood pressure and inner workings.

He built the new house right on the sea, and Nora and Feargal live a bit back, in the property's older cottage. His expensive new lawn has big dead patches where winter storms sprayed saltwater across it. He ripped down a hill behind the house, moving hill and dale to build a virgin peninsula of boulders and dirt with grass on top, to push out more shoreline in front of his house, to create money by minting new shoreline, but his pot of gold, this ersatz point of land under the sacred mountain, tempts the gods and is being patiently picked clean by the sea.

"He had some workmen come at 6 a.m., pounding and smashing on our cottage walls, and he didn't even warn us. Do you not think you could tell someone?" Nora says. "I've rarely seen Feargal mad — he's a very calm person and he's put up with a lot — but he tore a strip off the landlord and your man was in shock. He wants to subdivide his land to sell it off, but the local government turned him down. This will be another lawsuit for the rich landlord," she says. We have to laugh.

"When he lives there in the summer, *by contract* we must hide our Toyota well away from the gate because the landlord doesn't want to see our car when he's there. But when he is gone back to Los Angeles, *by contract* we must park the Toyota right at the gate so the place has an occupied look."

As if the dim locals won't twig to when His Nibs is there and when he's not.

If there's a problem during the winter, Feargal must call Los Angeles person-to-person with a code of sorts.

"Will you accept a call for Uncle Ernie?"

"No," the landlord says, "Uncle Ernie's not here right now." He hangs up. No charge to his bill.

Then the absentee landlord calls Feargal right back to see what the problem is, using his American plan. Saves himself a nickel.

Sharkey says, "Bad idea to come in with barbed wire and electric gates. Years ago we had no money, and Germans and Americans and English bought the coastline, then up goes the barbwire. Going to be trouble in the future."

The landlord has planted rows of trees, which sounds pleasing, but he's planted the trees to block his neighbours' views of the sea. If I was a neighbour I'd poison the line of saplings. If I was him I'd be more careful in a country with a tradition of torching the great houses, the rich landlords, a country with a resentment of foreign landlords, the absentee landlords.

"Where you see old trees means a Protestant landowner in the past," says Feargal. "The poor cut down all the trees they could for heat, but the Protestant estate owners could afford to keep trees for ornament."

"The British took all our trees for masts and ships," a man tells me in a pub.

"That's a myth," Feargal tells me.

The British navy did need millions of trees to build its wooden fleets. I'd bet a few came from here.

In *How the Irish Saved Civilization*, Thomas Cahill says that forests were cut down to deprive rebels of their hiding places. In 1602 Shakespeare was writing *Hamlet*. In 1602, eyewitnesses in Ireland said Elizabethan forces fired the rebel's corn to famish them, and they saw rebel soldiers eating horseflesh and unsavoury kites, and saw small children eating their dead mother's entrails, and old women hiding out in the bog to kill and eat children. There never seems to be one easy story.

Big black cows plough through my first morning of my visit, hoofs smashing huge round holes in the rich man's precious grass. Feargal and I shoo the cattle off the property. One cow nearly runs me down, but I wave my Edmonton Oilers cap and act like an idiot and the cattle turn back and run down the strand and plunge into the dark bay, where they stand and piss into the water while drinking from said water. A little like the loopy landlord.

Nora and Feargal take me to lovely deserted beaches on Clew Bay, white strands whipped to a froth in wind and rain, cold still in spring, and we motor under the eroded creases of the Devil's Mother and Mweelrea and Benbury and other western peaks with dangerous broken shale and limestone and quartzite and precipitous routes where it's dead easy to start rock slides and hit climbers below, get beaned in the head or taken right off your little foothold ledge.

Feargal tells me of a famous Irish climber who spent time on the dolomite heights we drive under. "Like a cat, scramble up anything, fearless." He risks his life scaling wrench-fault cliffs and castellated peaks and is then killed, not on a quartzite mountain (the divil you know) but sitting on a boat when a taut tow-cable snaps and, like a steel cobra, whips him in the head dead.

"A good friend of ours just died climbing in Kerry. She wasn't even climbing really — four of them going up steps cut into rock, and one person above her tumbled down into the others and two went over a cliff. Gone."

Follow the ruins, the roads, Murrisk, the megalithic tomb, the Partry Mountains, the Maumturk Mountains, and glowering fjords knifing deep inland to touch a tiny crossroads village where we stop for a dark pint and attempt to order sandwiches, but the young barman is on the phone and irritated by us wanting food and drink, and the sandwiches that finally arrive don't match what we ordered.

"Well, as he didn't specify," says Barman-on-a-phone.

"What do you mean, 'Didn't specify'?"

Feargal picks the ham from his bread and gives it to me. Feargal went climbing in Nepal and came back a vegetarian. The buses in Nepal — sides streaked with vomit.

Nora announced, "I'm not going to bother cooking any more if there's no meat involved; it's not worth it." And she was a good cook, according to Sharkey.

"I get depressed," Nora says. She sees a doctor at times. "After my first child I was depressed."

"Postpartum?"

"Thirty one years ago in Ireland there was no such thing as postpartum depression. I got better eventually. I was taking fertility drugs, became pregnant again, but we lost the baby. I was depressed over that, got a bit better, then we had our daughter. Postpartum again. The doctor put me on Valium."

Rose says she can't understand — Nora has a good life, a nice home in a beautiful part of the world, and a good husband and bright children doing so well. Maybe depression runs in our family. Maybe it's the climate here — the west of Ireland is harsher than Howth's palm trees and California tiles or London's sunny bowl of a valley in the south of England. The west is far more exposed, far more rain, greyer, colder.

"I moved from my father's house to my husband's house, and I wonder now if I should have had a life in between, wonder if I missed something important."

Nora says that she was terrified of her father's temper. "Anything could spark it off." She remembers, one childhood Christmas, driving across wide O'Connell Bridge in downtown Dublin, and a bus beeped its horn at them and Brendan jumped out of the car in the middle of traffic and was out shouting and shaking his fist at the huge bus above them. Rose was upset.

While Nora tells me this I think, I have some of this family temper, as do all my brothers. I've jumped out of cars to shout and fight. One man met me with a silver ratchet. I am trying to be better. I remember my uncle Brendan getting mad at us in 1981, shouting at us to shut up because he couldn't hear his radio program as we gabbed loudly at the kitchen table, but that was because he could hear out of only one ear at that point.

Rose gave me an old-fashioned ledger book of his when I needed a notebook. Most pages were blank, but several still had his long division in blue ink and lists of sales of Harp and cigars and hot whiskeys. Brendan did the books for a pub after his early retirement. No one seemed to know what he had. The decline was slow enough that the close family almost didn't notice. When Padraic and Sharkey saw photos of him dancing at a wedding just a year before, they realized the change; no way he'd dance now. I am glad I met him.

Throat cancer, I was told, but the symptoms also seemed like a stroke, as one side of him was stricken. Brendan had an eye patch hiding one eye, and he couldn't hear out of one ear and had great trouble swallowing food. Rose cut up his food as much as she could, but Brendan could hardly eat, had become as thin as his older brother Dermot.

"I was afraid of Josie too," Nora says. I'm surprised, as I associate my aunt Josie in Philly with polite visits in Germantown with tea served us. I'd deliberately get Josie and Marty arguing about the Kennedys just to liven things up. "She was a terror to us," says Nora. "We visited Philadelphia one Christmas when we were first married, and Feargal was growing a beard. This was in the Sixties.

"'You're not going to midnight Mass like that,' said Josie.

"'I am,' said Feargal. This quiet lad standing up to her. There was a huge row. We were lying in bed the first night, planning excuses to leave. But it was all right after that."

Nora is very happy after her first grandchild arrives (a great source of joy for us), and her younger sister has a baby too, Nora sending me cheerful e-mails about births, nappies, who has whose eyes, crowded birthday parties, and hectic family trips to Dublin and Portugal, Morocco and France and Spain (life is very good at the moment).

In 1997 Padraic and I discussed Lizzie and her hospital stays. Many times I had heard that she'd sign herself into St. Patrick's Hospital for a rest, paid for by a Guinness plan, and my uncle Dermot would come in the door from work to a note on the kitchen table and the kids his to look out for. Padraic was the only one in the family who sympathized with Lizzie.

"That poor woman," Padraic said, "she was clinically ill." He surprised me with a point of view diametrically opposed to that of most family members, who felt she was malingering, abandoning her children, and making life harder still for her husband.

I asked my mother about Lizzie's stays in hospital, and she said, "Wouldn't get her feet out of bed. That *nonsense* soon stopped after Dermot died." My mother is prone to depression (look at that grey sky) but not tolerant of it in anyone else.

Bridie visited Lizzie, and Marty was good to Lizzie, wrote her: "That's my brother's wife," he said. "Uncle Marty was a real gentleman despite his crusty exterior," comments my cousin Peggy in Philly.

Lizzie wrecked trips all of us planned to the country. Dermot had the car, so if at the last minute she said, "No, we're not going," then no one could go. Lizzie wouldn't invite you in. When people were over she'd slam pots or doors in the kitchen or stay upstairs and they wouldn't even see her — I heard versions of these stories from many relatives in the family.

But Padraic, a bit of an outsider himself, saw something else in the narratives. Padraic surprises me, but then I am also surprised to find that Lizzie is not dead.

Is she buried in Glasnevin, where Dermot is?

Lizzie's still alive.

An odd feeling, just assumed Lizzie was dead. My uncle Dermot dead so long, almost forty years. Has she been shunned? Buried alive? No one ever said, "Come, let's go see Lizzie." All my visits and never knowing she is alive somewhere in Dublin, her bed moved to the front parlour, a cold house falling to bits around her ears.

Look at that grey sky. My mother thinks the bottle is a problem with Nora's depression. But then my mother thinks we all drink too much. My mother never allowed our family to be sick, and I worry that a little of this disdain of visible weakness, this lack of sympathy, has rubbed off on me. In the university hospital my mother won't take her "tablets" and yanks out her IV.

"I think I've had enough," she says. They strap my mother to a chair and a security guard watches over her. A view of a cement wall.

A lovely, lonely view from Nora's kitchen sink, the best view in the cottage, looking south and west out to Croagh Patrick and sunsets and stones and low peninsulas and islands in a leaden sea. Nora doesn't drink, but she has Guinness and Heineken in the fridge for me. Feargal sips single malt. We talk and at night watch *Sex, Lies and Videotape* and *Sliding Doors*, rented movies about infidelity with a couple together more than thirty years.

Nora tells me that the travelling folk she works with are very religious, which surprises me. I thought as outsiders they'd be the opposite.

"Travellers are like in our grandparents' day: strong faith, traditions, deference to the tenets of religion. They may not go to Mass very Sunday, but they're very religious. Family is important to them — big families, no birth control. Travellers marry very young, marry at thirteen. Some of the women are abused. They have few choices. I've met a woman with thirty-eight grandchildren; she can't keep up with First Communions and confirmations to attend and she has to, an obligation, she gets very upset. At First Communion some traveller children run wild up and down the aisles, not used to staying still or quiet in a church. Huge expenditures on weddings, and big, garish headstones for funerals. It's important to them. If someone's sick they *have* to visit. They all go, and the crowds cause problems in the hospital. A lot of travellers in the west. Tuam is mostly travelling folk. Some want to settle, some don't. They're good gas. I like them."

The radio always on during the day, talk radio popular in Ireland and many stations to pull in. Radio Limerick 95 FM, Radio Kerry, Tipperary Mid West Radio, Galway Bay FM, Raidió na Life, Anna Livia 103 FM.

"People come from other countries to study Irish radio, see why it's sucessful," says Feargal. Feargal has a shelf of books on climbing in Wales, England, Ireland, and the Himalayas, and also has a collection of local poetry. Feargal shows me a poem he wrote after Padraic's death, an elegy that ends with Padraic urging us to quit grieving for him and get on with the dance.

"I miss Padraic," says Nora. "We agreed on politics. Both of us are more socialist than the others. Sharkey is like his father and the rest of our brothers, more right-wing. I miss Padraic." Named after a saint.

Chapter Twenty-six

THE GENIUS OF BOTOX

WE GET UP SATURDAY MORNING TO CLIMB the Reek, confront a mountain's crooked architecture. A decent day for hiking: not too hot, some cloud cover.

"Nora, you coming with us?"

"I've done it once — never again!"

I wonder if I can keep up with Feargal, the expert. This is not a real climb, *à la* the Himalayas, more a steep walk, though some end up crawling on hands and knees. Some pilgrims use sticks; at the base, by the white welcoming statue of St. Paddy and the souvenir shop, Feargal hands me one collapsible ski pole and keeps one pole for himself.

As we work our way up the rough watercourse path he tells me of recent cases where climbers ran into a little trouble.

"Not nice to find a body," Feargal says as we climb. (What is it with my cousins and dead bodies?) "One man had a heart attack while climbing, collapsed. His friend put him into a bivvie bag, hiked down, and called us."

"A bivvie bag?"

"Most experienced hikers carry one, like a big garbage bag, crawl into it in a storm. It was too late that day, so we had to wait and retrieve him the next day."

"How many of you does it take?"

"Eight, twelve, depends. Three on each side of the body and one at each end, and in steep terrain we have to take turns. Strange thing was, by the end of the trek down I had become very attached to the body we were carrying. A relationship, not like a parent to a child, but a relationship of some kind. Odd. I didn't want to hand him over at the bottom. And the others with me all said the same. They all felt something similar. Didn't want to hand him over to the ambulance boys." I wonder, was there someone like Feargal in 1113 A.D. to haul down the thirty bodies after the lightning strike up top?

The lower part of the path up the Reek follows a grassy stream bed. Higher up, the mountain is rough quartz rubble, treacherous the step and bleak to the eye, a chaotic felsenmeer, a sea of rocks. What forces broke these rocks loose? A small white chapel floats in the clouds where St. Patrick is supposed to have stayed forty days and forty nights and cast out the snakes and frogs over a cliff. Patrick a slave in Ireland six or seven years, escaped by boat, supposedly a shipload of Irish wolfhounds, and came back a bishop to convert the pagans. This mountain is a portal. Some pilgrims go barefooted on the rocks for penance, some on their knees. Some don't make it. "I've bandaged many feet here," says Feargal. Some red-faced pilgrims look like they'll have heart attacks. "But you'd be surprised at the ones that make it." In the thirteenth century a king of Connaught lopped off the hands and feet of a yobbo who tried to waylay a pilgrim en route to this spot. Pilgrims come from all over the world.

On the mountain we meet up with Tony, a climbing friend of Feargal's. Tony and Feargal are both whippet-lean from years of mountain climbing and cycling. Tony is escorting his boss's boss, a man who makes Botox in California. The Botox people have a branch plant in Westport, and Tony is showing him around.

Tony points to Feargal and says, "This man saved my life. We were climbing in Scotland in a whiteout, can't see your hand in front of face."

"I've heard of that," Botox Man says.

"I went out on a cornice, not knowing it was a cornice — you know, like an overhang, a ledge of snow that builds up in the wind — it broke away where I was standing. I wasn't tied in and fell a hundred metres. Lost my pickaxe, my compass, different bits of gear."

Feargal says, "I couldn't see anything, couldn't hear anything. He was just gone. This was right after our friend died in Kerry. Is this another one? I had to go backwards over the edge blind." Bent over, he mimics stepping in reverse with his ass out. "Can't even see where the edge is, just keep stepping backwards and then over the edge and down. About thirty feet down I heard, 'Feargal!' I was very happy to hear it."

St. Patrick was born on the west coast of Wales. At sixteen he was kidnapped by pirates and sold into slavery, a chieftain's shepherd alone on a hill. In his book *Confession* he calls himself unlearned, a sinner, least of all the faithful.

Tony and Feargal debate faith as related to going barefoot up the Reek. Feargal says that bringing shoes, just in case, demonstrates greater faith than not bringing shoes along. Tony disagrees. I say faith involves doubt, but no one listens. Tony and Botox Man are faster and pull ahead of us, which is fine by me because I like talking to Feargal.

"Look down there," says Feargal. "That's the way we drive up on a search. There's a road gets us 200 metres higher than the parking lot, so we can get up that much faster." The road below travels through bog and what looks like a tree farm.

Feargal steers me off the main route, a way he knows with no one else on the rocky path. If we climbed here on the last Sunday in July we'd have to deal with twenty-five thousand other people crawling to Mass at the summit chapel.

"A Sligo woman died over that way. Her car was found in Murrisk, so we weren't even sure she was on the mountain. The guards searched one side, we did this side. Nothing. Even brought in a search dog from Northern Ireland. She was found four weeks later by people walking down the other side with a dog. We didn't look that side because we were told it had been swept. Learned a lesson from that one."

"Do birds get at the bodies?"

"Birds, maybe foxes. They go for the eyes, nose, ears, the soft parts of the body. A travelling woman died up here at night. The travellers are very religious, and there's a belief that if you climb Croagh Patrick three times, doing all the stations, a dangerously ill person will recover, dispensation from God. There was a child very sick in her extended family, so this woman wanted to do the climb. This was October, days getting shorter, dark earlier. The woman did the mountain twice, then disappeared on the third climb. We found her body down some steep scree. She probably wandered off the trail and fell in the dark."

"What happened to the child?"

"The child died."

Climbing the Reek reminds me of hiking with Padraic in the Rockies, though I don't see any bears or bighorns. Amazing view at the very top, especially once the clouds lighten and finally blow off. Then we can see sandy beaches and the bay below and sunken glacial drumlins. Stand on a sea of rocks and see a real sea, water green and blue, different depths and stripes, a drowned coast. It's almost better to be blind, then have it revealed, a curtain torn back.

Tony and Botox Man are at the chapel, and we devour chocolate biscuits and blackberry-flavoured fizzy water: all of it tastes amazingly good after the climb. An American walks past me, saying into his cellphone (can you guess?), "I'm on the mountain now." The new gods. I wonder if the Celts killed people up here, human sacrifices to the old gods. I have a few candidates. Botox Man tries but his phone won't work up here. Funny that he makes Botox because he has a very expressive face, dark eyebrows wiggling up and down like Groucho Marx's.

"It's a perfect product," the chemist says, "because the customer has to come back for more. That's the genius of Botox. A teacup is all I make every few months. We don't need any more, but we found it more efficient to keep the factory up anyway; it's harder to mothball it and then do start-up. My crew wear full respirator suits, the stuff is so poisonous. A teacup, then we dilute it to sell." Like St. Patrick, we're all slaves, slaves to an idea, to chemicals, to fashion, to hormones and genetics.

A steep, rocky descent, patches of mud and bog. "Take your mountain bike down this?"

"Oh yeah, no problem," says the chemist.

Feargal and Tony look doubtful but can't say anything because he's the boss's boss.

A local politican wants to light the path up the mountain, says Feargal, like lights at your feet in a movie theatre.

Back from our little hike, Nora says, "You must be fit," which makes me happy. I am glad Feargal took me; I feel a sense of accomplishment. Odd regimen: cycling miles, walking miles, and drinking gallons of tea and Guinness. Maybe I should write a diet-and-fitness-and-beer guide. *The Skinny on Stout.*

Is there gas in the car? In the car in the rain, not far from Joyce's Country, Feargal tells me of a Beckett play, a small local production. Two men and a woman in three barrels; one male says a wrong line, a line from later in the play, and the second male responds with a line that follows the wrong line, and they mistakenly jump a section, jump the scene where the woman pops up from her barrel and speaks. Her lines are gone, her part is ruined, she is livid. She leaps out of her barrel and storms offstage furiously.

Feargal says he heard two men walk out discussing the play.

"Typical of Beckett, isn't it?" says one. "Woman hidden in a barrel the whole time and not a single line. Typical Beckett."

Doolough Valley, what I think of as a famine valley, clenching a dark lake with its closed hard history, seething rain a solid level force. It's lashing, they say on the radio; it's lashing, Nora says on the phone, and it is like being lashed, like being whacked with a thin stick. The rain's power reminds you that the ice-cold Atlantic is there riding in the distance. In the horizontal deluge I snap pictures of the valley and its monument to the dead, then sprint back to shelter in the car. The rain seems turbo-injected, filled with invective.

Imagine starving in the famine and, in this cold, sodden climate, with desperate tenants trudging to landlords or gombeen men for food, walking down to see Lord Sligo at Delphi Lodge for help but turned back to die by the hundreds on the path home through this valley. Sorry, can't help you. Bodies in the wet ditches and fields of stone and bodies on straw in cottages, the vacant blue eye, mouths green from eating nettles and weeds, and the living lining up into work houses or creaking coffin ships like the *Brig St. John*, the *Bolivar*, the *Looshtauk*, the *Richard White* to sail west to the pesthouses on Partridge Island or Middle Island, to see who will keep living, to hoist the yellow flag as a warning of typhus or ship fever or Asiatic cholera or smallpox, to hoist the yellow flag when their ships drift into Saint John's harbour or a bit north up on the Miramichi, the New Brunswick doctors treating the sick

Irish until the local doctors take sick as well and are buried in double-lined lead coffins in the Loyalist Burial Grounds.

"Do you see up that hillside?" Feargal points out faint evidence of old potato ridges on a steep slope above, empty now, no more people planting potatoes, the ripples in the earth grown over green and the history hidden on misty slopes: old trails through passes and bogs, stone circles like those the Plains Indians left, pre-Christian standing stones, Bronze Age burial sites, pagan gods like bloody little monsters in stone, secret outdoor altars from when Catholic Mass was forbidden, cuckoos at old wells, poteen stills, grottos to St. Bridget or the Virgin Mary, foundations of farmhouses and lost villages that Feargal and Tony stumble upon while hiking, and Dark Ages abbeys where people once lit lamps in a window. Once these were called the Congested Districts. There was more life in these valleys a thousand years ago.

We stop the car to see a deserted Augustinian abbey destroyed after the penal laws were enacted. "Sharkey and Padraic, when they were small boys, liked to explore here in the ruins," Nora tells me. "One time Feargal snuck along a bedsheet in the car's trunk." The boys enter the stone ruins first, down in the dark chambers and walls, and Feargal appears before them, a ghostly apparition. "Sharkey was scared the most," Nora says, "despite putting up a braver front."

Ireland is booming in the cities, but it is a ghost world out here. It's the old days, but it's not the old days. Cattle rub themselves on pagan standing stones, the way buffalo rubbed themselves against glacial erratics in southern Alberta. Sheep graze on the old potato ridges. There is European Union money to keep sheep, but the sheep cause erosion, so you can also be paid *not* to keep sheep. Beckett might appreciate that.

New houses in town or along the seaside all seem constructed of cinder blocks, reminding me of Mexico. "There isn't the trust of wood here," Nora says.

A hurricane this past winter was named after a saint's day, many trees lost, as were lost on the West Coast of Canada this same stormy winter. A big oak came down on the hill behind my house, wrecked my elbow and shoulder chopping up rock-hard oak. Feargal shows me where the hurricane lifted heavy square flagstones from the rich man's front patio facing the sea. I can barely shift the stone with two hands. The Atlantic hurricane levitated the flagstone like a weightless Weetabix.

"The gales we get now," says a man in the pub. "Didn't before. Turn of the season it would be windy, October or March, but now it's gale after gale, January, February, March. Get one, and two or three days later another."

Leenane is the setting for a series of plays by Martin McDonagh, including *The Beauty Queen of Leenane*, so I'm interested in seeing it, and then I'm surprised how small a town it is. Near Leenane we drive past the waterfalls and singularly bright green field featured in the movie *The Field*. Very odd, it seems to me, that in John Keane's play a local man fights an outsider, an Englishman, and in the later movie it's an American businessman who wants the field — while the true story it's based on involved two local men. They'd known each other a long time; one ambushed and killed the other in a feud over a piece of bog. All three versions have a kind of truth regarding Irish history.

Rose saw *The Field* at Dublin's Abbey Theatre.

"Oh, they'll fight over land, all right. Land is everything," comments Rose. "Whinge, whinge, whinge — farmers always whinging and crying. How big is your farm? Ah now, it's just a very small one. Never met anyone who says he has a big farm. Always after money. Now, if I open a shop and someone down the road opens a shop and my business is down, I can't go to the government for more money, but they expect to. I know some

Limerick farmers who bought an apartment block in Spain, and they let it out and take their holidays there when they're not busy. A woman gave me the phone number if I ever want to stay there. Whinge, whinge, whinge."

"Look, look!" Feargal points out fenceposts that he likes; he is excited, telling me and pointing as we motor past. Nora has seen them before. The newly milled posts were planted in the wet ground and then the naked posts sprouted branches and leaves, came back to life, walked again among us, so to speak.

Like Feargal, I love this living fence, its blooming, its resurrection. A shrine, a miracle site. I wonder if spy satellites can spot it. This is my favourite moment of this trip.

Well, I also liked the pubs in Leenane, and how the small dogs herd cattle with their noses down, and the freckled, long-haired redhead walking the windy white strand all by herself near Roonah Quay.

Chapter Twenty-seven

THE WAY THEY SAY AMERICA

QUITE SOME TIME BACK EVELYN WAUGH allowed (I believe we were having watercress sandwiches in Raffles Hotel) that an Irishman faced only two final realities: Hell and the United States. This is no longer true, if it ever was true, but America *is* where millions were forced to flee in coffin ships with typhus and smallpox, and it's where Padraic's friends moved for jobs even into the mid-1990s. America was green cards, Blue Cross, the uncle in Boston, and America sent back greenbacks and rifles to the isle of saints and kings and poteen and Armalites.

The Irish say "America," and in their accent resonates a serious breathy note, a note they are not aware of, a note connoting a mystical place far across a once dangerous ocean.

Canadians say it flatly, "the States," as if one is heading to the store for milk or walking the mutt. "Going to the States." It's not "America" to us. Canada is too close to the USA for reverence or romance, too close for a special tone of voice. We mean two different countries.

I see a new "lifestyle magazine" here called *SPEND*. Most

Irish mock Americans, yet here they are zestily becoming the new Texans. Ireland converted once, Ireland converted again. It's a new Irish lifestyle of big wallets, big stomachs full of fried chicken and lard shakes (the average weight in Ireland is going up, and teen suicides are also up), a new world of big roads for German cars with Keith Richards jamming with the Chieftains on the tape deck and Turkish heroin cradled in duct tape, a racehorse's leg taped, a famous female journalist shot dead in her car by the underworld gangsters she was writing about and the police allowing the IRA to take out a local gangster they don't like and the pro-British Red Hand Defenders shooting a journalist while he walked with his wife on a Friday night, shooting him because he wrote about paramilitaries and drug money, and the Royal Ulster Constabulary accused in a female lawyer's assassination, a lawyer they didn't care for.

It's a new world of complicated crimes and weird bedfellows, a world of hostile takeovers, scary monsters, soft mist, soft money, leveraged buyouts, ironclad dot-com investments, seed money and speed from a lab, endless lineups at the Temple Bar in-spots, pills the bright colours of artificial flowers, and lovely Irish boobs once covered and now overflowing from low-cut scarlet sheath dresses as disposable Detroit techno pumps in your less-than-innocent ears, and no more doloroso "bedads" and "begobs" from the drunken jarvey driving your jitney, your open hack, your spider phaeton. No jarvey in a jitney now unless it's in a Merchant-Ivory production.

Bernadette used to cross herself on the bus passing the church — everyone on the bus crossed themselves — and minutes later Bernadette and I'd make out in a churchyard close to her parents' house, hands exploring, get wound up.

"Didn't know what I was missing," she'd say, breathing hard as we toiled and moiled, but never all the way. Saving herself for the guard, a peeler posted to the west. A nice little world, quaint and frustrating.

When I mention Holy Hour, my cousin Sharkey says he'd forgotten all about Holy Hour, surprised to think that not long ago all Dublin pubs closed their doors in the afternoon. I have a 1981 photograph of men sitting on the grimy sidewalk outside Kelly's, waiting out the black clock hands, waiting on Holy Hour to turn less than holy.

All these years given to Christ and novenas to Mary the Virgin, and now we pray not for our soul or salvation but for a flat stomach, to look good in our new clothes and silky underwear. A bog creeps over the old village, hides it.

"Real estate is through the roof in Westport." Wealthy outsiders are resented for inflating prices. Some locals, finding it too dear, are forced to live in nearby villages (beyond the pale), and they commute the thorny hedgerows to their jobs looking after those who don't find the prices so dear.

Chapter Twenty-eight

MY POLONIUS ROOKIE CARD

A TRAIN IN SUNSHINE IS A DIFFERENT CREATURE from a train straining under night clouds and mountain shadows. I can't see the mountain I climbed. I leave Westport on an evening train and realize later that I left that station once before, left the west, riding that same seat back to Dublin with Padraic and Bernadette. Do I recall echoes of that time? Flirting with flippant Bernadette or planning our secret escape to southern France to be together on our own? Padraic and his mirthful mask, his saucerful of secrets? I try to recall but draw a blank. In my next life I'll have a memory, steel-trap model.

I can't remember leaving Westport, yet Dingle peninsula two decades ago is still so clear in my mind, especially the beautiful countrywoman staring out to sea from the slippery ramp of the stone dock, the slippery slope, her sweater, the triangular shape of the Blasket Islands, the shape of her sweater, which I hardly touch, the sweet country, the damp curls of her hair and the confabulation and fabrications from everyone I asked about the boat to the Blaskets.

Problems with the gears, hit a whale, engine trouble, crew is sick, a mermaid sorely vexed them.

Only Cait gives me the truth; Cait knows the crew, knows they've all hightailed it to watch a big match in Kerry, so no boat will run today. While they watch the match she will watch me and kiss me on the lips. What does she stare at?

Cait works in Dublin all week, but she takes the cross-country train back to this end of the Dingle peninsula on weekends — I am amazed by her strong ties to home. She isn't taken with Dublin — it's a good job — but she wants to come home each weekend. She doesn't want to go shopping. We walk the windy cliffs together, and sun comes between clouds, alters the chameleon landscape, colours the sea, and we sit talking and drinking in Kruger's pub where locals still speak Irish, and we're watched like hawks all day and night. We are allowed little time alone, but I feel happy just being close to her, my apparition on a dock.

We're the couple who make onlookers ill, holding hands or arm in arm, strolling around, relaxed and excited, looking into each other's eyes and smiling. It seemed ordinary at the time, but now that I'm older this seems rarer, of greater value. Walking through a patch of clover I check for a four-leaf clover, but Cait stops me. "We're lucky," she says.

But we aren't lucky. I study her on her bike as she leads the way. We're lucky. I haven't lost her address yet, my pack not stolen yet.

We watch a bird tuck in its wings and dive straight down the cliff like it's a game, a sleek little rocket going down.

"If I came back I'd like to be a bird," she says to me at the misty cliffs.

I like the idea of flying, but birds seem to freeze on wires or fly into windows, not to live long and prosper. I think of my old tabby cat's long life of luxury.

"I'd like to be a cat next time," I say.

"*My* cat," she says without hesitation, and I am thrilled, would love to be her lap-cat, a shape-shifting god out of Irish mythology. We drink for hours at night and meet for breakfast. "I have butterflies," she says, patting her stomach. The elderly woman in black seems out of a Mediterranean milieu; she reminds me of our proximity to Spain. An old-fashioned world still in 1981, with reputations, duties, and consequences.

I wondered if the boat sticks to a stricter timetable now, thinking it sad if it does, but when I finally went back to Dunquin I still couldn't get out to the Blaskets — water too rough to land on them, the magic islands still out of my reach. Monks used to go out there to suffer in exile, to get closer to God. The woman with the cane is now dead. In the pub there is a photo of her sweeping with a broom, steel glasses and her white hair pulled back, the same severe look my grandmother Mary took on late in life. The woman in the pub kept us apart and sent me to bed when she wanted to close the little pub, whacking my chair and leg with her cane — the Old World ways and I was a carpet-bagger, a blow-in with one thing on his mind, and now the dear woman's dead as Polonius.

Air in my lungs and mist glassing my sweater, I rode Dingle peninsula, where I fell in love so swiftly. Stone beehive hovels hunch above the road, misty cliffside shrines with Kerrymen asking for money to see them. Riding my old-fashioned rental bike to look up miles to mountains in mist, look down miles at men patching curraghs, tiny tarred boats the size of kayaks by a cove at the bottom of cliffs where St. Brendan the Navigator rowed out to the New World, my New World.

"This hand is mine," said Cait, holding my right hand. "You still have one; you can use that one." I never know what clutter will stay in my brain or which poster will fall when the tape gives up. Ireland in history was often portrayed as a woman. Cait is my Ireland. Our head at the mercy of aged adhesives, a memory faulty and random as dreams. Rita Mae Brown says one of the keys to happiness is a bad memory.

"Hey, you got anything like the Burgers and Beer place we got back home in Cleveland?" 1981, a loud voice in the pub in Dingle, the loud voice for dealing with foreigners. I go quiet while sitting with several Irish women in Irish sweaters; I don't open my mouth for fear of my own stupid accent. The man looks at me, sensing something, hoping I'm American. I let him down. I keep my mouth shut, avert my eyes, pretend to be a Fenian hillsider from way back.

"Back home, get a triple burger and a pitcher of Bud for $3.49. You folks got anything like that around here?"

One of my favourite spots in the world and he wants it to morph into Cleveland, wants a strip-mall grill, craves the king of bad beers. This is the way the world ends — not with a bang but with a Wimpy burger.

For two decades I wanted to travel back to that far end of Dingle but worried that I'd just be depressed. I heard that a Club Med was going in and tourists flocking to see the famous dolphin that cruises the bay. Uncle Marty was stationed in Hawaii during the war, and he never wanted to go back, not wanting to see it covered in high-rises and 7-Elevens. A *New York Times* travel piece talked of Dingle becoming like Lower Cape Cod in terms of cost and crowds. I wanted to keep it the way it was arranged in my head.

"You can go back," an expat Irishman told me. He runs gaze-hounds in Eden Mills, Ontario. We chat in campfire light, a yard party. "It's fine still; you can go back. I go back to Dingle every year." And he's right. I didn't see any Club Med and the dolphin in the water just off the Norman watchtower charmed me, and I didn't think I was a fan of traditional music (diddly-aye), but I ducked into O'Flaherty's for one pint and stayed listening to music for hours and hours, no stage, the band beside my table, a talented woman from Cambridge sitting in on violin with the locals playing accordion, guitar, drum, recorder, and a weirdly tuned banjo, band playing "The Devil's Reel," a mad fast mandolin, black pints down my throat, getting *lanngerd* with my feet on a floor of big slate slabs and the red-faced singer explaining Gaelic songs to me: "Her mother loathes you because you got drunk and violent, but the girl, she just loves you." Here he looks heavenward and hits his heart with his fist. Why is he telling me? "And this is a song about being far away from home and sick and no mother or father to lift your head."

Later the crowd stands to applaud the English violinist as she walks out into the misty night. One of my two favourite pubs in the world, and both on the same peninsula in the west. And a bike ride in light rain is just the ticket for a hangover the next day, clears out the cobwebs. I want to come back here. Ireland is my Botox: after a while I need it again.

On my first trip to the west, an old rolling fishboat took me to Inishmore, biggest of the Aran Islands. The usual ferry wasn't running. A young Englishman beside me kept bad-mouthing the Irish, echoing Princess Margaret's assertion that the Irish are animals, all animals, assuming I was in complete agreement. A rough crossing.

"You're turning green," I said happily. "This is the first time I've actually seen someone turn green."

The Aran Islands used to be cut off for weeks and months in stormy weather, cliffs and rocks ringed by white, harbourside water lifting in a frenzy of spray. No chopper flying in from Galway back in those days. No mountain bikes, no silky gears, no Rock Shocks. Where are the clunker bikes of yesteryear?

I was the only person lying on the sand of a beautiful strand in the Aran Islands. Walking the prehistoric cliffside fort at

Dún Aengus, crosscut rock, a world tipped sideways, and people crawling to peer over the square edge of the scary cliff, dropping deep into a dark blue world below.

A spooky night alone in a huge abandoned hotel up the coast. And where on the map is that sun-bright, seedy seaside holiday town that seemed out of the 1930s? In a chemist's shop I bought a cheap camera when my Russian camera jammed, wanting photos of the west. All a waste of money and effort — every photo, every bit of film, stolen in Spain.

Irish dogs always snapping at my ankles on the rental bikes. "Hey, boyo," I'd say in a soft voice, and that seemed to calm the dogs. Maybe they smelled food, the big B & B breakfasts. When no one at the table was looking I'd wrap some of my Irish bread and sausage in a napkin, maybe cheese, a banana, and keep this later for lunch, stretch my budget, stop my bike at a nice spot to stare at the sea and eat a sausage or two wedged in Irish bread. I eat and Bobby Sands starves himself to death in the H-Block prison where the walls are smeared with shit and a kindergarten teacher marries and is transformed into a princess, Irish streets vacant, surprising me, everyone indoors watching the royal wedding.

Now I stop my bike to stare at a spooky life-size crucifixion scene in the sharp, high rocks above the sea, cycling to the crucifixion, a sharp turn, a weird white Christ high on a cross in his crown of thorns, rust smeared down his white leg like blood, and Mary and her roses and the mourners in striking white against black rock arrowing up behind in the middle of nowhere. The old faith, the old rugged cross.

A German woman in O'Flaherty's vows, "I'll move here to Ireland after my children grow up." Her hand up to show the height they must reach. "I can't be in Germany," she says. "It's too cold. People are very clean. I can't *be* there."

I laugh, ask her, "As in *Hamlet*? To be or not to be?"

"Exactly," she says. "Ireland is good for — what is the word? — my seale."

"What?" I ask. She points at herself, at her ear or neck. "Ear, nose, and throat? Good for your sinuses?" I ask. She looks up a word in her tiny dictionary.

"Soul," she says. Oh, not sinus.

My train ticket seems cheap: twenty-one Irish pounds (punts) for a ride across a country and back again. A certain kinship among those who ride all the way from Westport, though most seats are empty at first, so there is less talk than on the train going west, less buzz on the rocking train. This changes as we pick up people en route to Dublin, the car soon packed.

"Jumped-up little cunt. Jumped-up little cunt." A young woman on the train keeps repeating this. Is she rehearsing? Imitating what someone said to her? Jumped-up little cunt. It doesn't seem aimed at anyone in her group of friends. Passengers puff away in the non-smoking carriage, blowing smoke over the tiny baby a young couple from Knock has perched on my table, miraculous Knock, where the Virgin Mary appeared in

1879 and the lame leave their crutches. Be a miracle if I survive this train trip.

Sun beating in our windows and heaters turned up high in the broiling carriage and we can't shut them off.

"Freeze to death in these cars in the winter."

"I'm melting," says a young drunk behind me, behind his tableful of Bud bottles.

Back in the days when Sharkey was in uniform (airport duty is plainclothes) my cousin was riding a night train, young drinkers on the suburban train snickering, making pig sounds, oinking at him.

Ignore them, he thinks, but when they clamber off at Bayside, Sharkey slips off as well and follows them, unnoticed. The two young drunks stop to take a leak after all the pints of creamy porter in the lovely seaside town of Howth, a harbour town full of fishing boats and drugs. Sharkey sneaks up behind and deftly whacks both boyos across the back of the knees with his timber. Both fall right over on cue, urine flying up and dousing their jeans.

"Did you have something to say to me?" Sharkey asks innocently.

"No! No!"

He whacks them a bit more and they flee, still peeing on themselves.

"Willy out," says Sharkey sagely. "Can't fight when your willy's out."

Sharkey tells me of busting a heroin addict and his parents dropping in to see him soon after. To attack Sharkey? To get their son off? To ask for mercy?

The parents say, Please lock him away. "We can't go on vacation. We come back and he's sold the telly and clock and camera and all, sells anything he can. We're prisoners, we can't leave our home."

Sharkey has been lucky to stay close to home, close to Dublin; perhaps this is because his mother is a widow. Usually you move around in the police, are not allowed to work near where you're from. For decades Dubliners have complained of big country louts out of their element working as gardaí in their city.

Sharkey has moonlighted as a bouncer (worked the door at Malahide). Bouncers lurk outside most bars in Dublin and Howth. "Now we keep the junkies away," one says to me. Some bouncers look like thugs (t'ugs, in the Dublin accent) or homicidal skinheads, scaring tourists with their long, black leather coats and shaved heads, some on steroids, but they nod like old pals to me: "Goo' noite, see youse."

They stand outside in the wet and cold while crowds inside are warm and dry and having fun. No bouncers outside brew pubs where I live, but they are fixtures here.

"A lot of the doormen are IRA or Sinn Féin," says Sharkey. "Hundreds of doormen over the city, and a cut taken every night. Some don't know who they work for, some do. We don't need a doorman, says the bar. Yes, you do need a doorman, they say. Some of them get violent, hammering a drunk something awful at the end of the night."

Sharkey and I meet for a final pub crawl, starting at Declan's puce pub, Hogan's, where we decide to go to the George again, have a drink to Padraic, a sentimental visit to Jurassic Park.

Doorman: "Know it's gay?" (How does he know we're not gay?)

Us: "Sure, no problem." (We're so tolerant, *moderne*.)

Doorman: "Five pounds to get in."

Us: "Five pounds to go in and then pay for a beer?" Forget that shite.

So much for our sentimental journey. I feel guilt for being mad at a dead person, for being mad at Padraic for taking off for Spain, for having a life. What would his grandfather make of him, make of the lot of us? What will floor us in seventy years? Your liver, the size of a duck, is full of blood and bile, the largest, most metabolically complex organ inside our fine skin. I gave Rose my photos of her son in Montana in 1980, including the goofy ones with flowers behind his glasses. The family seem to enjoy them. Has HIV but is fine, then gets a transfusion at the hospital and they give him hep C and that wrecks his liver. The liver is the road to health, says the old 1922 newspaper.

Smack versus booze: Sharkey and I discuss this on our pub crawl. Heroin and alcohol on his mind, but his take is different from two years before; he's changed his views a bit. Sharkey eyes the patrons at the public house, and I follow his gaze down the bar, the line of usual suspects. Your eye changes in policework: you check out faces, you view people differently.

"Heroin use is up," he says, "but *this* is still what causes trouble," pointing at our pint glasses. "Alcohol is worse than anything else. These fellows seem fine in the bar, polite to us, cheery to the staff — bye, guv; bye, lads — then they get home and mad, lashing out at the little ones or the wife, smashing the place all to bits. That's when we get called in. It's *drink*. Heroin goes from maybe 2 per cent to 4 per cent over the years, visible jump, makes the papers and telly, seems like a bloody epidemic, but it's drink that's the bigger problem. Any hospital, they see it."

Car crashes, joyriders, thieves, domestic disturbances, donnybrooks, public disorder, fights, broken bones, head injuries. Drink is still number one with a bullet.

On our last night we walk about to the Porter House (they make their own beer), the Funnel (*My Drug Hell* playing live), Hogan's, the Long Hall, the Foggy Dew, and the Mercantile. Dear Reader: I toil and moil in the name of research.

I was so much closer to my cousin Padraic, but now that Padraic is dead I spend my time talking and drinking with my cousin the policeman. I've grown to really like Sharkey. He's always been funny and irreverent, but he's also evolved into the one who watches out for the others, who gives you a lift to the airport or comes over when your leg is broken and you can't make the stairs. He's become a new Uncle Dermot, the one who takes care of things.

The gangsterish bouncers guarding the pub portals clap their hands to keep warm and call out as if we are dear relatives: "Cheers. God bless." I like these skinhead gatekeepers. St. Patrick heard a voice: "Look, your ship is ready."

And I'm gone.

Chapter Twenty-nine

AFTER ANGEL STATION

A PREGNANT WOMAN IS KILLED BY A NAIL BOMB, London's third nail bomb in a week. The IRA is blamed at first, but it turns out it's not their work (*What could anyone think of the IRA?*). Too amateur, this bomb is a lone wolf. The pregnant woman was in town to see my cousin Judy's ABBA musical, *Mamma Mia!* Her show is a huge hit first in London's West End, then all over the world, and now she is a multi-millionaire.

The nail bomb was planted in a gay pub. I think of the George in Dublin. That could be me and my Irish cousin they're patching together on the bloody sidewalk. A neighbourhood animal trying to pull something out of your leg, shiny new nails rocketing through space toward your table of drinks; you're walking the city, the market, or you're visiting London for my cousin Judy's feel-good musical, and then someone is trying to open you up, see what you're made of. "It took me off me chair," said a man named Joyce drinking in a pub close by.

At the boisterous London theatre an older woman, a good friend of the family's, observes that I don't seem nostalgic for

ABBA. Perhaps I don't look joyful enough.

"Before your time?" she asks.

England makes me feel as if I can't let my guard down, and Ireland does not. They are both my parents. London's smart red miles awe me, but London also humbles me, puts me on edge. London calling, but I'm an outsider, a voyeur. Dublin's sunset brick is more human in scale. Slouch past the imposing, sooty bulk of London's British Museum, my feeble brain afraid to take it in, I will be crushed by civilization's giant posterior. *Roma quanta fuit ipsa ruina docet.* Her ruins teach us how great Rome was.

I think of Dublin's elfin slum-kids right this moment riding huge-haunched white horses in the vacant spaces around the Connolly Station railway yards. Can't do that in central London: no elbow room, no chance of cow-byes and injuns here under Big Ben's shadow (I thought it'd be bigger, says a tourist). No leafy trees in the overpriced mews I drift through, not a twig for a bird to plant its tiny ass and claws, not a blade of grass. Dingle's raw cliffs and Feargal's green valleys and blooming fenceposts seem a million miles away.

Chapter Thirty

SWISS ARMY KNIFE

WITH PLANES FROM TURKEY, SINGAPORE, KUWAIT, we taxi the planet, taxi endless Heathrow runways, roving hunks of aluminum painted in a bright Babel of different languages, but all of us seeking the strange path home.

A towpath beside the canal, my grandfather Michael taking the path home, the canal's slow curve to the horizon engineered like a railway. Padraic lives close to the centre of town, northside, renovating a Victorian rowhouse, Dublin brick and stone and iron.

He walks his path to the hospital, knows his platelet count is down a bit, checks himself in with a smile, jokes with the nurses, who love him, asks for a better bed. My sunburned plane lifts in a path of contrails, my sunburned grandfather dips into the cool canal, and Padraic drowns in a coma, liver not taking out the toxins, poison leading to psychosis, blood overwhelming his stomach, an udder full of blood.

I fly a little rocketship and Sharkey flies to Amsterdam or Paris, escorting his alien choirs, St. Patrick (tough on crime) casting out of the country our snakes: back you go to the enchanting Snakeheads and Coyotes, see if they give a refund, back to the drawing board. Under stuttering foreign stars, our garda Sharkey walks a foreign city and gets locked, *lanngerd*, seeks the Irish pub's good craic and dark pints (*wild nights!*), Amsterdam's Irish pub, Paris's Irish pub, Madrid's Irish pub, Siberia's Irish pub. Guinness opens its fake Irish pubs like fast-food stands (Would you like ballads with that?) with the mandatory black-and-white photo of Flann O'Brien glowering out from his frame on wall after wall after wall in the weary Western world, poor Flann (my hero), pissed off knowing the jackanapes and cockerels drinking Schlub Lite haven't the foggiest who those beetled eyebrows might belong to.

My plane's 1940s shadow bisects England's bright fields and hedges, April skies (bogeys at three o'clock), and I spy the X of a small airstrip near sandy beaches, near glittering water, the ocean below an endless gymnasium deep with sleeping shadows, our plane's shadow a cross, a Celtic rood (*Lord that I may see you today*).

I spy tiny peaks like miniature versions of the Blaskets off Slea Head and Dingle, an edge of a world in gold and blue and green and granite, the colours of beautiful eyes. My eyes can't take it in, sight burning my retina, too much sun.

Sun in my eyes, sunset on Waterloo Bridge the night before, the Kinks song "Waterloo Sunset" possessing the inside of my skull. Standing alone at a rail, a beautiful dusk, a beautiful metropolis spread out so I can see how far I've walked from the city's other shores, and what is that object speeding at me in the muddy red water of the Thames?

A wooden barrel spinning past fast (no lie, GI), a dead cooper's work, an old world gyring under my feet and zipping under the London bridge, rivers to the sea and things fall apart and things don't fall apart, the centre will not hold and the centre does hold, and the dour old Orangemen keep beating their drums on the Glorious Twelfth and marching for King Billy and King Rat in their Clockwork Orangemen bowler hats.

Worst Sectarian Violence in Years

IRA Refuses to Disarm

Fear Rises as Catholic Teen Shot

Dozens Injured in Clashes

More Troops Sent into Northern Ireland

Ulster Returns to British Rule

What the outside world watches casually and casually remembers of Éire — the rib cage found on the downtown roof days after a blast, seagulls drawn to your bones, the murals, rubber bullets to a child's face, the dark night's Molotov cocktails floating by, flung by invisible hands over the wire barrier, flaming comets in a beautiful arc, some comets skimming off the fence and altering direction or splitting in two on the wire, flame spreading like lava in liquid colour on the ground and on a car hood, and in the foreground the silhouetted snout and high windshield of a burning Euro-van and then the stuttering notes of automatic fire and someone yelling to get down (*Doon! Doon!*).

We scan the violent Irish images over and over; we can call them up, call up the Troubles without effort. Even so, my less-than-reliable intuition tells me that the green Irish countryside and cobbled Irish streets pose far less visceral danger, less *trouble*, day to day than their knife-happy and gun-happy counterparts elsewhere. There is a better chance of a brick to the head or a knife to the liver in London or Glasgow or Marseilles or Moscow or Atlanta or New York City than there is walking the worst parts of Galway or Dublin. Several friends have been attacked in sunny Los Angeles, none in damp Ireland.

I was warned in 1997 to avoid O'Connell Street, the once elegant thoroughfare; history and statues and bulletholes become kips and crappy T-shirt shops. Rose said, My God, take your life in your hands. Padraic laughed at this, and at night we walked without incident past the male hustlers, past the post office where Pearce and the rebels rose up in 1916 as my mother was born.

Army Watchtowers Dismantled in Bandit Country

IRA agrees to Disarm

Explosion in Northern Ireland, Blamed on Terrorists, Caused by Meteorite

American Student Wins Irish Public House

Roman Catholic residents in south Belfast put up signs pledging there would be "no Orange feet" marching on Lower Ormeau. About 50 Protestants, mostly women, dipped their feet in orange paint and walked peacefully down the road late Tuesday, leaving a trail of orange footprints. The ploy elicited chuckles from the Roman Catholic residents, who normally are wary of annual Protestant marches that celebrate 300-year-old battlefield victories over the Roman Catholics.

Scandal and Change Leave Irish Church Adrift

IRA Agrees to Truce

Public Apology for 30 Years of Terror

Jet engine cowling like an elegant barrel beside me, its round maw will eat the air admirably for the next twelve hours. My ship is ready, the tunnel is open, I must go home to discover that lump in her breast. My loyalties smaller than to a nation. The plane leaving Europe behind is always less festive than the one that takes you there, our plane spewing not petals but brown exhaust.

I think of my first flight from Edmonton International decades ago, Swiss Army knife a talisman from my sister Maria and her friend Sheila, who I had a crush on, secret scissors and tweezers, in a neat blue folder my hostel membership and Eurail pass. I was sure our plane was going to crash, that *feeling*, but I was stoic about it, a melancholy romantic looking at wheatfields the bright shade of lemon peel, looking out the Oldsmobile windows en route to the sad airport, then shoved back in my seat by the surprising thrust, the banshee jets, and I peeked around grinning — did the other passengers hurtling to Europe feel it too? Liftoff still such a visceral thrill and, in my brute perception, somehow sexual.

My trips are blurring into one another, united by nostalgia and frustration and my quaint hatred of everyone else on the plane.

Uncle Marty would say, "You didn't pick that up off the ground." Marty was on a plane from Dublin to Philadelphia with my aunt Bridie when a passenger in front put his seat all the way back and Marty yelled in his booming Irish voice: "YOU'RE LYING ON TOP OF MY SISTER!" As kids we were embarrassed by such family scenes; now I admire such care and bravado, now I need him to yell at the person who puts her seat all the way back while I'm still eating, shoving the tray of food into my chest and lap and gee whiz it's only going to be like this for ten more hours.

My father and the English side of our family, raised to avoid raised voices or calling attention to themselves, would avoid such fuss. Like my dog I am a mongrel, I have traits of both crowds; I am quiet and loud, stuck inside the glove of my family DNA the way we are shoehorned inside our sweaty plane, our floating migrant motel.

I try to stare out from my plane at the sheets of light laid like blinding metal on the enormous sea, my eyes drawn to water, to tales of drowning. Shoeless and speechless, I sit above the beautiful, overwhelming Atlantic — I imagine a lone figure tumbling all that way down to that seascape glittering like needles (Hallooh, grand ya, I'm just after falling into the winedark sea), imagine our suitcases and long-sleeved shirts spilling down; I wrench my stiff neck staring backwards at the Hebrides' last hard edges, midget peaks and beautifully barren shores receding, and some longing grasps me, some worry that I may not ever be back (need my Botox).

I want to travel back, buy another ticket and find that exact curve of sand by the glittering sea *there*, find that exact patch of sunlight, that X of an airstrip, for X marks the moment that must be acted on later.

I know it won't happen, the notion will pass, though not without some pain. Somewhere else life is more exotic and exciting, a beloved smiling at us, a sunny strand, a shady lane, a jolly corner, a Hopper porch, a paradise, another possible life if we just jump up, if we act now. But we stay hunkered in our seats, Sinn Féin, ourselves alone.

I think of the woman at the end of Dingle peninsula, staring out to sea from the ancient pier (like a model on a runway but not a model, a complex person in a colourful sweater, and what was she staring at when I approached and screwed up my courage), then my pain-in-the-ass backpack stolen in Spain because I was careless, Cait's lost address, her long hair lost, and my cousin Sharkey dispatched by me to find her, Sharkey's futile search for her in a trad Dublin nightclub to give her my message two decades ago. She wanted to see the Wolfe Tones play live. She didn't get my message. She wouldn't remember me now, wouldn't recognize me.

A person standing alone on stone, in Dingle, on Cook Street, a mute shadow laid on the windswept landscape, at a canal, on a cliff, in a car, altering it by being there, altering it by not being there. It looks Edenic down there, but I know it's not Eden, know I'd find something to curse and dismiss and be depressed and nostalgic about. I'm the eel after a body, the sow that eats its farrow; I'm the gull drawn to the rooftop rib cage. But I can't stop wondering, can't stop my gaze, wanting to live nine lives, a conquistador wanting to make mine a tiny part of what I see.

The last stones stoics in the North Atlantic and waves work over their scarred gilt faces, eat at the last bits of granite like kibble, hard old world receding into mottled file folders, and waves walk in like slow tinker horses, and though it kills my eyes, I keep gazing into the beautiful light spread on the sea.

I am not looking forward to the meal or moronic movie or the irritating couple who always sit in front of me, not looking forward to Iceland's trance-trip-hop hotspots or Greenland's abandoned whaling stations and that lost bomber squadron covered in transluscent years of ice.

I am looking backwards, eight miles high in X-rays and accents and sunspots, craning my neck to watch the last spike of lit granite in blue dreaming waves (if it were possible to look into the sea), and the last pyramid slips under and we move on, and across the 767 aisle a nervous woman downs multiple Scotches and Xanax while a man with a face like a gargoyle's and a loud Cockney voice complains in her ear, in our ear: "'E's always saying, 'It makes you fink, it makes you fink.' So finally I says to him, I says, '*Naaah*, it don't make you fink at all!'"

At night I close my eyes and see faces and landscapes, images that itch at my sleep, ghostly blue outlines of the beautiful buildings I've seen above my head that day: Portland stone, flash-pale palisades, and cornices and plaster grape clusters; ivory bank pillars lit by fireflies; tall wooden windows and speckled spires; Georgian mansions and haunted statues and gargoyles; peach bridges and skinny metal bridges arching their backs and orange lights shaking down the River Liffey; high houses lining walled, sectioned quays that look a little like Bourdeaux or sidewalks along the Seine; and wet air washing in my aunt's window from the bog hills and milky sea. And I close my eyes, my head a host, hidden outlines hovering in my head like blueprints, my imprinted ghosts, my noisy lanes and yellow stone walls and the oval faces of my children and ancestors lit like brief chemicals and then held fast.

ACKNOWLEDGEMENTS

BARRELS OF LOVE TO MY RELATIVES who put up with me and fed me and may not be crazy about the end result (being a funny kind of book guaranteed to send you stupid).

Thanks to Betty, Leslie, Jonathan, Judy, and that grog shop in Mill Hill.

Thanks to Lily, Jimmy, Fran, Martin, Helen, Jean, Liam, Seamus, Maura, Colm, St. Patrick, and the Irish Historical Picture shop on Ormond Quay in Dublin.

Thanks to Declan, Maria and Bob, Leighton and Kay (*you'll be a football*), Leo, Liam, Bridie, James, Mary, Michael, Kitty, and Mary.

Thanks to Peggy and Jack, Josie and Marty, Bob and Bettie Jo and Jeanessa.

Thanks to Bernie, Billeh (*shaved them yet?*), Vera, Susan, Tracy, Roger, Ross, Sean, Dr. Len Frankenstein, the KV67s, all the bartenders, all the waitresses, Propeller Bitter, Big Rock, Felicita's happy hours, Barbara Moon, Michael Ignatieff, and everyone at the Banff Centre, BC Arts Council, and Canada

Council for the Arts. "Put the Moan on Ya" won the Maclean-Hunter Endowment Award for Creative Non-fiction from *Prism International* and was cited in *Best American Essays 2001*.

An excerpt called "The Eye of Ireland" was a winner of *Event Magazine*'s Creative Non-fiction Contest.

"Wankers and Widows and Chancers and Saints" was published in the Banff Centre anthology *To Arrive Where You Are*.

The Reader (Saint John *Telegraph-Journal*) published an excerpt called "The Canal."

Thanks to these editors.

Thanks also to Scott Griffin, Jack Stoddart, Martha Sharpe (good mud-wrestling), and love to Sharon, getting up with the larks and taming the animals while I fly about and stay up half the night and scribble with a smart Christian drop and take over every surface in the house and sleep in like a lazy lout.